Cohabitation in Europe

Originating from discussions about the reasons for, and regional variations behind, the remarkable rise in cohabitation that started in the 1970s – a rise that continues to this day – this book explores the main stimuli behind cohabitation. The variation in levels of cohabitation cannot be explained solely by regional differences, religious affiliation, nationality, levels of education, or by the varying rate in which contraceptive measures spread across Europe. The book also focuses on the ways in which cohabitants are legitimized or rejected by certain communities. Did communities develop specific terms to define cohabitation and because of which underlying reasons were these different terms created?

Illegitimacy is another phenomenon inseparably tied to cohabitation, based on the hypothesis that the understanding of marriage differs between societies and regions. In 1971, Shorter, Knodel and Van de Walle found that children born in rural Slavic communities in unlawful but stable, consensual unions were not recognized by civil law and the Church, and were registered as illegitimates, but in a cultural perspective were considered as legitimate. They also found more or less the same pattern in Scandinavian countries. This book explores the correlations that exist between illegitimacy and cohabitation across space and time in Europe?

This book was originally published as a special issue of *The History of the Family.*

Dalia Leinarte is Professor of History at Vytautas Magnus University, Lithuania, and a Fellow Commoner at Lucy Cavendish College, University of Cambridge, UK. She is a Chairperson of the UN CEDAW Committee. Leinarte is the author of *The Lithuanian Family in its European Context, 1800–1914: Marriage, Divorce and Flexible Communities* (Palgrave Macmillan) and *Adopting and Remembering Soviet Reality: Life Stories of Lithuanian Women, 1945–1970* (Brill).

Jan Kok is Professor of Social, Economic and Demographic History at Radboud University, Nijmegen, The Netherlands.

Cohabitation in Europe

A Revenge of History?

Edited by
Dalia Leinarte and Jan Kok

Routledge
Taylor & Francis Group

LONDON AND NEW YORK

First published 2018 by Routledge

2 Park Square, Milton Park, Abingdon, Oxfordshire OX14 4RN
52 Vanderbilt Avenue, New York, NY 10017

Routledge is an imprint of the Taylor & Francis Group, an informa business

First issued in paperback 2019

British Library Cataloguing in Publication Data
A catalogue record for this book is available from the British Library

ISBN 13: 978-1-138-73274-2 (hbk)
ISBN 13: 978-0-367-23434-8 (pbk)

Typeset in Times New Roman
by RefineCatch Limited, Bungay, Suffolk

Publisher's Note
The publisher accepts responsibility for any inconsistencies that may have
arisen during the conversion of this book from journal articles to book chapters,
namely the possible inclusion of journal terminology.

Disclaimer
Every effort has been made to contact copyright holders for their permission to
reprint material in this book. The publishers would be grateful to hear from any
copyright holder who is not here acknowledged and will undertake to rectify
any errors or omissions in future editions of this book.

Contents

Citation Information

The chapters in this book were originally published in *The History of the Family*, volume 20, issue 4 (October 2015). When citing this material, please use the original page numbering for each article, as follows:

Chapter 6

Spatial variation in non-marital fertility across Europe in the twentieth and twenty-first centuries: recent trends, persistence of the past, and potential future pathways
Sebastian Klüsener
The History of the Family, volume 20, issue 4, (October 2015), pp. 593–628

For any permission-related enquiries please visit:
http://www.tandfonline.com/page/help/permissions

Notes on Contributors

Marė Baublytė is based at the Demographic Research Centre, Vytautas Magnus University, Kaunas, Lithuania.

Anca Dohotariu is an Associate Professor at the Faculty of Political Science, University of Bucharest, Romania.

Ginger S. Frost is a University Research Professor at the Department of History, Samford University, Birmingham, AL, USA.

Sebastian Klüsener is a Research Scientist and the Deputy Head of the Laboratory of Fertility and Well-being at the Max Planck Institute for Demographic Research, Rostock, Germany. He holds a Visiting Professorship at the Vytautas Magnus University, Kaunas, Lithuania.

Jan Kok is Professor of Social, Economic and Demographic History at the Department of History, Radboud University, Nijmegen, The Netherlands.

Dalia Leinarte is Professor of History at Vytautas Magnus University, Kaunas, Lithuania, and a Fellow Commoner at Lucy Cavendish College, University of Cambridge, UK. Leinarte is a Chairperson of the UN CEDAW Committee.

Ineta Lipša is a Senior Researcher at the Institute of Latvian History, University of Latvia, Riga, Latvia.

Aušra Maslauskaitė is a Professor at the Department of Sociology, Vytautas Magnus University, Kaunas, Lithuania. Her research topics include family sociology, family demographics, and gender sociology.

Andrejs Plakans is Professor Emeritus at the Department of History, Iowa State University, Ames, IA, USA. His main research interests are European social history, as well as population and family history.

Liv Johanne Syltevik is a Professor in the Department of Sociology, University of Bergen, Norway. Her research interests are family practices, lone motherhood, street level bureaucracy, and the development of the Norwegian welfare state.

INTRODUCTION

Cohabitation in Europe: a revenge of history?

Jan Kok and Dalia Leinarte

Unmarried cohabitation is often seen as a radically 'new' phenomenon, originating in the 1960s, but in fact it has long historical antecedents. The question is, however, whether traditional and modern cohabitation are comparable and whether we can speak of persistence. This article offers a literature review on cohabitation in Europe, with the focus on persistence over time, integrating the results of a 2013 conference on this topic. What sources are available to confirm or reject such persistence? How should we understand persistence? In terms of the motivations of unmarried cohabitants? Or in terms of the acceptance of the community at large? And if no real persistence is found, does this mean that European cohabitation since the 1970s truly represents 'new' behaviour? We show that, on the regional level, the legacy of the past is still visible in factors affecting the timing and frequency of marriage of cohabiting couples. These factors are a mixture of regional socio-economic constraints, the relative cultural importance attached to marriage, the religious history, and the level of secularization.

1. Introduction

Often, studies of unmarried cohabitation in contemporary society begin with a reference to its historical origins. However, these origins are almost always placed in the 1960s or 1970s when specific groups of divorced people and highly educated, urban youths began to refrain from (re)marrying (e.g. Kasearu & Kutsar, 2011, p. 309; Martin & Théry, 2001, p. 135). However, several authors have noticed that the areas where modern cohabitation seems to have been 'invented' were also the areas where it had been prevalent in the past, especially in the nineteenth century. Ron Lesthaeghe describes this overlapping of old and new patterns as 'a revenge of history' (Lesthaeghe, 2010, p. 214; in a similar vein see Therborn, 2004, p. 193). In fact, cohabitation has a very long history which is, by definition, intimately tied to the history of marriage and marriage regulations. What kind of history can be written on the roots of modern cohabitation? Is it a social history of more or less marginal groups of people who, for one reason or another could not meet the costs of a wedding or could not comply with the exigencies of official marriage? Or is it a cultural history of regionally different perceptions of the meaning of marriage and of the stages of courtship leading towards marriage? In other words: what does 'a revenge of history' mean? Can we really find continuity of cultural perceptions or even 'path-dependent' repertoires of family formation which somehow survived the supposed 'golden age of marriage' in the mid-twentieth century?

Censuses are of little help to study persistence and change in the patterns of regional variation and in the levels of cohabitation. In most countries, direct questions to accommodate common law unions did not appear in the censuses before 2000 (Spijker, Esteve, & Cusidó, 2012). In some countries, surveys exist that make it possible to go back a few decades earlier (e.g. Casper & Cohen, 2000). Before the 1970s, one would have to infer cohabitation from the fact that unmarried persons were living together, but this may also include housekeepers, boarders, etc. Thus, data on illegitimate births are often the only source used to estimate the occurrence of cohabitation in the past. However, cohabitation is only one of the explanatory factors of illegitimacy, and estimates of its share are notoriously unreliable. Even more important is the relative meaning attributed to marriage and cohabitation in different periods and different regions. Did communities develop specific terms to define cohabitation that were created with different underlying reasons? In several countries children born in unlawful, but stable, consensual unions were not recognized by civil law and the church, and were therefore registered as illegitimates, but in a communal perspective they were considered as legitimate. Examples are children from 'irregular marriages' in Scotland and 'incomplete marriages' in Sweden (see below).

The articles collected in this special issue originate from a conference, held in September 2013 at the Gender Studies Centre at Vilnius University, Lithuania. The meeting brought together social historians, historical demographers and social scientists working on contemporary cohabitation. The aim of the conference was to study the issue of persistence in cohabitation over time. What sources are available to confirm or reject such persistence? Can we find persistence in the motives to cohabit? Can we find it in the communal norms on what constitutes 'proper' marriage? And if no real persistence is found, does this mean that European cohabitation since the 1970s represents truly 'new' behaviour, and that its surge reflects the sweeping change towards tolerance and 'self-actualization' that the theory of second demographic transition describes (Lesthaeghe, 1995; van de Kaa, 2001)?

In this introductory essay, we will try to answer those questions. We will briefly discuss the history of cohabitation in both Western and Eastern Europe, since the late sixteenth century. The Council of Trent (1545–1563) forms a good starting point, as it stipulated that a public ceremony performed by a priest, in the presence of witnesses and after consecutive proclamations of the banns, constituted a valid marriage. Next, we will discuss to what extent historical patterns have persisted and are still traceable in the current forms and regional variations of cohabitation. In our review, we integrate the findings in the papers collected in this Special Issue. Finally, we will conclude with an inventory of future research questions and prospects. We will begin, however, with the problem faced by all scholars working on this topic: the lack of reliable sources.

2. 'A dark area': methodological problems in the history of cohabitation

In his seminal work *For better, for worse* John Gillis (1985) presents estimates of the numbers of consensual unions, although he frankly admits that it is 'a dark area that cannot easily be determined' (p. 111). More recently, Pat Thane (2013) is just as cautious: 'The best we can say is that, as yet, we simply do not know how many people lived together in unmarried relationships before the recent past' (p. 246). Why is it so difficult to find cohabiting couples?

Cohabitation can be defined as marriage-like relations in which there has been no marriage ceremony but in which the partners live together. As said, the obvious source to look for such relations is the census, but this is not of very much use. First of all, an unmarried couple could co-reside with others and not be recognizable as such. Second, they could easily hide their status by claiming to be already married, or by describing one of the partners as servant, housekeeper, boarder or lodger (Brunet, 2010; Matovic, 1986, p. 405). Brunet and Bideau (2010) even found a couple in nineteenth-century Lyon who presented themselves to the census-takers as mother and son. Another source is the civil registration of vital events. In countries which retained the French civil codes after the Napoleonic era, or adopted them afterwards, clear and comparable administrative procedures and documents of birth and marriage exist, including the recognition and legitimization of children born out of wedlock. By recognizing a child, a father claimed paternity and accepted the obligation of maintenance of the child, who, in turn, could inherit from him (although less than a fully legitimate child). Some scholars have thus deduced the frequency of cohabitation from the percentage of illegitimate children that were recognized by their fathers (Berlanstein, 1980, p. 365; Frey, 1978, p. 20; Kaplow, 1978). Shorter (1971, p. 255), however, saw recognition as an easy way for men to abscond and to avoid their family responsibilities. In his view, only subsequent marriage, by which the children were legitimized, offers insight into premarital cohabitation. However, cohabiting couples could decide not to marry or to recognize their child (Brunet, 2010). Some couples placed their children in other homes, e.g. with their parents, only to legitimate them much later (Matovic, 1986, p. 409). 'Legitimizing' marriages could take place many years after the birth of the children, which might also indicate that a man other than the biological father married the mother and 'adopted' the children through recognition. Furthermore, several studies of the addresses on certificates of 'legitimizing' marriages indicate that such marriages offer no conclusive evidence for cohabitation. Kok (1991) found that only half of the couples legitimating a child (in the city of Haarlem 1825–1833) shared the same address. But even those who did share an address might not have lived together *before* their marriage. Brunet and Bideau (2010) tried to link 498 Lyonese marrying couples (1876–1886) who had indicated the same address on their marriage certificate (out of a total of 8100 couples) to census listings of 1876, 1881 and 1886. Only 200 were actually found, and 123 of them could be described as cohabitants (also Ratcliffe, 1996). Population registers, which existed in the nineteenth century in Belgium, The Netherlands and Italy, can be seen as continuously updated censuses. Thus, addresses of single mothers mentioned in birth certificates can be checked for signs of cohabitation. For The Netherlands, this procedure yields a range of 3% (in rural communities) to 20% (in large cities) of unmarried single mothers living in a consensual union in the nineteenth century (Kok, 1991). The illegitimacy ratios in The Netherlands were very low, with just a few percent of all children born out of wedlock. Thus, it is not surprising that among all single women (with and without children) in the city of Haarlem in the first half of the nineteenth century less than 1% were found to be cohabiting (de Haan & Stam, 1986).

Several scholars assumed that single mothers who gave birth to more than one child must have been cohabiting (e.g. Fine, 1988, p. 433). Such mothers were often responsible for a large share of all illegitimate children (e.g. Blaikie, 1993; Viazzo, 1986). But studies of 'repeaters' show that, when the fathers of their children were known, they were often from different men (Brunet, 2010, p. 53; Kok, 1991, p. 53; Reay,1996, p. 187). Also, fathers of children of 'repeating' women were not more likely to declare the child than other fathers of illegitimate children (Kok, 1991, p. 53).

Even with proper administrative systems of housing and declarations of births and marriages in place, we will not be able to arrive at reliable estimations of the frequency of cohabitation, at least not covering long periods of time and large areas. Clearly, this is even more difficult in the period before the nineteenth century. Furthermore, percentages tell us little about the actual motivations of people to forgo marriage in a period of moral condemnation. Scholars therefore have often used other sources to study the background, characteristics, and motives of cohabiting couples.

When cohabitation was a criminal offence, which was the case in many Western European countries until around 1800, we can find prosecuted couples in the court records (e.g. Sogner, 2003; van der Heijden, 2014). Churches continued the surveillance of morals much longer, and information is to be found in the minutes of, for instance, Calvinist Scottish or Dutch presbyteries (Mitchison & Leneman, 1989; Roodenburg, 1990) or in the files of the English Church ('bawdy') courts (Tarver, 1995). In the nineteenth century, charitable organizations bent on 'civilizing' the poor became interested in the situation of cohabiting couples. One of the most successful was the *Société de Saint-François Régis* that put an end to thousands of Parisian concubinages. In the period 1826–1854, this society alone was responsible for more than 7% of all marriages in Paris (Ratcliffe, 1996, p. 323). In The Netherlands, as in other countries, this organization was also active, but it operated on a smaller scale. In Amsterdam the volunteers assisted with only several dozens of marriages per year. The records of the organization contain interesting information on cohabitants, but perhaps even more on the mindset of the volunteers. For instance, in 1868 the chair of the department in the town of Hoorn proudly reported to the head office having succeeded in separating an elderly couple, who had lived together for 20 years with several children, and added that 'we hope that with God's blessing they will secure a legal wedding within a couple of days' (Kok, 1991, p. 80). Information on characteristics and motives can also be found in court cases of couples that secured a (bigamous) marriage (Frost, 1997) or that committed serious crimes (Frost, this issue). Finally, information can be found in contemporary surveys into the situation of unmarried mothers and their children. From the late nineteenth century onwards, many nations collected statistics and organized surveys to prepare or monitor laws intended to improve the health and well-being of children. For instance, publications in Sweden (1916, see Hwang & Broberg, 2009) and The Netherlands (Centraal Bureau voor Maatschappelijk Hulpbetoon, 1923) reported on remarkable studies on life courses of illegitimate children. The situation of their mothers (married, cohabiting, single) was included. Other surveys offer less information on cohabitation, as they focus on single mothers with information culled from institutional records (e.g. Kammerer, 1918) or from paternity suits (e.g. Overdiep, 1955). Overall, sources providing information on the lives of cohabiting couples are rare, disparate, and suffering in differing degrees from selection bias. Couples that stayed under the radar of church control, that remained childless, did not commit crimes, and did not need social assistance, remain largely unobserved.

As in Western Europe, Eastern European researchers have access to very limited quantitative data bases and statistics on cohabitation. It appears that Hungary and Poland are the few rare exceptions in this regard. During the census of 1970 in Hungary, a special family status category, 'partners in life' was introduced which identified cohabitating people. Thanks to this identification, today we have the numbers of cohabitating couples in Hungary from the 1970 and 1980 censuses and the microcensus of 1984 (Carlson & Klinger, 1987, p. 89). The mentioned censuses in Hungary give us statistics about married, divorced and single cohabitating men and women. Some of the censuses conducted in

Poland also identified informal unions that in 1988 made up 1.3% of all marriages, 1.7% in 1995 and 2.2% of all marriages in Poland in 2002 (Matysiak, 2009, p. 216).

After the Second World War and up to the demise of the communist regimes, statistical data about cohabitation in East European countries practically did not exist, as this kind of marital form was unacceptable and unregistered. An example of extreme negative attitudes towards cohabitation is Albania, where even after the fall of the Communist regime cohabiting couples were stigmatized, and where short-term cohabitation was akin to prostitution. According to Albanian researchers, women who had cohabitated and did not marry ended up choosing emigration and resolved never to return to their homeland (Murzaku & Dervishi, 2003, p. 251). As Plakans and Lipša (this issue) note, the censuses held in the Soviet Union after the Second World War in 1959, 1970, 1979, and 1989 contained only traditional married life categories and as such cohabiting couples were left uncategorized: 'married'/'single'/'widower', with 'divorced' as a possible category in some cases.

A similar situation regarding lack of statistical registration data remained in Eastern Europe after 1990 which is why the absolute majority of studies about cohabitation are based on qualitative studies, surveys, interviews, individual-level rates and so on (see Gerber & Berman, 2010; Hoem, Kostova, Jasilioniene, & Mureşan, 2009; Kasearu & Kutsar, 2011; Legkauskas & Stankevičienė, 2009; Leinartė, 2012b; Liefbroer & Dourleijn, 2006; Sobotka, Šťastná, Zeman, Hamplová, & Kantorová, 2008; Stankūnienė, 2003; etc.). Often, such surveys about cohabitation involve tens of thousands of people. For example, in Hungary in 2001–2002 a total of 16,363 people were surveyed (Aassve, Billari, & Spéder, 2006, p. 137). Although the various kinds of non-census surveys and specialized 'sociological' inquiries are instructive on these diverse cohabitation situations, they do not allow for the analysis of cohabitation processes in the long-term perspective.

Illegitimate children, on the other hand, were always much better registered in Eastern Europe, starting with nineteenth-century statistics. That is why researchers often use these statistics as a reference point for the analysis of cohabitation. Yet these statistics rarely distinguish between children born to cohabiting couples and children born to single women (Perelli-Harris & Gerber, 2011).

The most important source for determining the numbers of cohabiting people in nineteenth-century East European Catholic communities, at least in Tsarist Russia, are the so-called 'Trials on Depraved Lifestyles' that were scrutinized by the Consistory's ecclesiastical court. Cohabiting families who were in illegitimate marriages for certain objective reasons put forward their cases: due to obstacles in Canon law, legally binding earlier marriages or current separation which banned one from forming a new family. The plaintiffs in the 'Trials on Depraved Lifestyles' cases were usually legal spouses. Seeking the assistance of spiritual leaders or the police, they aimed to punish their former spouse, to tear apart their new family, and to return them to their earlier (legally binding) family. The 'Trials on Depraved Lifestyles' cases are especially important in estimating the number of cohabiting couples and their prevalence over time.

Meanwhile, common census-like materials from the nineteenth century like *Status Animarum* only identified the traditional family form, or people's relationship with the head of the family. Informal marriages were reflected neither in household composition lists nor in the first tsarist Russian census of 1897. Plakans and Lipša (this issue) say about the tsarist Russian province of Latvia: 'most of these eighteenth- and nineteenth-century microdata about coresidence come from fiscal censuses called "revisions of souls", and the enumerators who prepared the revision had little interest in probing the subtleties of personal relationships within a coresidential unit'. It can be assumed that a similar mist hangs over cohabitation practices from the eighteenth and nineteenth centuries in other regions of Eastern Europe as well. In the next sections we will discuss how historians, despite the lack of proper statistical material, have interpreted cohabitation in Western and Eastern Europe.

3. The experience of cohabitation in historical Western Europe

3.1. Motives for marriage and cohabitation

Notwithstanding they are rare, disparate and selective, qualitative sources, in combination, do provide us with information on the most common motives of people to cohabit. From the late sixteenth century until well into the twentieth century, churches and governments actively persecuted, or at least discouraged, cohabitation. Couples skipping the official and unofficial *rites de passage* that made them full members of their communities had a lot to lose, so it seems. What were the reasons for choosing cohabitation instead of marriage? In this section, we provide a brief overview of the history of cohabitation in Western Europe, focusing on two questions. First, which factors affected the *desirability* of official marriage in comparison with cohabitation? Second, which factors affected the *feasibility* of official marriage? We assume that the higher the relative desirability of marriage and the higher its feasibility, the lower the incidence of cohabitation in a given period or region will be.

Why and when was official marriage more *desirable* than the alternative of cohabitation? First, marriage offered social as well as legal status to spouses as well as their children, which was, until recently, mostly denied to cohabitants. Second, marriage allowed couples to avoid state and church sanctions against cohabitation. Third, the state could offer specific material benefits to married couples and withhold them from cohabiting ones. Last, marriage might be perceived as being more stable, offering more security, and being proof of a greater commitment than cohabitation. In other words, the symbolic value of an official marriage was higher. And when was official marriage more *feasible*? First, when there were no legal obstacles to getting married. Such obstacles ranged from stipulations on prohibited degrees of kinship to laws against marriages of the poor. Second, marriage was more feasible when the costs of a wedding were rather low, which depended on the expectations of the community and the real wages of the couple. Third, marriage was more feasible when the official procedures were relatively simple, and, for instance, also facilitated access to marriage for foreign migrants. Last, the feasibility of marriage increased when it was not tied to the life cycle transitions of other persons, for instance to the relinquishing of headship of a household in old age (or even at death) of the parents. Below, we will discuss these factors in greater detail.

3.2. The desirability of marrying officially

Getting married was, for a long time in human history, a major *rite de passage* and marker of adulthood. Permanent celibates were often subjected to the derision of their peers (Chambers-Schiller, 1984; Froide, 2005; Israel, 2002; van Poppel, 1992). The issue at stake here, is, of course, what defined a proper marriage in the eyes of the community? And who exactly constituted the community? Did sub-communities exist with different norms and sanctions with respect to marriage?

After the Council of Trent (1545–1563), a properly proclaimed public ceremony performed by a priest in the presence of witnesses came to define an official and valid marriage, but in various European regions older notions of marriage survived for several centuries after Trent. Betrothals or vows of marriage, especially in a public ceremony, may have given a couple the same social standing in their community as those that went on to church to repeat their vows in front of a priest, but what about legal status? Official marriage defined the statuses of husband and wife, and of children versus their parents, in terms of obligations and rights, e.g. to one another's property. Illegitimate children had no access to property, and therefore had lower chances of marriage. Moreover, illegitimate boys were not accepted as apprentices in the guilds, although governments such as in Denmark tried to outlaw this exclusion (Telste, 2009). The negative consequences of an illegitimate status lasted well into the twentieth century. For instance, in The Netherlands illegitimate sons could not be exempted from military service (Overdiep, 1955, p. 49).

Within Western Europe, there is a distinction between countries where the rules of Trent were followed quickly and strictly and other nations where it took more time. In England the canonic rules of Trent had never been formally backed up by legislation, leaving room for cohabiting couples. However, their common-law marriages, outlawed by Hardwicke's Marriage Act of 1753, appear to have enjoyed no legal status (Probert, 2009, pp. 75–76). In Scotland, 'irregular marriages' based only on the mutual consent of couples persisted and were considered valid. It seems to have been a rare but accepted recourse for couples who did not wish to be married by the clergy, which was the only legal option until 1940 (Smout, 1981). Especially in Lutheran countries, children from betrothed couples held the same rights as children from married couples, at least for a long time (Fauve-Chamoux, 2011). An example is the case of Sweden. The church tried to incorporate the betrothal in one single ceremony, but in practice betrothals and church weddings remained parallel forms of marriage until the eighteenth century. The marriage code in the Act of 1734 made the church ritual the only lawful form of marriage, but still the (public) betrothal followed by copulation was respected in the curious legal form of 'incomplete marriage' (Sellin, 1922). This means that deserted partners as well as the children were treated as if the intended wedding had actually taken place, thus they were given the same rights to property inheritance as legally married partners and legitimate children (Lundh, 2003; also for Norway, Sogner, 2003). In the perception of local communities in several regions in Sweden, betrothal remained the crucial transition. In northern Sweden, the actual living together of an unmarried couple was celebrated by a village feast called *skjuta på björn* (shooting at the bear) (Marks, 1994).

The consequences of not marrying were different for men and women. On the one hand, not being married was riskier for women than for men. Until the eighteenth century, women made pregnant after a promise of marriage could still have their honour restored, and their child financially supported, through a paternity suit. But many countries tightened the procedures proving that promises had been exchanged. For instance, Norway accepted only public promises after 1734 (Telste, 2009, p. 177). Countries that adopted the French Civil Code banned paternity suits wholesale. In many areas, these suits were reinstated in the first decades of the twentieth century, on behalf of the children. Possibly, the lack of possibilities to enforce legal claims on the male partner might have made women more reluctant to enter into cohabitation (Leffingwell, 1892, p. 48). On the other hand, a woman might have had good reasons to choose cohabitation over marriage if she had more assets or more income than her prospective husband. Through marriage, men became the legal guardians of women, and gained the right to control their wives' savings and income. In the Swedish so-called 'incomplete marriage' form (see above), the husband did not become the legal guardian of his wife and children and could not exercise the right of the master of the household (Matovic, 1986, p. 27). In England as well, women had been made legally incapable by Hardwicke's Act, and by not marrying they could retain control over their property (Burguière & Lebrun, 1996, p. 136)

In every Western European society, sub-communities existed which had their own definitions of marriage and cohabitation. When travelling groups of pedlars or workers such as chimney sweeps consisted of men and women, sexual relations would be regulated through customs of their own. Dutch navvies working on canal digging or land reclamation were accompanied by women doing their washing and cooking. Their common-law marriages were sealed by 'jumping the well-hook', which became one of the terms for cohabitation in The Netherlands (Kok, 1991). Likewise, people such as Dutch knife grinders had their own practice (the 'marriage under the oaks' with a special knife grinder's formulary), and a study of illegitimacy in one inland province (1912–1940) revealed that more than a third of cohabitations could be ascribed to the small group of itinerants (Overdiep, 1955, p. 35). Sogner (2003, p. 225) stresses the similarities between vagrant and 'ordinary' marriages, but 'The economic, or maybe rather the cultural, incentive to set up an ordinary [...] marriage was evidently lacking'.

Avoiding sanctions against cohabitation has been a powerful stimulus to seek official marriage. Countries, such as the Calvinist Netherlands, adopting the Church's vision of a morally pure community could be very severe in their prosecution of cohabitation as a form of 'fornication'. Dutch couples caught would have to pay a heavy fine, but they were often acquitted when they could prove that their intended marriage had been delayed and they then married quickly. However, those that persisted were banished for 10 to 12 years (Van der Heijden, 1998; 2014). In France, and other Catholic countries, cohabitation was also punished harshly, in contrast to England, as we have seen (Laslett, 1965). Cohabitation was no longer deemed a criminal offence in countries following the French Civil Code (early nineteenth century), but authorities still had many ways of disciplining cohabitants. For instance (Dutch) juvenile courts threatened out-of-home placement unless the parents married (Overdiep, 1955, p. 51). In Scandinavian countries illegitimacy and cohabitation remained punishable for a longer period. A Swedish 'guilty' couple had to pay a fine to the church which corresponded to about one month's pay for a farmhand (Matovic, 1986, p. 26). In Norway, persecution of cohabiting couples was, after 1812, limited to those who had more than two children. Interestingly, cohabitation remained in the Norwegian Penal Code until 1972 (Sogner, 2003). In her contribution to this issue, 'Cohabitation from illegal to institutionalized practice: The Case of Norway 1972–2010', Liv Siltevik describes how Norway abolished the concubinage paragraph and moved on to become one of the world's first nations to realize institutional equality between cohabitation and marriage.

The churches had their own ways of punishing cohabiting couples, apart from informing the police (when this was still possible). For instance in Sweden, unmarried mothers had to be 'purified', which means she had to admit her sins to the parishioners in the church. In 1741, this was changed to a private ceremony, in which she had to face only the minister. The system was abolished in 1855 (Brändström, 1996). In Calvinist countries, such as The Netherlands, couples found guilty of fornication were banned from the Eucharist, and were excommunicated when they persisted (Roodenburg, 1990). According to Ehmer (2002, p. 319) the strict control of premarital sexuality by several religious groups (Calvinists, Catholics in Ireland and southern Europe, Muslims and Jews) had been very successful, in the sense that people had internalized the norms.

Cohabitants could also face sanctions from their community (e.g. through *charivaris*), their kin, and their employers. For instance, in small French industrial towns, such as Le Creusot, employers put pressure on their workers to marry (Fauve-Chamoux, 2011). On the other hand, in many European working-class communities cohabitation was not frowned upon, as long as one behaved as ordinary couples, as is shown in Ginger Frost's contribution in this issue '"As If She Was My Own Child": Cohabitation, Community, and the English Criminal Courts, 1855–1900' (also, Abrams, 1993, p. 89). European family systems differ to the degree in which adult children depended on parental approval and support (Reher, 1998). It is likely that in regions with strong family ties the diffusion of cohabitation in the twentieth century was delayed, until the parents themselves had accepted or even experienced it (Di Giulio & Rosina, 2007).

Cohabiting couples missed many of the material benefits available to married ones. Unmarried partners could not benefit from pensions or allowances, such as provided to the dependants of soldiers. In the first half of the twentieth century, social and family policies were geared to improving the situation of families. Sometimes, the aim was to give a boost to the nation's birth rate, sometimes to reinforce traditional, patriarchal relations (Therborn, 2004). The benefits, such as marriage loans, maternity leave and child allowances were not granted to cohabiting couples. Cohabiting couples in, for instance, The Netherlands and Scotland were not eligible for social services, such as public housing or unemployment allowances for dependants (Overdiep, 1955, p. 50; Smout, 1981, p. 227). However, some policies had the unintended consequence of stimulating consensual unions. Examples are laws removing married women from public service and ending widows' pensions on remarriage.

Apart from having social, legal and financial advantages, official marriage had symbolic value and promised more protection, stability and endurance, if only because getting divorced was costly and difficult until the second half of the twentieth century. Especially for women who, after divorce, had no income to support themselves, this might have been an important reason to press for marriage. Frost (1997) describes how English women tried to get their relationship (with separated men) legalized, even at the risk of being persecuted for bigamy: 'The ceremony, then, must have had an attraction beyond the mere practical, giving a sense of permanence, public proof of a partnership, and community acceptance' (p. 295). In the 1970s when divorce rates surged and marriage lost its aura of stability and permanence, it may also have lost its comparative advantage of offering more permanence. Indeed, some social scientists see cohabitation as a 'strategic long-term response' to the prevalent divorce culture (Hiekel & Keizer, 2015, p. 213).

3.3. The feasibility of marrying officially

Many cohabiting couples, perhaps the majority, would have been perfectly happy to marry, were it not for insuperable obstacles preventing them from doing so. One obstacle could be the parents, who, in several countries, still had to consent to the wedding of their adult children. Also, marriages were prohibited among kin (either consanguinal or affinal) by elaborate rules on forbidden degrees. The rules were sometimes hard to comprehend and state and church authorities sometimes interpreted them differently. For instance, in seventeenth-century Netherlands, the church and the state debated whether marrying the widow of a brother of one's late wife should be prohibited (van der Heijden, 2014). More common was the situation of widowers with young children, who were often assisted by – but could not marry – their sisters-in-law (Overdiep, 1955). In Roman Catholic countries a divorce could not be obtained, and remarriage after separation was not possible (Fauve-Chamoux, 2011). Cohabitation of couples of which one or both of the partners was still married was treated as adultery. In protestant countries, it was somewhat easier to obtain a divorce, especially after adultery was proven or admitted. However, remarriage with the person deemed guilty of adultery was still forbidden (in The Netherlands until 1970, de Smidt & Gall, 1985). Another obstacle was the disappearance of a partner, which happened frequently to sailors' wives. It meant the woman had to wait at least five years before remarrying. The law also put obstacles in the way of mixed couples (especially Jews and Christians), couples who for religious reasons did not accept civil marriage (such as Italian Catholics during the conflict with the Vatican in the 1860s), professional military (because of the limited funds for widows' pensions) and, in several regions of Europe, the poor. In Germany, Switzerland and Austria governments aiming to curtail the expansion of pauperism subjected marriages to strict conditions. Applicants had to prove themselves to be of impeccable moral conduct (which could mean pregnant women were not allowed to marry), they had to demonstrate sufficient means of sustaining a household, and the officials had to be convinced that there was demand for their labour (Head-König, 1993). Districts with such marriage restrictions were also the districts with the highest levels of illegitimacy. In Germany these restrictive laws were repealed in the 1860s, out of concern for the staggering illegitimacy ratios. Indeed, the ratios fell off rapidly after that (Guinnane & Ogilvie, 2014; Kraus, 1979).

For poor people, the costs of a wedding could be prohibitive, especially when a lavish feast was expected. In the Swedish countryside, weddings could sometimes attract as many as several hundred guests. Thus, couples might have to save a long time for the wedding (Lundh, 2003; Matovic, 1986). In addition, church and state officials had to be paid for their services. Governments of, for instance, France and The Netherlands, reacted to the nineteenth-century rise of proletarian cohabitation by creating the option of free marriages (Burguière & Lebrun, 1996; Kok, 1991). However, for some workers, already the costs of renting a suit and of forgoing a day's wage could be a reason not to marry (Kok, 1991, pp. 54–55). In Scotland, 'irregular marriages' became more popular after 1870, as they offered more privacy, were cheaper, and could be arranged quicker, which all suited the needs of a mobile workforce (Smout, 1981, p. 226). Economic necessity, for instance of pooling the rent, might have been a motive to start the cohabitation in the first place (Matovic, 1986, p. 398). The very high levels of illegitimacy in the first half of the nineteenth century in cities such as Stockholm, Prague and Paris have been attributed to low standards of living. When real incomes started to rise, especially after 1875, illegitimacy rates began to drop, indicating that the cultural value of marriage had not diminished, and was even spreading among the lower classes (Ehmer, 2002, p. 320).

Other barriers were of a purely bureaucratic kind. Before a marriage could be secured, the French Civil Code stipulated that documents were shown proving one was of legal age, not still married, that parents had consented to the wedding, that one was not in the military, etc. All in all, the number of different documents to be amassed could amount to more than 20. Meeting these requirements was especially problematic for foreign migrants, who had to enter into prolonged communication with bureaucrats in their native communities. The already mentioned society of *Saint-François Régis* was very helpful in dealing with problems of this kind.

Finally, farming couples in the stem family regions in Scandinavia or the Alps frequently waited for marriage until they came into landownership, as successor to a farm (e.g. in Norway, see Sogner, 2003). Marks (1994) noticed that when, in the 1930s government regulations facilitated agricultural credits, illegitimacy declined rapidly in Northern Sweden. In Austria, the designated heir and his future bride lived on the parents' farm, awaiting succession and marriage. Illegitimate births were accepted and often even welcomed (Kytir & Münz, 1986).

4. Cohabitation in the Eastern European past

4.1. Marrying officially versus motives for cohabitation

Up until the beginning of the twentieth century, in terms of at least one aspect, the history of cohabitation in Eastern Europe differed from the West European examples. It appears that in the past in East European countries, cohabitation was rarely or never justified as a prelude to marriage. Cohabitation in East European communities was often caused by bigamy, as usually one or both of the men and women in cohabitation were already married. In many cases cohabitation in Eastern Europe in the nineteenth century and earlier can be treated as an informal and alternative way of resolving legal problems where it was impossible to officially enter into marriage or to dissolve a marriage.

The history of cohabitation and bigamy in the Grand Duchy of Lithuania (GDL) can be traced back to the fifteenth century (by then, the GDL was the largest state in Europe. Until 1772 it included Lithuania, Belarus and a larger part of Ukraine). In the GDL it mostly stemmed from the legal confusion between custom law, the canon law of the Orthodox Church and the secular legal code outlined in the Statute of Lithuania. According to the Polish historian Juliush Bardach, this legal confusion allowed Orthodox believers in the GDL to marry on the grounds of custom law. In such cases marriages took place in a home environment, not in a church, and not in the presence of a priest. Wanting to dissolve such a union, it sufficed to declare one's desire in public. In this way, marriages formed according to customary law opened the way to cohabitation as marriage and divorce essentially did not require legal validity (Bardach, 1970). In the seventeenth century, among the Orthodox population of Vilnius city there were also cases of cohabitation/bigamy where marriages or divorces were carried out according to customary law (Frick, 2013, pp. 229–248).

Cohabitation in Eastern Europe is particularly closely related to the history of marriage. For example, according to the 1836 Law on Marriage as well as the Civil Code of Tsarist Russia, marriage and divorce matters were handled by the Church, while property issues of the separated couple were deliberated in the civil courts. So in the Tsarist Russian Empire, Catholic marriages and separations were regulated according to the Council of Trent norms. According to the canon code of the Catholic Church, dissolution of a legally binding marriage was impossible and only the death of one of the spouses could terminate the marriage sacrament. The only form of complete judicial divorce that was sanctioned by the jurisdiction of the Catholic Church was the acknowledgement of a legally invalid marriage as void, that is, recognizing its annulment. In the everyday life of Catholics, this meant that canon law testified to the very limited opportunities for separation and divorce (annulment of marriage) up until 1917 when civil registration was introduced in Soviet Russia (Leinarte, 2012a). In 1863–1904 in the Kovno governorate, which was the largest Catholic part of tsarist Russia, only 89 requests for annulment of marriage were registered, and out of these, 77 court rulings handed down a negative verdict. At the time, the Kovno governorate had a population of around a million inhabitants.

In cases of failed family life, cohabitation in tsarist Russia was practically unavoidable. It is interesting that in Tsarist Lithuania, Latvia and Estonia, cohabitation was accepted and justifiable even though the surnames of men and women in cohabitation were different, and their children would be registered as illegitimate. Even in their appeals made to the ecclesiastical court for separation or the annulment of an earlier legally valid marriage, the plaintiffs would usually indicate that they had now 'formed a new marriage', despite being fully aware that the sacrament of marriage had not been granted and that they were indeed living in illegal cohabitation (Leinarte, 2012). In the nineteenth century, priests themselves would justify unavoidable cohabitation or bigamy to some extent. In presenting the ecclesiastical court information about cohabiting couples in their parish, clergymen would often come across as confused: 'I have the honour to inform the consistory about the illegal life of the lesser noble Herbertas Gedgaudas, who married the already married peasant Domicelė Daubarienė' (Marcinkevičienė [Leinarte], 1999, p. 171).

Catholics in Tsarist Russia were also forced into cohabitation in cases where a spouse had disappeared. Men and women who were abandoned by their other halves and who wanted to form new legal families faced enormous bureaucratic hurdles, because they had to prove that their missing husbands (or wives) had died or could not be located throughout the entire Russian Empire. Searches for missing spouses were conducted in a centralized way, a task which demanded great outlays of time, effort and financial means. As a consequence, the abandoned husbands and wives usually entered into cohabitation arrangements, just because work had to be done on the farm.

In late eighteenth- to early twentieth-century tsarist Russia, belonging to different religious communities often led to cohabitation. The different religions and confessions had different regulations for marriage and divorce. Jews recognized only one form of divorce – a complete legal divorce; this did not demand a complicated divorce case, and depended entirely on the personal will of the couple. From the moment when a husband would give his wife a divorce act in the presence of a rabbi and witnesses and declare: 'You are hereby divorced from me and available to any other man', the formalities of a Jewish divorce would be completed. From that moment on, both the wife and the husband could enter into new, legally valid marriages. But that does not mean that Jewish divorces were a flippant matter, as strict regulations applied to the property relationships of the separating couples. Having this freedom of choice in their personal lives, Jews could make conscious decisions and avoid cohabitation. Naturally enough, in Tsarist Russia official legal divorce amongst Jews was a common phenomenon. Based on the data of the 1897 census, in the Kovno governorate, there were 434 divorced individuals amongst the Jewish population, and 846 both separated and divorced amongst the Lithuanian and Polish speaking population (Catholics and Protestants) combined. It can be assumed that Jews entered into cohabitation on fewer occasions than did Catholics. The Evangelical Lutheran, Reformist and Old Believer churches recognized several reasons for divorce; however, obtaining a divorce was nevertheless a difficult procedure. The statistics for illegitimate newborns are inadequate to determine cohabitation numbers because there is no way of finding out how many were born into cohabiting families and how many were born to single mothers. Nevertheless, the number of Catholic, Orthodox and Lutheran illegitimate newborns is relatively larger than the same figure for Jews. When comparing the data on illegitimate children born to the contemporary main faiths in Lithuania, the numbers are as shown in Table 1.

Shorter, Knodel and Van de Walle (1971) raised the hypothesis about cohabitation as a usual form of married life among Slavic peasants (though, so far there is no clearer data concerning this aspect). According to these scholars, children born in unlawful but stable consensual unions were not recognized by civil laws and the Church, and were registered as illegitimate, but were considered as legitimate by their Slavic communities. They assumed that in the nineteenth century, among Slavic rural communities, the understanding of marriage was different to that in Western societies. However, they presented a similar example from Western Europe. According to Italian scholars a majority of children born between 1866 and 1871 were registered as illegitimate because their parents only had had a religious marriage, which was not registered in accordance

Table 1.   Illegitimate births in Lithuania per 1000 of total population, by religion.

1899	Total population	Total illegitimate children	Number of illegitimate children per 1000 inhabitants
Catholic	1,158,530	1906	1.6
Jewish	301,224	21	0.1
Orthodox	39,490	71	1.8
Lutherans	46,577	89	1.9

Source: *Памятная книжка Ковенской губернии 1899 года*. Ковно: Ковенский Губернский стат. ком., 1900. [Translation: Statistics on Kovno governorate for the year 1899. Kovno: Statistical Committee of Kovno governorate, 1900.]

with the usual civil procedures. In this regard, Shorter, Knodel, and Van de Walle (1971) did not mention how nineteenth-century Italian society viewed these officially unregistered but stable unions and the children born into such families. We are safe to conclude that in some cases the existence of cohabitation in Eastern Europe is similar to the experiences of Western European societies.

In Tsarist Russia cohabitation was punishable and if a couple living in cohabitation was exposed, they would be forced to separate. In such cases, the police would demand that even families raising several children that had lived together for even a dozen or more years would still have to part ways. The exposed cohabitating men and women would be sentenced to perform penance by the ecclesiastical court, a situation that remained basically unchanged throughout the entire nineteenth century. The condemned individuals would have to spend seven or 14 days at the parish and pray every day: in turns, one day kneeling, the next day lying in the shape of the cross. On Mondays, Wednesdays and Fridays they had to follow a strict fast allowing only water and bread, and in this way prepare for 'the confession of their lives'. In addition, the priest had to hand down the strict precept that in the future the couple would not start to live together again (Marcinkevičienė [Leinarte], 1999, p. 167).

Financial calculations were another reason for cohabitation in Tsarist Russia, as annulment of a marriage required a fair sum of money. Plaintiffs had to present their request for divorce on armorial paper, which was expensive. Otherwise the consistory would not even consider their request. Each time the consistory replied to the plaintiff in writing, the latter had to pay for the paper used – 80 kopeks for two sheets. In addition, if the couple that had lived in an illegitimate marriage (i.e., one formed not abiding by Canon law) received an annulment, they would have to pay the court a fine ranging from 6 to 270 roubles. Strict norms and obstacles for Catholic marriages also pushed people into cohabitation. For example, cohabitants or former lovers could not validate a marriage. In this regard, neither penance nor the death of one's legitimate spouse granted the opportunity to move from cohabitation to marriage. Marriage was also forbidden if the couple were expecting a child as Canon law forbade marriage between former or existing bed-mates. Canon law also prohibited marriage between individuals having so-called religious bonds. These would include association between a godfather/godmother and their godchild.

Meanwhile, cohabitation in nineteenth-century Romania could be explained by early and often arranged marriages, a large number of unsuccessful marriages, as well as particularly difficult separation processes. For these reasons, mutually separated spouses and widows/widowers often started living in new, unregistered marriages (Bolovan & Pădurean, 2005). Strict wedding customs and custom law in Macedo-Romanian communities (A-Romanians and Megleno-Romanians) required that weddings be planned even before the couple's birth. In these communities, marriage planning, organization and the selection of a spouse had to follow strict rules and thus unavoidably encouraged cohabitation (Țîrcomnicu, 2009). Meanwhile in Transylvania in 1853 the Austrian Civil Code was accepted, as well as several other family-related laws that laid the foundation for different and more egalitarian wedding and interpersonal relationships. Unlike the Romanian Civil Law, the Austrian Civil Code foresaw much broader rights for married women (Pinca, 2009).

Cohabitation in Hungary in 1875–1914 can be explained by several factors, among them specific marriage registration rules and the mandatory registration of marriages, births and deaths introduced in 1895. Scholars believe that before 1895, young people from different religious backgrounds registered their marriages according to civil procedures in areas where there were facilities for this to take place. Yet when the newlyweds returned to their homes, their marriages would not be recognized and the children born to such unions would be registered in church birth registers as illegitimate. In Hungary, the status of cohabitation was almost equal to that of official marriage. Such consensual unions were recognized by village communities as a couple that happened to live together. They would be invited to village community festivals, and the children would be identified in the name of the father (Ajus & Henye,1994).

Bolshevik Russia was the first modern state in the world which consciously encouraged cohabitation. A free union of two people based on romantic love, unbound by obligations, property relations or official registration became one of the state's symbols (Goldman, 1993, p. 34). Immediately after the Bolshevik Revolution in 1918 the Code on Marriage and the Family was passed which legalized *de facto* partnerships and divorces without identifying a reason (Wood, 1997). That is why already in the mid-1920s Russia had the highest number of divorces in Europe: it was 3 times greater than in Germany, 3.56 times greater than in France, and 26 times greater than in Wales or England. In 1926 in Moscow, every second couple that had registered their marriage ended up by divorcing, and could then freely enter into a new marriage or cohabitation. In 1926 a new Code on Marriage, the Family and Guardianship was passed in Russia, which continued to recognize *de facto* partnerships and further simplified the divorce procedure. Now an officially registered marriage could be dissolved at the request of one of the spouses without even announcing their decision to their other half. The book of biographical interviews by Anastasia Posadskya-Vanderbeck and Barbara Alpern has recorded numerous testimonies from Russian women who spent their married life in the 1920s and 1930s in Russia. The women recalled how easily men left their *de facto* partners and their common children (Alpern Engel & Posadskya-Vanderbeck, 1998). Cohabitation and bigamy in Bolshevik Russia of the time surprised no one, as the highest leaders of the Bolshevik party encouraged unregistered partnerships. Lenin's comrades in arms Inessa Armand and Aleksandra Kollontaj dreamt about the nationalization of motherhood in Russia, where women would be liberated from caring for children through the creation of children's towns and communal apartments with state-trained house-mistresses. However at the beginning of the 1930s, ever stricter commentary could be heard in the Soviet Union against such unbridled interpersonal relationships between men and women. That is, relationships without certification of an officially registered marriage and cohabitation were condemned more and more often. In 1936 in the newly passed Law on the Family, *de facto* partnerships were abolished, and only officially registered marriages were recognized, while the divorce process was tightened.

Meanwhile, the religious form of marriage remained in place in Lithuania until 1940. As Lithuanian society grew more modern in the interwar period, cohabitation developed into a relatively widespread phenomenon. More and more frequently, when faced with the issue of divorce or a new marriage, Church norms would be violated or confessional changes would occur, or marriage in another country. According to the data of various authors, there were from 8000 to 30,000 cohabiting men and women in interwar Lithuania (Marcinkevičienė [Leinarte], 1999).

4.2. Cohabitation after the Second World War

After the Second World War, the laws of a majority of East European countries regulated private and family life and limited the possibility of cohabitation. Nevertheless, regardless of the laws on marriage and divorce, the spread of cohabitation in Eastern Europe, i.e., in the Soviet Union and the Soviet bloc countries, was not identical. For example, in Soviet Estonia cohabitation could be compared to what was happening in Sweden or Denmark at the time. We should also note that the term cohabitation was used interchangeably with bigamy as was the case in earlier historical periods, as often cohabitating people were actually married. In some East European countries, for example in Hungary, cohabiting couples were identified by the special legal term 'partners in life'. This term meant that one or both partners in cohabitation could be married.

The spread of cohabitation after the Second World War in the USSR can be related to and explained in terms of not only the laws regulating marriage and divorce, but also the social policies in place. Welfare distribution in the USSR was centralized. That is, the arrangements for provision of citizens with a place, plots of land for the construction of an individual house, cars and some exclusive items were regulated by the state. When it came to the distribution of goods and services, families had priority. That is why cohabitation interfered with the organization and the normalization of everyday life, which generally required significant efforts in the USSR as it was (Legkauskas & Stankevičienė, 2009, p. 23).

From the early 1950s onwards, an increase in cohabitation in several Soviet republics could be noticed. This trend was confirmed by the changing approaches of Soviet citizens towards sexual relations before marriage. For example, if in 1972 45% of women in Russia had had sexual relations before marriage, by 1990 this figure had grown to 80%. Russians' attitudes towards cohabitation also changed. In 1990 98.2% of men aged 18 and 23, and 95.8% of women had a positive view of cohabitation (Legkauskas & Stankevičienė, 2009, p. 23). Family behaviour in Russia changed significantly after 1965 when the strict divorce law was liberalized. After changes to the law were introduced, around one-third of marriages ended in divorce, which also probably encouraged cohabitation. According to demographers' data, 20% of Russians born between 1920 and 1960 were in cohabitation arrangements during their first partnerships. On the other hand, around half of them would get married within one year, while two-thirds of cohabitating couples would register their marriage within three years. It is believed that unlike Estonia and Latvia where cohabitation grew from the beginning of the 1960s, in Russia it started to increase markedly only after 1984 (Gerber & Berman, 2010, p. 5).

Yet cohabitation in the European part of the USSR was not evenly distributed over the area. Cohabitation obviously flourished in Soviet Estonia and Latvia where from the 1950s the number of children born out of wedlock constantly grew. By the end of the 1980s, 25% of all newborns in Estonia and 18% of all newborns in Latvia were children born out of wedlock. Scientists explain that this is exclusively the byproduct of cohabitation, as children born to single mothers in Estonia and Latvia comprised no more than 6–10% of the total number of children born (Katus, Puur, Põldma & Sakkeus, 2007, p. 272). At the time in Soviet Lithuania, children born out of wedlock comprised around 7% of all newborns. Similar numbers of illegitimate children were recorded in pre-war Lithuania (Katus et al., 2007, p. 272). In the context of the Soviet republics and communist countries, Estonia was an exceptional case, as here cohabitation was more of a tradition than an exception. Two-thirds of Estonians born in 1924–1938 entered into marriage during their first partnership. Meanwhile over 50% of Estonians born in the 1940s and who formed their first partnerships sometime in the 1950s and early 1960s cohabitated. And cohabitation was a regular phenomenon among Estonians born in 1969–1973: only 11.2 men and only 5.9 women of this generation entered into marriages without having cohabited first (Katus et al., 2007, p. 267). According to cohabitation indicators from 1985, the three Baltic states could be attributed to traditions existing in different West European countries. Estonia and to some extent Latvia reflected the Scandinavian cohabitation model, whereas Lithuania could be grouped with Spain, Italy and Poland where cohabitation as a path to marriage was neither popular nor accepted (Katus et al., 2007, p. 270).

After the Second World War in Bulgaria, Hungary and Romania, much like in Russia, cohabitation started spreading after the 1960s with a marked increase noticeable from the 1980s. In effect, this cohabitation trend can be explained using the Second Demographic Transition (SDT) theory (Aassve et al., 2006, p. 130; Hoem et al., 2009, p. 242). During the census of 1970 in Hungary, 61,170 women were registered as living in cohabitation, or, by the legal term as 'partners in life'. This number made up 1.4% of all Hungarian women aged over age 15. In 1984 this percentage grew to 9%, when amongst the 92,350 registered cohabitating couples or 'partners in life', one-quarter (20,950) were couples of which the man or woman was still married (Carlson & Klinger, 1987, pp. 86, 89). This legal duality in effect means that at least until 1970–1984, cohabitation in Hungary was often identified as bigamy.

Opposite examples were Socialist Romania and Albania. The 'Law on Family' of the Republic of Albania did not contain any discriminating provisions against children born out of wedlock. The law of 1982 provided that 'Children born of unmarried parents enjoy the same rights and obligations as children born of married parents' (Murzaku & Dervishi, 2003, p. 245). However, cohabitating couples and their children were particularly discriminated against in Albania. They could risk losing their jobs or even punishment from living in the capital and other larger cities in Albania. In addition, cohabitating parents and their children experienced enormous stigmatization from their closest circle of friends and relatives, which is why they would try to hide this episode of their lives (Murzaku & Dervishi, 2003, p. 245). It appears that in Albania the family was understood as the foundation for a patriarchal order, whereas in Romania the family was seen as one of the essential tools of the communist ideology. The Family Code of Romania contained the main socialist principles on labour and family that were confirmed at the Eleventh Congress of the Romanian Communist Party in 1974. Cohabiting couples opposed the communist morale and could be summoned by party institutions. Cohabitation was also discouraged by the famous Decree no. 770 of 1 October 1966, named 'On regulating pregnancy interruption' (Padurean, 2009, pp. 521–542).

The spread of cohabitation across the map of Eastern Europe can be followed not by the political boundaries that were formed after the Second World War, but more by the traditional ethnic entities that were present in pre-war Europe. In the USSR, cohabitation first of all spread in Estonia and Latvia. In the Federation of Yugoslavia,

Slovenia was the leader in cohabitation, while in Czechoslovakia cohabitation had found its niche in northern Bohemia. In Communist Poland, this was the domain of those territories that had belonged to Germany before the war. Cohabitation spread in western Belarus and western Ukraine, i.e., in those territories that had belonged to Poland before the war. According to demographers, during the Second World War the population in these territories experienced major changes in family structure and thus became more open to non-traditional forms of establishing family relations (Klüsener, Perelli-Harris, & Sánchez Gassen, 2013, pp. 149, 152). Yet this cohabitation hypothesis does not explain why the scale of cohabitation was unreservedly greater in Estonia compared to Lithuania, even though both countries shared a practically identical history.

5. The revenge of history? Contemporary trends and historical legacies

From the late 1960s onwards, cohabitation began to spread rapidly in western countries, and is still on the increase. According to many social scientists, this remarkable development is part and parcel of the so-called Second Demographic Transition, a revolution in demographic behaviour leading to large and unpredictable demographic changes (Lesthaeghe, 1995; van de Kaa, 2001). Supposedly, this Transition is caused by value changes in society as people begin to realize 'post-materialist' needs, such as recognition, freedom of expression, and self-realization. Individualism and self-realization imply breaking free from restrictive interpersonal ties; people begin to divorce more often, to live alone more often, to cohabit, to have fewer or no children, etc. The possibility to fulfil these post-materialist needs stems from a number of important changes in post-war societies. First, it arises from the rise of the welfare states with their improved living standards and security through social legislation. Second, it is related to the arrival of efficient means of contraception (e.g. the pill), which disconnected sexuality and procreation. For couples who could control the arrival of children, their social and legal status (see above) was no longer part of the equation (Sweeney, Castro-Martín, & Mills, 2015). Third, the sexual revolution which disconnected marriage and sex played a role. Fourth, it was associated with women's economic and legal emancipation, which strongly reduced their dependency on their husbands. Women following a professional career tended to postpone having children (and marriage), which made cohabitation a logical option. Finally, the ongoing secularization removed, for large parts of the European populations, the moral objections to cohabitation. According to Lesthaeghe, the rise in cohabitation 'depends more strongly on moral acceptability and legitimacy rather than on the calculus of advantage' (Lesthaeghe, 2010, p. 227).

If cohabitation is indeed an integral part of the value changes described in the theory of the Second Demographic Transition (SDT), what does this mean for its recent and future development? Many social scientists working on SDT theory tend to extrapolate from the recent history of cohabitation in Scandinavia. In Scandinavian countries, three distinct stages could be discerned. First, a stage of diffusion in which cohabitation, still mainly a prelude to marriage, spread from small groups (e.g. urban intellectuals) to virtually all groups in society. Second, a stage of permanency, in which cohabitations lasted longer and were less often converted into marriage. Finally, there was a stage in which cohabitation and marriage were, for all intents and purposes, no longer distinguishable from one another (e.g. Kasearu & Kutsar, 2011; Matysiak, 2009; Sobotka & Toulemon, 2008). SDT theory predicts that all countries will, eventually, follow this sequence and that an international convergence in behavioural patterns will occur. Indeed, the spread of cohabitation is unmistakable and, in terms of percentages cohabiting and of ratios of illegitimate children, convergence can be detected (Lesthaeghe, 2010, 2014).

Several papers in our special issue contribute to the debate on whether the timing and geographical spread of the increase in cohabitation indeed prove the SDT claim that value changes are leading to the disappearance of all (demographic, social, legal, and cultural) differences between marriage and cohabitation. This debate revolves around (a) the impact of economic crisis, (b) the evaluation of values and attitudes), (c) postponed demographic behaviour), (d) the interpretation of life course patterns, and (e) the valuation of marriage. Below, we will elaborate on these issues.

(a) A first issue concerns the effect of economic crisis. Various scholars suggest that the spread of cohabitation in Eastern Europe, in terms of timing and the social groups in which it occurred, can be explained by economic crisis and social disruption in the post-Soviet era, rather than by the spread of individualistic values (Aassve et al., 2006, p. 148; Coleman, 2004; Kalmijn, 2007; Rotariu, 2009). One indication is that illegitimacy and cohabitation are especially prevalent among people with low levels of education living in the countryside. This 'pattern-of-disadvantage' interpretation of cohabitation (Lesthaeghe, 2014) suggests that it is, just as in the past, a proletarian reaction to adverse circumstances. However, some researchers claim that the crisis in Eastern Europe had already started in the 1980s. In addition, if the economic upheavals had a great impact on the decrease of marriages and the growth of cohabitation, then in Russia the number of marriages would have had to increase immediately after 1999 when the crisis lessened (Gerber & Berman, 2010, p. 7).

(b) A second question is how to evaluate attitudinal change. Scholars working on Eastern Europe do find, for instance in interviews, that cohabitants display modern values and attitudes (Hoem et al., 2009). However, this is not necessarily the same as SDT-type self-fulfilment. In her article 'The Unmarried Couple in Post-Communist Romania: A Qualitative Sociological Approach' Dohotariu (this issue) claims that after the decline of the communist regime in Romania, cohabitation was most likely affected neither by the SDT that had started back in the socialist times, nor by the socio-political and economic upheavals of the 1990s. In the author's opinion, cohabitation in post-communist Romania can be viewed as a completely new social phenomenon that has no link with the past and which has been initiated by democracy and gender equality. According to Dohotariu, in post-communist Romania cohabitation became a new form of interpersonal relationship.

(c) Third, the rise of cohabitation has been interpreted as a form of 'postponed behaviour'. The theory of 'Developmental Idealism' sees the spread of cohabitation as a postponed form of Western European family formation patterns (Thornton & Philipov, 2009). In their article 'Stigmatized Cohabitation in the Latvian Region of the Eastern Baltic Littoral: Nineteenth and Twentieth Centuries', Andrejs Plakans and Ineta Lipša support this theory on the transmission of the cohabitation process from Western to Eastern Europe. In their view, cohabitation in Latvia can be termed a twentieth-century social phenomenon that was accelerated by opened borders and the crumbling of Soviet ideology. According to the authors, the Latvian censuses after 1991 give evidence of this. On the other hand, the article by Aušra Maslauskaitė and Marė Baublytė, 'Education and transition from cohabitation to marriage in Lithuania' opposes the

Development Idealism theory. In these authors' views, in Soviet Lithuania there were all the necessary features of SDT: declarations of gender equality; a large number of women in higher education institutions, often outnumbering men; universal participation of women in the labour market; and the very weak influence of religion in society. Accordingly, the authors say that the spread of cohabitation in Lithuania after the fall of the regime in 1990 could hardly be explained as a delayed process from the West, as similar processes already existed in Soviet Lithuania.

(d) A fourth research strand looks at life course patterns to study whether cohabitation behaviour is converging across Europe. Several scholars study the sequences of cohabitation, pregnancy and marriage, and investigate to what extent transition rates from one stage to another become similar across countries. Does pregnancy everywhere accelerate the transition to marriage (Perelli-Harris et al., 2009)? It turns out that there are very different trajectories within Europe. For instance in The Netherlands, Germany, Switzerland and Flanders, marriage is still the preferred situation for the planning of children. In Eastern Europe, the rapid transition after pregnancy to either marriage or cohabitation points at limited access to reliable contraceptives, in other words, to the limited role of (efficient) planning. In England, pregnancy, especially of teenagers, often leads to cohabitation. Thus, the rise of illegitimate births across Europe is not the unequivocal outcome of the rise of 'modern' cohabitation. Cohabitation is associated with different stages in the life courses in different countries, and certainly does not replace marriage everywhere. A convergence of European life courses – in the sense that the 'choice biography' will dominate everywhere is not (yet) visible (Billari & Wilson, 2001). The research of Maslauskaitė and Baublytė (this issue) shows how in Lithuania, one of the countries with limited cohabitation traditions (along with Romania, Russia and Hungary), after 1990 as many as 80% of cohabiting couples went on to register their marriages. Their findings confirm those of other researchers in whose opinion cohabitation in Lithuania and Latvia generally ends in marriage (Katus et al., 2007, p. 270). In Poland as well cohabitation has become an important prelude to marriage, although the country did not have cohabitation traditions. After 1990, as many as 89% of cohabitating couples in Poland would marry within the course of three years (Matysiak, 2009, p. 223). Another example is the Czech Republic. Between 1975 and 1989 only 20–25% of couples in the Czech Republic cohabitated in the first year of their partnership. However, in the 1980s and the beginning of 1990 more than half of the married women in the Czech Republic did so when they were expecting their first child (Sobotka et al., 2008, p. 429). On the other hand, the situation in Russia and Bulgaria is very different, as almost half of the cohabitating couples in Russia in 1999–2003 and around 40% of cohabitating couples in Bulgaria did not marry (Philipov & Jasilioniene, 2008, p. 2078) which confirms that cohabitation was not a prelude to marriage in these two East European countries (see also on reasons for cohabitation in Russia: Potârcă, Mills, & Lesnard, 2013).

(e) Finally, researchers debate the valuation of marriage. A recent comparative project based on interviews with focus groups suggests that in most European countries (Eastern Germany being a noteworthy exception) marriage is still seen as qualitatively distinct from cohabitation. Marriage is perceived as a higher level of commitment; it stands for 'the real deal', the most durable expression of love. Cohabitation, either as a trial for testing compatibility or as a temporary recourse, is seen as subordinate to the marriage ideal (Perelli-Harris et al., 2014). The increase of cohabitation therefore does not imply a growing rejection of marriage. Marriages seem to be postponed more often, probably as a result of the global economic crisis. Prolonged cohabitation is thus a response to financial constraints and increased instability and insecurity. But there are still many regional differences in the value attached to marriage relative to cohabitation. Religion, especially Roman Catholicism, still colours the valuation of marriage. And we have seen that in familistic countries the opinion of the parents weighs heavier than elsewhere. Institutional path dependency may also play a role. In Western Germany and Austria, cohabitation is seen as a free, but premature, stage in the life courses of young adults, whereas marriage stands for adult responsibility. Perelli-Harris et al. (2014, p. 1055) suggest that this may reflect 'the long-standing reliance on the breadwinner model, which relies more heavily on women's dependence on men, especially through marriage. Marriage is a form of protection, and policies aimed at preserving marriage and the breadwinner model, for example, exempting married couples from taxes, reinforce the strength of the marital institution'.

Can we still trace the legacy of the past in the current developments in European cohabitation? This question is central in the analysis of geographic distribution of extramarital births in Sebastian Klüsener's 'Spatial Variation in Non-Marital Fertility across Europe in the 20th and 21st centuries: Recent Trends, Persistence of the Past, and Potential Future Pathways' (this issue). He concludes that, in the past 100 years, continuity is certainly visible, although it is fading. Moreover, the observed continuity seems to have different causes in different regions. Klüsener links regional family systems, the national differences in welfare arrangements (with breadwinner models associated with lower levels of illegitimacy), and different processes of secularization. In some regions, strong divergence from historical patterns has occurred, most notably in Bulgaria. Also, Eastern Europe seems to be witnessing a form of 'de-secularization' in which a revived interest in and power of the Church is associated with a return to traditional marriage.

It is clear that after, say, 1970, very much has changed. Marriage no longer constitutes the exclusive access to sexuality, reproduction, inheritance rights, adult status and social recognition. The meaning of marriage has been reduced to its symbolic role of representing lasting commitment. But that is not a negligible legacy. Furthermore, history seems to play a role in determining how long cohabitations will last, whether pregnancy will stimulate a conversion to marriage, and what social gradients exist in the duration and sequences of cohabitation and marriage (see also Maslauskaitė and Baublytė, this issue). Having children while cohabiting seems to have been much more accepted in Lutheran countries than in Roman Catholic or Calvinist ones as the distribution across Europe shows (Therborn, 2004, p. 201). We have seen that in Lutheran countries, premarital unions, especially those based on the formal betrothal, were legally recognized for a long time after the Council of Trent, and undoubtedly even longer in the popular perception. The valuation of marriage is also affected by the institutional benefits created in the era of the male breadwinner family. Cohabitation has spread over all social classes. However, the highly educated are no longer its forerunners. The fact that in various countries the poorer and lower educated sections of the population postpone a subsequent marriage the longest brings to mind the survival strategies of the nineteenth-century poor. Thus, prolonged 'proletarian' cohabitations may be yet another legacy of the past.

Summing up, the 'revenge of history' can be found in factors affecting the timing and rate of conversion of cohabitations to marriages. These factors are a mixture of socio-economic constraints, of the relative cultural importance attached to marriage, the religious history of a specific region and the level of secularization.

6. Research prospects

Now that cohabitation has become such a prominent stage in the life courses of young adults across the globe, it is surprising that we know so little about its antecedents. Although illegitimate fertility in its variation across European societies of the past has attracted ample attention (e.g. Laslett et al., 1980; Mitterauer, 1983), the incidence, importance and meaning of cohabitation are still largely unknown. In some countries, cohabitation is even still an uncharted field (for example in Latvia, see Plakans & Lipša, this issue). The most important reason is the lack of proper sources, as cohabitants tended to disguise their relationship. Often, they can only be glimpsed when their 'fornication' was persecuted by Church or State, when they committed a crime, or when a child was born out of wedlock and information on both parents was provided (e.g. because the father declared, recognized or legitimized his child). But even then, the duration of and reasons for the cohabitation remain unknown, as well as the community's reaction to it. The papers in this issue have made some progress in describing new sources, such as homicide cases (Frost, this issue) or the Latvian 'revisions of souls' (Plakans and Lipša, this issue), but there is still much to be discovered in the archives, as has been demonstrated by, for instance, Romanian scholars (Bolovan & Pădurean, 2005).

Future qualitative research into the motives of cohabitants should address more explicitly the issue of gendered strategies and gender bargaining involved in cohabitation. Currently, the literature is not very conclusive on this topic. On the one hand, cohabitation is sometimes interpreted as a survival strategy of poor women, who needed to pool incomes or rent, but did not have enough bargaining power to press for marriage which would offer them more status and relative security against desertion. On the other hand, cohabitation supposedly gave some women an advantage over marriage, as they avoided legal guardianship of a husband. On specific male motives for choosing cohabitation over marriage we know next to nothing.

To assess the *likelihood* of people entering and ending cohabitation, and to see how this differs across social groups, regions, and periods, we will have to rely on rare life course reconstructions. This presupposes that we can follow people in their different household configurations over the life course. Recently, the accessibility and interoperability of various large European databases containing historical life courses are being improved (Alter & Mandemakers, 2014). This might offer opportunities for a comparative history of cohabitation. A longitudinal approach will also make it possible to study the implications for children. Did their parents' concubinage affect their health, occupational positions, and marriage choices, for instance compared to children of single mothers, widows and children of married couples (van Poppel, 2000)? And how did temporary or permanent cohabitation affect the health (e.g. Koskinen, Joutsenniemi, Martelin, & Martikainen, 2007) and career prospects of the cohabiting men and women themselves?

Disclosure statement

No potential conflict of interest was reported by the authors.

References

Aassve, A., Billari, F. C., & Spéder, Z. (2006). Societal transition, policy changes and family formation: Evidence from Hungary. *European Journal of Population / Revue Européenne De Démographie, 22*, 127–152. doi:10.1007/s10680-005-7434-2

Abrams, L. (1993). Concubinage, cohabitation and the law: Class and gender relations in nineteenth century Germany. *Gender & History, 5*, 81–100.

Ajus, F., & Henye, I. (1994). Illegitimacy in Hungary 1880–1910. *Journal of Family History, 19*, 369–388.

Alpern Engel, B., & Posadskya-Vanderbeck, A. (Eds.). (1998). *A revolution of their own: Voices of women in Soviet History*. Boulder: Westview Press.

Alter, G., & Mandemakers, K. (2014). The intermediate data structure (IDS) for longitudinal historical Microdata, version 4. *Historical Life Course Studies, 1*, 1–26.

Bardach, J. (1970). *Zwyczajowe prawa małżeńskiego ludności ruskiej Wilekiego Księstwa Litewskiego, in Studia z ustroju I prawa wielkiego Księstwa Litewskiego XVI–XVII wieku* (pp. 261–315). Warszawa: Panstwowe Wydanictwo Naukowe.

Berlanstein, L. R. (1980). Illegitimacy, concubinage, and proletarianization in a French town, 1760–1914. *Journal of Family History, 5*, 360–374. doi:10.1177/036319908000500402

Billari, F. C., & Wilson, C. (2001). Convergence towards diversity? Cohort dynamics in the transition to adulthood in contemporary Western Europe MPIDR WORKING PAPER WP 2001–039.

Blaikie, A. (1993). *Illegitimacy, sex, and society: Northeast Scotland, 1750–1900*. Oxford: Clarendon Press.

Bolovan, I., & Pădurean, C. (2005). *Concubinage, illegitimacy and morality on the Romanian territories between the 17th and 20th Century*. Arad: Editura Gutenberg Univers.

Brändström, A. (1996). Life histories of single parents and illegitimate infants in nineteenth-century Sweden. *The History of the Family, 1*, 205–226.

Brunet, G. (2010). Célibataires et mères de nombreux enfants. Parcours de femmes à Lyon au xixe siècle. [Celibates and mothers of many children. Courses of women in Lyon in the 19th century]. *Annales de Démographie Historique, 119*, 95–114.

Brunet, G., & Bideau, A. (2010).), Épouses et concubines. La cohabitation pré-maritale à Lyon (France) au IXe siècle. [Wives and concubines. Premarital cohabitation in Lyon (France) in the 19th century]. In M. P. Arrizabalaga, I. Bolovan, M. Eppel, J. Kok, & M. L. Nagata (Eds.), *Many paths to happiness ? Studies in population and family history. A festschrift for Antoinette Fauve-Chamoux* (pp. 465–480). Amsterdam: Aksant.

Burguière, A., & Lebrun, F. (1996). The one hundred and one families of Europe'. In A. Burguière, C. Klapisch-Zuber, M. Segalen, & F. Zonabend (Eds.), *A history of the family, vol. 2. The impact of modernity* (pp. 11–94). Cambridge Mass: Harvard University Press.

Carlson, E., & Klinger, A. (1987). Partners in life: Unmarried couples in Hungary. *European Journal of Population, 3*, 85–99. doi:10.1007/BF01797093

Casper, L. M., & Cohen, P. N. (2000). How does POSSLQ measure up? Historical estimates of cohabitation. *Demography, 37*, 237–245. doi:10.2307/2648125

Centraal Bureau voor Maatschappelijk Hulpbetoon. (1923). *Onderzoekingen naar de levensom-standigheden der in 1911 en 1912 te Amsterdam buiten echt geboren kinderen en hunne moeders. Geschriften van den Armenraad te Amsterdam VII.* [Investigations into the living conditions of children born out of wedlock in 1911 and 1912 in Amsterdam and their mothers]. Amsterdam: Armenraad.

Chambers-Schiller, L. V. (1984). *Liberty: A better husband: Single women in America: The generations of 1780–1840*. New Haven: Yale University Press.

Coleman, D. (2004). Why we don't have to believe without doubting in the "second demographic transition" – some agnostic comments. *Vienna Yearbook of Population Research, 1*, 11–24. doi:10.1553/populationyearbook2004s11

de Haan, F., & Stam, D. (1986). *Jonge dochters en oude vrijsters. Ongehuwde vrouwen in Haarlem in de de eerste helft van de negentiende eeuw*. Haarlem: Haerlem Studies.

de Smidt, J. Th., & Gall, H. C. (1985). Recht en gezin [Law and family]. In G. A. Kooy (Ed.), *Gezinsgeschiedenis. Vier eeuwen gezin in Nederland* [Family history. Four centuries of family in The Netherlands] (pp. 31–68). Assen/Maastricht: Van Gorcum.

Di Giulio, P., & Rosina, A. (2007). Intergenerational family ties and the diffusion of cohabitation in Italy. *Demographic Research, 16*, 441–468. doi:10.4054/DemRes.2007.16.14

Ehmer, J. (2002). Marriage. In D. I. Kertzer & M. Barbagli (Eds.), *Family life in the long nineteenth century 1789–1913* (pp. 282–321). New Haven and London: Yale University Press.

Fauve-Chamoux, A. (2011). European illegitimacy trends in connection with domestic service and family systems (1545–2011). *Romanian Journal of Population Studies, 5,* 8–45.

Fine, A. (1988). Enfant et normes familiales [Child and family norms]. In J. Dupâquier (Ed.), *Histoire de la population Française. III De 1789 à 1914* [History of the French population. III From 1789 until 1914] (pp. 436–463). Paris: Presses universitaires de France.

Frey, M. (1978). Du mariage et du concubinage dans les classes populaires à Paris (1846–1847). [Marriage and cohabitation in the popular classes in Paris (1846–1847)]. *Annales E.S.C., 33,* 803–829.

Frick, D. (2013). *Kith, Kin, & Neighbours. Communities & Confessions in Seventeenth-Century Wilno.* Ithaca: Cornell University Press.

Froide, A. M. (2005). *Never married: Single women in early modern England.* Oxford: Oxford University Press.

Frost, G. (1997). Bigamy and cohabitation in Victorian England. *Journal of Family History, 22,* 286–306. doi:10.1177/036319909702200302

Gerber, T. P., & Berman, D. (2010). Entry to marriage and cohabitation in Russia, 1985–2000: Trends, correlates, and implications for the second demographic transition. *European Journal of Population / Revue Européenne De Démographie, 26,* 3–31. doi:10.1007/s10680-009-9196-8

Gillis, J. R. (1985). *For better, for worse: British marriages 1600 to the present.* New York: Oxford University Press.

Goldman, W. Z. (1993). *Women, the state and revolution. Soviet family policy&social life, 1917–1936.* Cambridge: Cambridge University Press.

Guinnane, T. W., & Ogilvie, S. (2014). A two-tiered demographic system: 'insiders' and 'outsiders' in three Swabian communities, 1558–1914. *The History of the Family, 19,* 77–119. doi:10. 1080/1081602X.2013.870491

Head-König, A. -L. (1993). Forced marriages and forbidden marriages in Switzerland: State control of the formation of marriage in catholic and protestant cantons in the eighteenth and nineteenth centuries. *Continuity and change, 8,* 441–465.

Hiekel, N., & Keizer, R. (2015). *Dutch focus group research on cohabitation and marriage.* Risk-avoidance or utmost commitment. *Demographic Research, 32,* 311–340. doi:10.4054/DemRes. 2015.32.10

Hoem, J. M., Kostova, D., Jasilioniene, A., & Mureşan, C. (2009). Traces of the second demographic transition in four selected countries in central and eastern Europe: Union formation as a demographic manifestation. *European Journal of Population / Revue Européenne De Démographie, 25,* 239–255. doi:10.1007/s10680-009-9177-y

Hoem, J. M., Kostova, D., Mureşan, C., & Jasilioniene, A. (2009). The structure of recent first union formation in Romania'. *Romanian Journal of Population Studies, 3,* 33–44.

Hwang, C. P., & Broberg, A. G. (2009). The historical and social context of child care in Sweden. In M. E. Lamb, K. J. Sternberg, C.-P. Hwang, & A. G. Broberg (Eds.), *Child care in context: Cross-cultural perspectives* (pp. 27–54). Hillsdale NJ: Lawrence Erlbaum.

Israel, B. (2002). *Bachelor girl. The secret history of single women in the twentieth century.* New York: Harper Collins.

Kalmijn, M. (2007). Explaining cross-national differences in marriage, cohabitation, and divorce in Europe, 1990–2000. *Population Studies, 61,* 243–263. doi:10.1080/00324720701571806

Kammerer, P. C. (1918). *The unmarried mother. A study of five hundred cases.* Boston: Little, Brown, and Company.

Kaplow, J. (1978). Concubinage and the working class in XIXth Paris. In E. Hinrichs, E. Schmidt, & R. Vierhaus (Eds.), *Vom Ancien Régime zur französischen Revolution: Forschungen und Perspektiven.* [From Ancien Régime to the French Revolution: Research and perspectives]. Göttingen: Vandenhoeck und Ruprecht.

Kasearu, K., & Kutsar, D. (2011). Patterns behind unmarried cohabitation trends in Europe. *European Societies, 13,* 307–325. doi:10.1080/14616696.2010.493586

Katus, K., Puur, A., Põldma, A., & Sakkeus, L. (2007). First union formation in Estonia, Latvia and Lithuania: Patterns across countries and gender. *Demographic Research, 17,* 247–300. doi:10. 4054/DemRes.2007.17.10

Klüsener, S., Perelli-Harris, B., & Sánchez Gassen, N. (2013). Spatial aspects of the rise of nonmarital fertility across Europe since 1960: The role of states and regions in shaping patterns of change. *European Journal of Population, 29,* 137–165.

Kok, J. (1991). *Langs verboden wegen. De achtergronden van buitenechtelijke geboorten in Noord-Holland, 1812–1914* [By forbidden paths. The underlying causes of illegitimate births in the province of North-Holland, 1812–1914]. Hilversum: Verloren.

Koskinen, S., Joutsenniemi, K., Martelin, T., & Martikainen, P. (2007). Mortality differences according to living arrangements. *International Journal of Epidemiology, 36,* 1255–1264. doi:10.1093/ije/dym212

Kraus, A. (1979). 'Antizipierte Ehesegen in 19. Jahrhundert; Zur Beurteilung der Illegitimität unter sozialgeschichtlichen Aspekten. [Anticipated marriage blessing in the 19th century. Towards an evaluation of illegitimacy from the perspective of social history]. *Vierteljahrschrift für Sozial- und Wirtschaftsgeschichte, 66,* 174–215.

Kytir, J., & Münz, R. (1986). *Illegitimität in Österreich. Demographische Informationen.* [Illegitimacy in Austria. Demographic information]. Vienna: Institut für Demographie, Österreichische Akademie der Wissenschaften.

Laslett, P. (1965). Personal discipline and social survival. With notes on the history of bastardy in England. In P. Laslett (Ed.), *The world we have lost* (pp. 135–158). London: Methuen & Co.

Laslett P., K. Oosterveen, & R. M. Smith (Eds.) (1980). *Bastardy and its comparative history. Studies in the history of illegitimacy and marital nonconformism in Britain, France, Germany, Sweden, North America, Jamaica and Japan.* London: Edward Arnold.

Leffingwell, A. (1892). *Illegitimacy, and the influence of seasons upon conduct.* Two studies in demography. London: S. Sonnenschein & Co.

Legkauskas, V., & Stankevičienė, D. (2009). Premarital sex and marital satisfaction of middle aged men and women: A study of married Lithuanian couples. *Sex Roles, 60,* 21–32. doi:10.1007/s11199-008-9497-0

Leinarte, D. (2012a). Cohabitation in imperial Russia: The case of Lithuania. *The History of the Family, 17,* 16–30. doi:10.1080/1081602X.2012.658146

Leinartė, D. (2012b). *Census-like material preserved in the archives of Lithuania, 19th century.* Rostock: Max Planck Institute for Demographic Research. http://195.37.34.109/publications/mosaicWP/MOSAIC-WP-2012-005.pdf

Lesthaeghe, R. (1995). The second demographic transition in Western countries: An interpretation. In K. O. Mason & A.-M. Jensen (Eds.), *Gender and family change in industrialized countries* (pp. 17–62). Oxford: Clarendon Press.

Lesthaeghe, R. (2010). The unfolding story of the second demographic transition'. *Population and Development Review, 36,* 211–251. doi:10.1111/j.1728-4457.2010.00328.x

Lesthaeghe, R. (2014). The second demographic transition: A concise overview of its development. *Proceedings of the National Academy of Sciences, 111,* 18112–18115. doi:10.1073/pnas.1420441111

Liefbroer, A. C., & Dourleijn, E. (2006). Unmarried cohabitation and union stability: Testing the role of diffusion using data from 16 European countries. *Demography, 43,* 203–221. doi:10.1353/dem.2006.0018

Lundh, C. (2003). Swedish Marriages. Customs, Legislation and Demography in the Eighteenth and Nineteenth Centuries. Lund Papers in Economic History 88.

Marcinkevičienė [Leinarte], D. (1999). *Vedusiųjų visuomenė: Santuoka ir skyrybos Lietuvoje, XIX–XX amžiaus pradžia.* [The Society of Married People: Marriage and Divorce in Lithuania, XIX – the beginning of XXth century]. Vilnius: Lietuvos istorijos institutas.

Marks, H. (1994). On the art of differentiating: Proletarianization and illegitimacy in northern Sweden, 1850–1930. *Social Science History, 18,* 95–126. doi:10.2307/1171401

Martin, C., & Théry, I. (2001). The PACS and marriage and cohabitation in France. *International Journal of Law, Policy and the Family, 15,* 135–158. doi:10.1093/lawfam/15.1.135

Matovic, M. R. (1986). The Stockholm marriage: Extra-legal family formation in Stockholm 1860–1890. *Continuity and Change, 1,* 385–413. doi:10.1017/S0268416000000333

Matysiak, A. (2009). Is Poland really 'immune' to the spread of cohabitation? *Demographic Research, 21,* 215–234. doi:10.4054/DemRes.2009.21.8

Mitchison, R., & Leneman, L. (1989). *Sexuality and social control. Scotland 1660–1780.* Oxford: Blackwell.

Mitterauer, M. (1983). *Ledige Mütter. Zur Geschichte illigitimer Geburten in Europa.* [Single mothers. Towards a history of illegitimate births in Europe]. München: Beck.

Murzaku, I. A., & Dervishi, Z. (2003). Albanians first post-communist decade. Values in transition: Traditional or liberal? *East European Quarterly, 37*, 231–256.

Overdiep, G. (1955). *Rechtsbescherming van de feitelijke verhouding tussen het onwettige kind en zijn ouders, gezien in het licht dier verhouding in Drente.* [Legal protection of the actual relation between the illegitimate child and his parents, viewed in the light of this relation in Drente]. Groningen/Djakarta: J.B. Wolters.

Padurean, C. (Supplement/2009). Family in Romania during the communist regime. *Romanian Journal of Population Studies, 3*, 521–542.

Perelli-Harris, B., Kreyenfeld, M., Sigle-Rushton, W., Keizer, R., Lappegård, T., Jasilioniene, A., Berghammer, C., Di Giulio, P., & Koeppen, K. (2009). The increase in fertility in cohabitation across Europe: Examining the intersection between union status and childbearing. MPIDR Working Paper 2009.

Perelli-Harris, B., Berrington, A., Berghammer, C., Keizer, R., Evans, T., Mynarska, M., & Vignoli, D. (2014). Towards a new understanding of cohabitation: Insights from focus group research across Europe and Australia. *Demographic Research, 31*, 1043–1078. doi:10.4054/DemRes.2014.31.34

Perelli-Harris, B., & Gerber, T. P. (2011). Nonmarital childbearing in Russia: Second demographic transition or pattern of disadvantage? *Demography, 48*, 317–342. doi:10.1007/s13524-010-0001-4

Philipov, D., & Jasilioniene, A. (2008). Union formation and fertility in Bulgaria and Russia: A life table description of recent trends. *Demographic Research, 19*, 2057–2114. doi:10.4054/DemRes.2008.19.62

Pinca, A. C. (2009). Aspects regarding the married Woman's condition reflected in the laic legislation of Transylvania in the second half of the 19th Century. *Romanian Journal of Population Studies, 3*, 507–520.

Potârcă, G., Mills, M., & Lesnard, L. (2013). Family formation trajectories in Romania, the Russian federation and France: Towards the second demographic transition? *European Journal of Population, 29*, 69–101.

Probert, R. (2009). *Marriage law and practice in the long eighteenth century: A reassessment.* Cambridge: Cambridge University Press.

Ratcliffe, B. M. (1996). Popular classes and cohabitation in mid-nineteenth-century Paris. *Journal of Family History, 21*, 316–350. doi:10.1177/036319909602100304

Reay, B. (1996). *Microhistories: Demography, society and culture in rural England, 1800–1930.* Cambridge: Cambridge University Press.

Reher, D. S. (1998). Family ties in western Europe: Persistent contrasts. *Population and Development Review, 24*, 203–234. doi:10.2307/2807972

Roodenburg, H. (1990). *Onder censuur; De kerkelijke tucht in de gereformeerde gemeente van Amsterdam, 1578–1700.* [Under censure. The church discipline in the Reformed parish of Amsterdam, 1578–1700]. Hilversum: Verloren.

Rotariu, T. (2009). A few critical remarks on the culturalist theories on fertility with special view on Romania's situation'. *Romanian Journal of Population Studies, 3*, 11–32.

Sellin, J. T. (1922). Marriage and divorce legislation in Sweden. PhD thesis University of Pennsylvania.

Shorter, E. (1971). Illegitimacy, sexual revolution, and social change in modern Europe. *Journal of Interdisciplinary History, 2*, 237–272. doi:10.2307/202844

Shorter, E., Knodel, J., & Van de Walle, E. (1971). The decline of non-marital fertility in Europe, 1880–1940. *Population Studies, 25*, 375–393.

Smout, T. C. (1981). Scottish marriage, regular and irregular 1500–1940. In R. B. Outhwaite (Ed.), *Marriage and society. Studies in the social history of marriage.* London: Europa.

Sobotka, T., Št'astná, A., Zeman, K., Hamplová, D., & Kantorová, V. (2008). Czech Republic: A rapid transformation of fertility and family behaviour after the collapse of state socialism. *Demographic Research, 19*, 403–454. doi:10.4054/DemRes.2008.19.14

Sobotka, T., & Toulemon, L. (2008). Overview chapter 4: Changing family and partnership behaviour. *Demographic Research, 19*, 85–138. doi:10.4054/DemRes.2008.19.6

Sogner, S. (2003). Looking for the principles of marriage by looking at non-marital cohabitation: A Norwegian parish in the eighteenth and nineteenth centuries. In C. Duhamelle &

J. Schlumbohm (Eds.), *Eheschliessungen im Europa des 18. Und 19. Jahrhunderts. Muster und Strategien* [Marriages in Europe in the 18th and 19th centuries. Patterns and strategies] (pp. 215–239). Göttingen: Vandenhoeck & Ruprecht.

Spijker, J., Esteve, A., & Cusidó, T. A. (2012). Census measures of union formation in the time of cohabitation. Paper presented at the European Population Conference. Stockholm, Sweden. 13–16 June.

Stankūnienė, V. (2003). *Šeimos revoliucija? Iššūkiai šeimos politikai.* [Revolution of the Family? Challenges for the family policy]. Vilnius: Socialinių tyrimų institutas.

Sweeney, M. M., Castro-martín, T., & Mills, M. (2015). The reproductive context of cohabitation in comparative perspective: Contraceptive use in the United States, Spain, and France. *Demographic Research, 32,* 147–182. doi:10.4054/DemRes.2015.32.5

Tarver, J. (1995). *Church court records: An introduction for family and local historians.* Chichester, England: Phillimore & Co Ltd.

Telste, K. (2009). Children born out of wedlock. Legal rights and social reforms in Norway from the 17th century to the present. In M. Durães, A. Fauve-Chamoux, L. Ferrer, & J. Kok (Eds.), *The transmission of well-being. Gendered marriage strategies and inheritance systems in Europe (17th–20th centuries)* (pp. 317–333). Bern: Peter Lang.

Thane, P. (2013). The changing legal regulation of cohabitation. From fornicators to family, 1600–2010. *Population Studies, 67,* 246–248. doi:10.1080/00324728.2013.788320

Therborn, G. (2004). *Between sex and power. Family in the world, 1900–2000.* London and New York: Routledge.

Thornton, A., & Philipov, D. (2009). Sweeping changes in marriage, cohabitation and childbearing in Central and Eastern Europe: New insights from the developmental idealism framework. *European Journal of Population / Revue Européenne De Démographie, 25,* 123–156. doi:10.1007/s10680-009-9181-2

Țîrcomnicu, E. (2009). Some topics of the traditional wedding customs of the Macedo – Romanians (A – Romanians and Megleno – Romanians). *Romanian Journal of Population Studies, 3,* 141–152.

van de Kaa, D. J. (2001). Postmodern fertility preferences: From changing value orientations to new behavior. In R. A. Bulatao & J. B. Casterline (Eds.), *Global fertility transition* (pp. 290–331). New York: Population Council.

van der Heijden. M. (1998). *Huwelijk in Holland. Stedelijke rechtspraak en kerkelijke tucht 1550–1700* [Marriage in Holland. Urban justice and church discipline 1550–1700]. Amsterdam: Bert Bakker.

van der Heijden, M. (2014). *Misdadige vrouwen. Criminaliteit en rechtspraak in Holland 1600–1800* [Criminal women. Crime and justice in Holland 1600–1800]. Amsterdam: Prometheus.

van Poppel, F. (1992). *Trouwen in Nederland. Een historisch-demografische studie van de 19[e] en vroeg-20[e] eeuw.* [Marrying in The Netherlands. A historical-demographic study of the 19th and early 20th century]. Wageningen: Landbouwhogeschool.

van Poppel, F. (2000). Children in one-parent families: Survival as an indicator of the role of the parents. *Journal of Family History, 25,* 269–290. doi:10.1177/036319900002500301

Viazzo, P. P. (1986). Illegitimacy and the European marriage pattern: Comparative evidence from the Alpine area. In L. Bonfield, R. M. Smith, & K. Wrightson (Eds.), *The world we have gained. Histories of population and social structure. Essays presented to Peter Laslett on his seventieth birthday* (pp. 100–121). New York: Basil Blackwell.

Wood, E. A. (1997). *The Baba and the Comrade.* Bloomington: Indiana University Press.

Cohabitation from illegal to institutionalized practice: the case of Norway 1972–2010

Liv Johanne Syltevik

The main objective of this article is to explore the institutionalization of cohabitation that occurred in Norwegian law in the period 1972–2010. From being (officially) illegal until 1972, cohabitation in its contemporary form has become majority practice, a child-rearing institution, as well as recognized in law in ways that blur the differences between cohabitation and marriage. Although cohabitation is common in many European countries, Norway is one of the few to have gone full circle. This article focuses on the changes in politicians' ideas and norms regarding intimate relationships during this period. The empirical analysis is based on political documents and debates in the Norwegian parliament about cohabitation, marriage, single motherhood and the family.

1. Introduction

Informal cohabitation – a purely consensual marriage – then, is an ancient Western European Christian practice, which was de-legitimized in early modernity, to surge forward in proletarianized and early industrial Europe, and then abandoned in the age of industrial marriage. In the last third of the twentieth century, simultaneously with the turn to de-industrialization, cohabitation was returning with a vengeance, primarily in its areas of historical origin. (Therborn, 2004, p. 193)

Norway is one of the countries that have followed the trajectory outlined by Therborn. Nowadays, cohabitation is majority behaviour as part of couple formation as in most of north-western Europe and North America (Kiernan, 2004; Nazio, 2008, p. 16f; Smock, 2000). The extent, significance and meaning of cohabitation are however different in different parts of Europe (Cherlin, 2010; Kiernan, 2004; Leinarte, 2012). In contemporary Scandinavia, compared to rest of Europe, cohabiting relationships last longer, more children are born in such unions and they are legally recognized. Cohabitation has long roots in Scandinavian history. In pre-Christian times, cohabitation was fully recognized morally as well as legally (Asland, 2005), and historians have pointed out the similarities between the present family formation pattern and the prolonged process with engagement followed by formal marriage in the seventeenth and eighteenth centuries (Elliassen & Sogner, 1981; Gaunt & Nyström, 1996, p. 489f). Therborn argues that several preconditions made this development in Scandinavia possible, namely being the most secularized and least religious region in Western Europe, having a tradition among young working-class women of cohabitation, an unbroken tradition of youth independence, and good opportunities to obtain housing and paid employment. In addition, Therborn also emphasizes the fact that the changes took place in connection with a more general process of informalization and deritualization in the youth culture in the 1960s and 1970s (Therborn, 2004, p. 197).

There are no statistics in Norway showing how common cohabitation was in the past, but evidence from several centuries ago points to the existence of stable non-marital unions in which children were born (Sogner, 2003). Historians have pieced together evidence that shows that in many parts of Norway it was more the rule than the exception in the seventeenth century that the bride was pregnant at the wedding ceremony (Elliassen & Sogner, 1981). This does not prove that cohabitation was common though, as it may have been a strategy used by youths so that their parents would allow them to marry. Such stable non-marital unions are found though well into the nineteenth century. The practice is portrayed most vividly by the Norwegian demographer and priest Eilert Sundt (1968) who found many such relationships during his fieldwork in different parts of Norway in the 1850s. The postponement of weddings until couples could afford wedding clothes and the feast that was appropriate in the local community was an accepted practice (Sundt, 1968, p. 119).

In the twentieth century and what has been termed the golden age of marriage (1960–1970), legal marriage became the norm and was almost mandatory. As an illustration, around 1970 only 4% of Norwegian women and 5% of men were unmarried at the age of 50 (Noack, 2010, p. 27), and around 97% of all children were born inside marriage in the period 1950–1965 (Noack, 2010, p. 30). However, sexual relations before marriage were common and the term 'having to marry' referred to the necessity to marry when pregnant.[1] The modern form of cohabitation took shape from the late 1970s; in a few decades, Norway went from high levels of marriage, with few births outside wedlock and few people living together outside marriage to becoming a land of cohabitation. This process has been called a silent revolution as it happened without much public debate (Noack, 2010). The evidence is inclusive as to where in the social structure cohabitation first took hold. Ramsoy (1994, p. 29) refers to research that argues that the practice began among university students and others who claim that it is a continuation of what the poor had long done, and suggests that the modern practice has multiple origins. The development was very rapid, and while cohabitation was considered unheard of just years before, at the start of the 1980s it was the dominant way of living together among the young (Noack, 2010, p. 9). The acceptance of such relationships also followed very quickly. While the majority (70%) of Norwegians were not in favour of cohabitation in 1977, just 47% were against it in 1982 (Noack, 2010, p. 170). Currently, 90% of couples have cohabited before they marry, and 43% of all children born in 2012[2] had cohabiting parents (SSB, 2012, 2013).

Norway is an interesting example of the institutionalization of modern cohabitation as the country has gone full circle legally with regard to regulation of cohabitation. The process started in the early 1970s with the abolishing of the so-called concubinage paragraph that made cohabitation illegal, and ended with major changes in the 2000s that minimize the differences between cohabitation and marriage. The main aim of this article is to discuss how this has occurred. How and why did cohabitation become recognized in law from the early 1970s onwards? The focus will be on the changing ideas, norms and attitudes among politicians towards intimate relationships and the family in the period 1972–2010. Ideas are important since they help to construct the problems on the political agenda, they affect the content of reform proposals and guide reform imperatives (Béland, 2009).[3] By comparing politicians' ideas about cohabitation, intimate relationships and marriage over time, we gain insight into the arguments that they considered relevant and how they viewed relations between couples, the family and the state, and how these ideas changed. The empirical analysis is based on relevant debates about the regulation of cohabitation in law, about single motherhood and social benefits, and about broader family policy issues as well as debates that explicitly deal with cohabitation.

2. Institutionalization and methodological issues

The title of this article implies that there has been an institutionalization in Norwegian society concerning cohabitation. Therborn (2004) makes a distinction between institutional change and 'change of an institution'; the latter is any alteration of a given institution (a disturbance or an erosion of its hold) while the former indicates:

> the establishment of a new institutional order and temporal equilibrium through a re-organization of the challenged institution, re-allocation of its place and significance in the broader social order, through its replacement by a new institution, or by its abolition into irrelevance. (Therborn, 2004, p. 299)

Institutional change then includes crucial moment(s) of normative decisions, when a process of deinstitutionalization or of institutionalization begins to move along one path and not the other. According to Therborn, such crucial moments occur on the macro-level moment of legislation, judicial verdicts or authoritative religious decisions. On the micro level, they are present when the breach of institutional norms ceases to cause offence and to lead to social marginalization.[4] With regard to cohabitation, cohabitation has been institutionalized as an (almost) mandatory part of couple formation. First, heterosexual cohabitation has become a normative feature of the life-course before marriage and remarriage, and the connection between having children and marriage has diminished, with marriage viewed as something that would eventually follow. Second, cohabitation is now clearly recognized and regulated by the state.

The process of the institutionalization of cohabitation is discussed as it is displayed in debates on legislation. I consider the debates and official documents on cohabitation from 1972 to 2010 as significant events in this process. In particular, I am interested in the cultural and ideological ideas and norms of marriage and cohabitation that are present in these political documents and debates. Three political debates have taken place where cohabitation as such has been the focus and it is therefore possible to follow all three:[5] the reports and debate about the abolishing of the concubinage paragraph in 1972, the reports about cohabitation in the early 1980s, and the report about cohabitation in the 1990s (NOU, 1999:25) and the white papers and debates that followed. The second and third of these debates were connected with two broader family policy discussions that took place in the Storting (the Norwegian parliament)[6] in the same period. When studying these debates, I found that 'negative' recognition (recognition of cohabitation as a reason for *not* getting rights) of cohabitation came with the idea of the cohabiting male provider; for this reason, I have included the debates in the period 1972–1998 about benefits for single mothers. Taken together, these documents and debates provide a broad insight into how Norwegian politicians framed the questions regarding cohabitation.

Political documents and parliamentary debates are an obvious and easily accessible data source if one is interested in the change in ideas about family issues over time. The texts are produced by bureaucrats, politicians and others who have been invited to participate. The debates are transcriptions of what Members of Parliament say when the policy is discussed in the Storting. Both data sources have a particular character as they form part of the political struggle about the issues on the agenda. They are meant to serve certain goals and their interpretation thus needs to take this into consideration (see Scott, 1990, for a discussion). Compared with the texts, parliamentary debates provide more room for arguments and differing views. They are a rich source of data since there has been considerable debate on issues in Norwegian policy about the family, gender equality and family policy (Vollset, 2011).

3. The regulation of cohabitation: from illegal to recognized in law

In the early nineteenth century, Norway was what Therborn (2004) called a family avant-garde. Patriarchy was weaker than in the rest of Europe, and this gave way to laws giving equal rights to husband and wife, and rights to children born out of wedlock, as well as no-fault divorce rights. However, Norway was somewhat more culturally conservative than Denmark and Sweden, and this may be one of the reasons why heterosexual cohabitation continued to be illegal in the Penal Code in 1902 contrary to the other Scandinavian countries.[7] Skevik (2004) has suggested that both the concubinage paragraph and the Children's Act of 1915 (giving rights to children born out of wedlock) were based on an understanding of extra-marital sex as 'something that men did to women', and that both laws were seen as means to strengthen the position of women towards men. It had already been suggested in 1925 and again in 1955 that the paragraph should be abolished; however, abolition was not supported by a majority of the Storting until 1972. Noack (2010, p. 114) argues that the existence of the paragraph was probably not widely known among the population and thus could be characterized as 'sleeping'. There were a few cases reported to the police most years though, and as late as 1954 one resulted in fines (Ot.prp. nr. 5, 1971–72).

The process of recognition after 1972 came in two versions. One was 'negative' recognition where cohabiting couples lost advantages they had by being treated as two single adults. The other was 'positive' recognition where cohabiting couples were given the same rights as if married or rights as cohabitants. The first period of regulation of cohabitation in Norway consisted mostly of 'negative' recognition and was associated with the benefits for single mothers/parents and pensioners. The first 'positive' recognition of cohabitation came in 1981, when the law on subsidized housing co-operatives made it possible for cohabiting couples to share a flat and take over that flat from the other in the eventuality of death or a break-up of the relationship. Then, in 1991, cohabitants were given the right to take over all types of shared flats/houses from the other after death or break-up, if they paid market price. The major positive recognitions regarding inheritance tax, inheritance and shared parental responsibility came during the 2000s.

4. Abolition of the concubinage paragraph

The concubinage paragraph was finally abolished in 1972. The paragraph stated that: 'A person, that even when warned by the authorities, continues to live in an immoral relationship concerning public offence with a person of the other sex, is punished with fines/fees or jail for 3 months or less' (Ot.Prp. No. 5, 1971–72, p. 10). In the Storting debate at the time, only the members of the Christian Democratic Party argued that the paragraph was still important:

> The abolition of the concubinage paragraph may have unfortunate and unintended consequences as it in short or longer terms will weaken the way of living that our society is built on.[8]

In their view, the abolition of the paragraph could be interpreted as a legitimation of cohabitation and a weakening of marriage. They also thought it right to use the law to strengthen moral conduct. Those in favour of the abolishment of the paragraph argued along two main lines. First, it was important to make a distinction between law and morality. Even if marriage was the best way of living together (and cohabitation immoral), it ought not to be established in law that ways of living together other than marriage were unacceptable. Second, they argued that the law had hardly been applied, and neither did the minority intend it to be used more. To have 'sleeping laws' could foster disrespect for the legal system.

The majority as well as the minority emphasized the importance of marriage. There was however a slight difference in the way they did so and this was summed up by one of the speakers in the following way:

> The majority will emphasize that Norwegian society is built on marriage as the best way of living together, and it is the responsibility of society to support marriage both practical as well as ethical [...] The minority states that marriage is the most common way of living together in our society. The most important thing is that parents whatever status – give their children a safe, harmonious and developing up-bringing.[9]

Many speakers used the opportunity to praise traditional marriage at the same time that they argued that they did not want to use the penal code to advocate the best way of living together. None spoke in favour of cohabitation.

Cohabitation was not mentioned at all in the white paper about family policy in the early 1970s 'The living conditions of families with children' (St. Meld. No. 117, 1972–73). The main message in this white paper concerns the change in women's role in the family. Women increasingly are supposed to want to have more employment outside the home and in particular part-time employment. The emerging family policy ought to make this possible (by expanding childcare provision outside the home and improving the opportunities for adult education) as it is a way of improving the economy of the family. The politicians thought most women still would become housewives. However, the decrease in the age at marriage, fewer children and easier housework tasks made employment possible for more women. In addition, the white paper focused on the needs of single mothers and the increase in the divorce rate. The increased divorce rate was also mentioned by one of the speakers in the debate in the Storting about the abolition of the concubinage paragraph. This is one of the few instances in this debate of the politician sensing something new emerging. Another speaker also referred to disturbing reports about the rise in the number of people living together in Sweden and Denmark.[10] A new issue was raised by two MPs[11] concerning the allowance for unmarried mothers (introduced nationally in Norway in 1964), which did not exclude unmarried mothers if they lived together with a partner. As we shall see in the next section, the understanding of this as an emerging problem resulted in the first 'negative' recognition of cohabitation the same year.

5. The emerging cohabitant (male) provider

The first 'negative' recognition came a few months after the March 1972 Storting Debate. Unmarried mothers living with the child's father (or someone who could be the father) were no longer eligible for the allowance for unmarried mothers. De facto partnership status and not formal civil status decided whether women had the right to receive support as a single mother from then on. Some MPs were reluctant to target this group (as seen in the Andersen quote below); however, there was general agreement that the benefits were not meant for couples who lived together:

> It is common knowledge that there are a lot of rumours among people – if we can call it that – that there is a lot of misuse of the allowances and social benefits we have today. But I have to say that I thought it strange that this little group was in focus. However, we have to act since this group could grow otherwise, and I do agree that we shall not use our benefits in this way.[12]

In practice, unmarried mothers who cohabited were treated as married, while their male partners were treated as unmarried. The consequence was that 1328 cohabiting unmarried mothers lost the allowance (Gulli, 1992).

In the early 1980s, the debate about single mothers and cohabitation continued. Now the challenge concerned cohabitation with men who were not the fathers of the children. Many argued that this kind of relationship ought to be treated as if the mother had married. The argument was that cohabitation resembled marriage, and that the rules made it pay economically not to marry:

> The allowances are a burden to us all. We want all who need support to get it. However, if you see that your neighbour gets support as a single mother even if she lives an ordinary family life, it just is not formalized, this will ruin the legitimacy of the allowance system.[13]

The discussion in 1980 did not end with a change in the rules. The main argument made by the majority was that cohabiting partners had no obligation to provide for their partner, and that their contributions to the household varied. In 1994 (extra child allowance) and 1998 (transitional allowance), the counter-arguments won, and cohabitation (defined as living together 12 of the last 18 months) became treated as marriage. The idea of marriage-like relationships with regard to obligations towards children had gained ground:

> The other argument [the first was the economic position of single mothers, the authors addition], that a cohabiting partner do not contribute economically to upbringing of his stepchildren, is ridiculous. In a stable marriage like relationship, there must be presupposed that there is a fellowship even for children who are not one's own. What fellowship would that be if not?[14]

The idea of the couple presented here is one where both contribute financially and practically, and where there is moral obligation and fellowship. These changes represented a strengthened control of relationships; since 1994, single parents who received benefits have been required to fill in a form annually for National Insurance about whether or not they are cohabiting (Skevik, 2001).

The same changes occurred in the rules for pensioners. Until then, unmarried pensioners received their whole pension, while married couples received a reduced pension on the basis that it is cheaper to live together. These rules were amended so that marriage and cohabitation were treated equally in 1994 (for pensioners who have children together) and in 1998 (for childless pensioners who are cohabiting) (Noack, 2010, p. 213).

6.   The debate about living together without marriage (1980s)

The first 'positive' recognition of cohabitation came in 1981 in the form of a minor regulation of the rules regarding a shared house/flat in housing co-operatives. This resulted from the first official report about cohabitation 'Living together without marriage' (NOU 1980:50), which appeared in 1980 as part of the work on a new Marriage Act. Cohabitation was understood as heterosexual couples living together without marrying, and the subtitle of the white paper was 'paperless marriages'. The committee members[15] making the report had different views on the issue. One of the members was against making a report at all:

> Marriage is not just a private matter. The marriage ritual, in church as well as in the civil ceremony, it is not just a matter for those involved, but something that concerns the whole society [. . .] It should not be indifferent for society what family form people choose since it is documented that looser ways of living together weakens the family institution. (John Lillestøl, headmaster, NOU, 1980:50, p. 8)

The rest of the committee was also divided. One member (the sociologist Erik Grønseth who at the time worked at the University of Oslo) suggested that cohabitation was a new type of engagement or trial marriage:

> We are here seeing a new type of dating and choice of partners, the temporary cohabiting relationship. This is a new type of engagement, while the more long term ones have the character of trial marriages. (Erik Grønseth, NOU, 1980:50, p. 37)

Others restricted themselves to emphasizing that they saw marriage as a good way of living together. The committee argued that cohabitants represented a very heterogeneous group, that there were many difficulties with regard to identifying who belonged to the category or not and suggested just a few regulations concerning laws on inheritance, owning a shared house/flat, and cohabiting women's loss of the right to alimony from ex-husbands.

The white paper about family issues in the early 1980s did not mention cohabitation apart from as a future challenge (St. Meld. No. 25, 1981–82, p. 5). In a white paper four years later, cohabitation was mentioned as one of the changes in the family:

> At the end of the 1960s the family structure changed. There was a rise in divorces, fertility decreased and we got a rise in unmarried cohabitation and women's participation in the labour force. These changes are significant but are not so dramatic as they can appear at first sight. The changes the last years with regard to divorce-rates and fertility have been relatively small. Still most people also marry and get children, if later in the lifecourse than a few years back. (St. Meld. No. 50, 1984–85, p. 5)

Cohabitation is still seen as a minority practice:

> Today there is relatively few people who live as unmarried cohabitants. The need for legislation to clarify the legal position in different situations, would partly depend on the development with regard to how many will be cohabiting over time. (St. Meld. No. 50, 1984–85, p. 89)

Nevertheless, cohabitation was one of the main issues in this white paper with the rights and obligations for married and cohabiting couples being compared. The conclusion was that from an economic perspective it was sometimes best to marry, and sometimes not. The white paper suggested several possible ways of regulating cohabitation in the future.

What became the most controversial issue in the Storting debate on this white paper was the definition of cohabitation: 'Two persons that live together in a marriage-like relationship in a shared household' (St. Meld No. 50, 1984–85, p. 73). This definition did not exclude homosexual relationships and nearly caused the collapse of the coalition between the Conservative Party and the Christian Democratic Party (Noack, 2010, p. 166). The Christian Democrats did not want to acknowledge homosexual relationships in any way. To avoid a governmental crisis, the debate on the white paper ended without any voting on the proposals concerning legal regulations of cohabitation.

Apart from the lack of conclusion, the debate on this white paper is interesting because it shows the many changes in the way politicians approached family politics. There was agreement that it was at last possible to introduce new reforms for families, mainly concerning longer parental leave and more public childcare. The main issue in the debate (apart from homosexual cohabitation) was women's work and how to make it easier to combine children and employment. The idea now was that men and women ought to contribute both at home and at work. To reach this goal changes as more support for parents as well as shorter working hours were needed (St. Meld. No. 50, 1984–85, p. 11). With regard to cohabitation, the Conservative Party presented their view in the following way:

> The Conservative Party wishes to support marriage as a way of living together. In our view all who live together ought to have a contract that regulates the practical things in a relationship. Here marriage is the best, the simplest and the most tested way of doing this. But since not everyone wish or are able to marry – we have to respect that and discuss some rules that secure unmarried cohabitants and their children in certain situations. We have chosen rules regarding housing and inheritance.[16]

The parties were divided with regard to cohabitation. The Christian Democrats did not support any (positive) changes that would make marriage and cohabitation more equal. The Conservative Party, the Centre Party and the Labour Party wanted legal regulations to secure children and the weaker party. The Socialist Left Party wanted to make marriage and cohabitation equal in most legal matters, while the right-wing Progress Party wanted to preserve the status quo, reasoning that it was their own choice if people did not marry.

7. From marriage to committed relationships (1990s–2000s)

At the start of the 1990s, many discussions came to a close. The second 'positive' recognition in law of cohabitants came in the 1991 Household Community Act.[17] In this law, cohabitants (heterosexual, homosexual as well as brothers and sisters and other persons who shared a house/flat and covered the daily expenses of the household together) were included (NOU, 1988:12, p. 7). The law was very limited, but secured some rights with regard to the shared house/flat and furniture in case of break-up in the relationship or the death of one of the partners. On the same day that this law was voted through the Storting, the new Marriage Act was also discussed. Here, alterations were made that were in tune with the new ideas about gender equality and changes in the family:

> A marriage is between two autonomous and equal partners. Each partner is free to do as they wish with regard to property they have brought into the marriage, and what they earn, with the exception of house and furniture.[18]

The new Marriage Act stressed the principle of independence, and also restricted the obligation concerning alimony after divorce 'since each partner is supposed to seek economic independence'.[19] These changes made marriage more like cohabitation in many ways. Another important change that came in the early 1990s was the law on partnerships for homosexual partners, which gave those who registered the same rights as married partners (with some exceptions).[20]

The government appointed a new committee with the task of going through the issues related to heterosexual cohabitation on a broad basis. This resulted in the report 'Cohabitants and society' (NOU, 1999:25). Cohabitation was defined as heterosexual couples living together for some time (two years) or having children together. The report concluded that this kind of cohabitation ought to be more regulated in law, but not equalized with marriage.

When the subsequent white paper on the family called 'About the family – committed relationships and parenthood' (St. Meld. No. 29, 2002–2003) was discussed in the Storting, there was a new aspect regarding how marriage and cohabitation were discussed. The statements about the importance and advantages of marriage were still there, but stable relationships and the interests of children were considered more important by the majority. There was more talk about the family in different forms, and less about marriage. The majority argued that the time had come to make changes in the direction of 'positive' recognition of cohabitation in many areas, and this now also included the Christian Democrats. Only the right-wing Progress Party continued to argue that people should be allowed to make their own decisions about their relationships, and that the differences between marriage and cohabitation ought to be upheld. The chairman from the Christian Democrats responded that children did not have a choice, and argued that it was important that the state supports ways of making relationships more stable:

> A marriage or a long cohabitation relationship is not just rosy. Everyday life is overbooked, with little time to each other, and we are often silent about what causes trouble for us. In a packed everyday life the benefits we have in our society; cash for care, public childcare and arrangements in the labour market – are very important for a good family life [...] It's therefore very promising that the majority today will vote for the Government's suggestion of a one-day course in living together.[21]

The picture the debate gives of the situation of the family is one of families with two incomes, time bind with regard to care and work, and where it is an important goal to increase the responsibility of fathers. The view that relationships have to be 'worked on' has gained ground. With the exception of the right-wing Progress Party, all voted for the course mentioned by the minister. The understanding of the family was as this quote in the white paper indicates:

> We live in times that even with great support for the family, is characterized by loneliness, broken relationships and broken relations. There is an increase in divorces and break up in relationships that demands an offensive family policy. (St. Meld. No. 29, 2002–2003, p. 5)

Regulating unmarried cohabitation is considered a part of such a policy. The government argued that it was necessary to regulate cohabitation since this was best for children and the weaker party, even if they still thought marriage best and would also support marriage.[22] The change received a positive response from earlier opponents, who also used the opportunity to express their viewpoints concerning homosexuality and the aim of even greater equality between ways of living together:

> We have a white paper from a minister from the Christian People's Party suggesting that marriage and cohabitants are treated alike. That is positive. The minister has seen that it is not important for children whether their parents are married or not, if only they have a good and stable home. And people could be good parents if they have the same gender too. The Christian Democrats ought to note this.[23]

> The Socialist Left Party wants to underline that the family is important for children's development, however children may have good childhoods also without being connected to their biological family. The family is a broad concept, including different ways of living together, they are chosen by the individual freely, and has to be seen as equal.[24]

The debate in 2003 was the last in the Storting of any length on these issues. In its aftermath, major changes were voted on in the Storting with little or no debate. In 2003, cohabitants were allowed to take their partner's surname if they had children together or had lived together for a minimum of two years. In 2006, cohabiting couples were automatically given shared parental responsibility for their children (before, the mother had to sign a document). In 2007, cohabiting couples splitting up had to go to mandatory mediation if they had children; in addition, such couples were treated as married couples with regard to tax issues. In 2009, the inheritance laws were amended so that cohabitants with children together automatically got the right to some inheritance if their partner died (in 2013, up to approximately 4250 euros). In addition, cohabitants with children together (and no children with other partners) were allowed not to give out any heritance to the heirs before both were dead. Wills that stipulate other conditions are possible (Jussformidlingen, 2010; Noack, 2010, p. 213). In spring 2014, a new Adoption Act is introduced (Prop. 171 L, 2012–2013), which proposes that married and cohabiting couples are to be treated alike.

In sum, this means that there are relatively few differences left between marriage and cohabitation. Cohabiting partners without children who have lived together for less than two years (or who are registered at the same address) are not however treated as if married in any legislation. Whatever the length of the relationship, cohabiting partners have no legal duty to provide for each other as married partners have. There is also one important difference regarding paternity. If not married, the father has to declare paternity, which is mostly done to a doctor or nurse, before or after birth. In addition, there remain all the symbolic aspects of marriage: the ritual, the public declaration and the wedding, which are very important social markers of the relationship.

8. Discussion

Ideas about cohabitation have obviously changed dramatically in the period we have studied. In the Adoption Act (spring 2014), cohabitation is defined in the following way:

> Cohabitation involves only two parties. They may be of the same or have different sex. There will be a concrete assessment whether the applicants [for adoption] are cohabitants in the sense that they live together in a marriage-like relationship. A shared address in the people register is important, but not an absolute condition. (Prop. 171 L, 2012–2013, p. 57)

The way cohabitation is understood has become neutral with regard to homosexual and heterosexual relationships. The term 'marriage-like' excludes friends or siblings living together and it has to be two persons; but apart from that, the definition is flexible. This is a great contrast to earlier discussions of cohabitation. The understanding of cohabitation has also changed from being seen as an emerging problem of relevance to the very few, to long-term cohabitation as a major change in couple-formations that require action from the state.

One idea that has not changed is politicians' insistence that marriage is a good way of living together. This is repeated in all debates and documents. However, marriage is no longer talked about as a cornerstone of society. How people live together is more thought of as a choice about which the state should be more neutral. Strengthening commitment and children's needs are placed at the top of the agenda, enabling the positive recognition of cohabitation in parallel with marriage. The Norwegian approach to cohabitation has been called pragmatic, because it has adjusted to demographic changes (Noack, 2001, p. 115). The institutionalization of cohabitation is also so far mainly for couples with children. An important factor that has made cohabitation and marriage more alike is also the change that has taken place in marriage in the period. The main change occurred in 1991 when the Marriage Act was amended to emphasize that marriage was a union between independent and autonomous partners. The new act also provided more opportunity to divide property unequally after divorce (Sverdrup, 1999). The other important change came in 2009 when same-sex couples were given the same right as heterosexual couples to marry, and the 1993 law of partnership (for same-sex couples only) abolished. When homosexuals were given the right to partnership and marriage, it became difficult not to regulate heterosexual relationships.

One interesting feature in the Norwegian process is that there has not been any major change in the expressed policy towards marriage and cohabitation. Emphasizing the importance of keeping marriage and cohabitation separate – discussing changes concerning cohabitation first 'negatively' and then 'positively', one by one – has made every move less dramatic. If a Cohabitation Act had been proposed as the end result at any point in time, the development could have taken other directions. This may well be one of the factors that have made the institutionalization process possible. Another factor is the way 'negative' recognition came about in the contextual framework of preventing allowance fraud and supporting marriage. The 'negative' recognition of cohabitation was based on the idea of the traditional male main bread-winner who opted out.

Sociological theories about changes in intimacy and personal commitment are broadly relevant to cohabitation in the sense that they address changes in the content and meaning of couple relationships on economic, practical, and emotional issues. On the one hand, some have viewed the rise of cohabitation as part of a general trend towards looser, less committed long-term relationships (Beck & Beck-Gernsheim, 2002; Giddens, 1992). Marriage as an institution has weakened and fewer people feel they have to marry; divorce is a real option and more couples live together without marrying. Traditional social structures have lost much of their influence. The individualization thesis and the detraditionalization thesis have focused on the increase in individual choice (May, 2011, p. 5). On the other hand, opposing theories have claimed that this emphasis on choice is grossly exaggerated and that people are still embedded in social structures and that relational considerations have a great impact on people's lives. They note the continuing importance of structural conditions (see, for example, Jamiesson, 1999) and how personal life also in contemporary Western societies is characterized by strong and emotional bonds (May, 2011; Smart, 2007). Modern cohabitation is then viewed as being more a type of connectedness than the opposite and the main difference is that there is no longer a moral distinction between marriage and cohabitation (Lewis, 2001). It could however be asked if this is a question of one or the other. My own research on cohabitation and marriage (Syltevik, 2000, 2010) supports this; people interviewed understand both types of union formations as ways of making commitments. However, my and indeed other research (Noack, 2010; Reneflot, 2010) demonstrate that many consider marriage as making an extra commitment and cohabitation as 'looser' and more of a step along the way.

The idea about the family that emerges among Norwegian politicians during the period studied is obviously one of more fragile and unstable relationships, which resembles the picture of the family that individualization/detraditionalization theorists give. Politicians have also taken up the ideology of couple relationships as being something that the partners have to 'work' to keep up (Giddens, 1992). On the other hand, they view the state as an important actor in the process of making committed, stable relationships possible and the present situation is an argument for an offensive family policy. In this context, the 'positive' recognition of cohabitation (mandatory negotiation after a break, the new inheritance laws, and so on) is seen as necessary regulation to protect children and their parents from the negative effects of not marrying.

9.   Concluding remarks

The political shift represents a change of focus from protection of marriage towards the protection of children. At present, both marriage and cohabitation are institutionalized in Norwegian society; they are both ways of making a commitment towards a partner. Cohabitation followed by marriage is in accordance with present norms of family formation; establishing relationships slowly, planning for a proper (and often expensive) wedding, as well as taking love seriously (Syltevik, 2010). Cohabitation makes it possible to develop relationships further before you eventually feel ready to marry. Cohabitation is a more gradual ways of making a commitment in an individualistic culture with ideals of gender equality and relationships between autonomous independent partners. One could say that the recognition and institutionalization of cohabitation in Norway have overruled this drive towards informality by regulating relationships, even if couples with children together do not marry, or they have been living together for some time.

Historically, cohabitation has gone from being an illegal towards becoming a worthy status. Nowadays, cohabitation in Norway is recognized in society both on the micro and macro level. An exciting question concerns what will happen from now on. The relationship between laws and behaviour is complex. First, it is not clear how well known these regulations are. Many couples will probably still act according to the old rules for many years to come. Second, even if the rules are known, their effect on behaviour could be manifold. Will people marry because of the wedding ceremony or the other differences that still exist? These differences may still have great symbolic meaning. Or will people stop bothering about getting married when there is nearly no difference?

Notes

1. In 1965, nearly every second Norwegian bride was pregnant (Ramsoy, 1994).
2. Among mothers who gave birth in 2012, 13% were single, 43% cohabiting, and 44% married (SSB, 2013).
3. This ideational approach does not imply that I think structural explanations are irrelevant. On the contrary, I agree with Ruggles (2012, p. 435f) that probably both changes in families and patriarchal ideology are related to the enormous structural changes of the Industrial Revolution and the emerging wage labour outside the household.
4. This became very apparent when Crown Prince Haakon moved in with his then-girlfriend Mette-Marit Tjessem Høiby in 2000. When the Royal Palace announced that she and her three-year-old son would move in with Haakon in his flat, the discussion was more about her suitability as a partner than about cohabitation. Representatives from the Church said: 'The church would have preferred that the Crown Prince did not follow the conventions of his own age group, but formalized the relationship through marriage' (The Norway Post, 2000).
5. The parliamentary debates and political documents are available at the home page of the Norwegian Storting from 1814 to the present (Stortingstidende 1814–2010, http://www. Stortinget.no/no/Saker-og-publikasjoner/Stortingsforhandlinger/). I used the search terms cohabitation, living together without marriage, family, and marriage to identify significant documents.
6. When laws are discussed, the Storting is divided into two chambers: the Odelsting and the Lagting.
7. To live together 'as if married' had been illegal and punished with fines and prison according to the Criminal Act of 1842. There were around 150–200 convictions each year between 1842 and 1885. From 1885 until 1900, there were around 50 yearly, while this decreased to just a few at the start of the new century (Solli, 2004).
8. All quotations are translated from Norwegian by the author. The debates are found in Stortingstidende 1814–2010, http://www.Stortinget.no/no/Saker-og-publikasjoner/Stortings-forhandlinger/ under the mentioned dates and the page numbers refer to the original documents. This quote is by Asbjørn Haugstvedt, Christian Democrat MP, the Odelsting, 21 March 1972, p. 307.
9. Rolf Furuseth, Labour MP, the Odelsting, 21 March 1972, p. 306. Citation from the Stortingstidende 1814–2010 website: http://www.Stortinget.no/no/Saker-og-publikasjoner/ Stortingsforhandlinger/.
10. Jens Haugland, Labour MP, the Odelsting, 21 March 1972, p. 318. Citation from the Stortingstidende 1814–2010 website: http://www.Stortinget.no/no/Saker-og-publikasjoner/ Stortingsforhandlinger/.
11. Olav Totland, Labour MP, the Odelsting, 21 March 1972, p. 309, and Bent Røiseland, Liberal MP, the Odelsting, 21 March 1972, p. 309. Citation from the Stortingstidende 1814–2010 website: http://www.Stortinget.no/no/Saker-og-publikasjoner/Stortingsforhandlinger/.
12. Liv Andersen, Labour MP, the Lagting, 14 June 1972, p. 116. Citation from the Stortingstidende 1814–2010 website: http://www.Stortinget.no/no/Saker-og-publikasjoner/ Stortingsforhandlinger/.

13. Gerd Kiste, Conservative MP, the Odelsting, 18 March 1980, p. 223f. Citation from the Stortingstidende 1814–2010 website: http://www.Stortinget.no/no/Saker-og-publikasjoner/ Stortingsforhandlinger/.
14. Kjellaug Nakkim, Conservative MP, the Odelsting, 9 December 1993. Citation from the Stortingstidende 1814–2010 website: http://www.Stortinget.no/no/Saker-og-publikasjoner/ Stortingsforhandlinger/.
15. Official reports are written by committees appointed by the government. Citation from the Stortingstidende 1814–2010 website: http://www.Stortinget.no/no/Saker-og-publikasjoner/ Stortingsforhandlinger/.
16. Annelise Høeg, Conservative MP, the Storting, 3 June 1985, p. 4227. Citation from the Stortingstidende 1814–2010 website: http://www.Stortinget.no/no/Saker-og-publikasjoner/ Stortingsforhandlinger/.
17. Odelstingdebate, 7 June 1991, pp. 604–611. The debate is found at the Stortingstidende 1814– 2010 website: http://www.Stortinget.no/no/Saker-og-publikasjoner/Stortingsforhandlinger/.
18. Wenche Frogn Sellæg, Labour MP, the Odelsting, 7 June 1991, p. 569. Citation from the Stortingstidende 1814–2010 website: http://www.Stortinget.no/no/Saker-og-publikasjoner/ Stortingsforhandlinger/.
19. Odelsting debate, 7 June 1991, p. 570. The debate is found at the Stortingstidende 1814–2010 website: http://www.Stortinget.no/no/Saker-og-publikasjoner/Stortingsforhandlinger/.
20. Odelsting debate, 29 March 1993, pp. 445–541. The debate is found at the Stortingstidende 1814–2010 website: http://www.Stortinget.no/no/Saker-og-publikasjoner/Stortingsforhan-dlinger/.
21. Dagrun Eriksen, Christian Democrats MP, the Storting, 27 November 2003, p. 732. Citation from the Stortingstidende 1814–2010 website: http://www.Stortinget.no/no/Saker-og-publikasjoner/Stortingsforhandlinger/.
22. Minister for children and the family Laila Davøy, Christian Democrats, Storting debate, 27 November 2003, p. 740. Citation from the Stortingstidende 1814–2010 website: http:// www.Stortinget.no/no/Saker-og-publikasjoner/Stortingsforhandlinger/.
23. Eirin Faldet, Labour MP, Storting debate, 27 November 2003, p. 733. Citation from the Stortingstidende 1814–2010 website: http://www.Stortinget.no/no/Saker-og-publikasjoner/ Stortingsforhandlinger/.
24. May Hansen, Socialist Left Party MP, Storting debate, 27 November 2003, p. 737. Citation from the Stortingstidende 1814–2010 website: http://www.Stortinget.no/no/Saker-og-publikasjoner/Stortingsforhandlinger/.

References

Asland, J. (2005). Norske rettsregler om ekteskap, samboerskap og partnerskap [Norwegian law regulation for marriage, cohabitation and partnership]. In B. Thorbjørnsrud (Ed.), *Evig din? Ekteskaps- og samlivstradisjoner i det flerreligiøse Norge [For ever yours? Marriage and cohabitation in the multireligous Norway]* (pp. 37–59). Oslo: Abstrakt Forlag.

Beck, U., & Beck-Gernsheim, E. (2002). *Individualization*. London/Thousand Oaks/New Dehli: Sage.

Béland, D. (2009). Ideas, institutions, and policy change. *Journal of European Public Policy, 16,* 701–718.

Cherlin, A. J. (2010). *The marriage-go-round. The state of marriage and the family in America today*. New York: Vintage Books.

Elliassen, J., & Sogner, S. (Eds.). (1981). *Bot eller bryllup: Ugifte mødre og gravide bruder i det gamle samfunnet [Punishment or wedding: Unmarried mothers and pregnant brides in the old society]*. Oslo/Bergen/Tromsø: Universitetsforlaget.

Gaunt, D., & Nyström, L. (1996). The Scandinavian model. In A. Burguière, C. Klapisch-Zuber, M. Segalen, & F Zonabend (Eds.), *A history of the family. Volume II: The impact of modernity* (pp. 476–501). Paris: Polity Press.

Giddens, A. (1992). *The transformation of intimacy*. Cambridge: Polity Press.

Gulli, B. (1992). *Moderskapets frigjørelse? Offentlig likestillingspolitikk på 1970-tallet [The emancipation of motherhood]*. Oslo: Universitetsforlaget.

Jamiesson, L. (1999). Intimacy transformed: A critical look at the pure relationship. *Sociology, 33,* 477–494.

Jussformidlingen. (2010). *Ugift samliv [Unmarried cohabitation]*. Stavanger: Jussformidlingen UniversityI of Bergen.

Kiernan, K. (2004). Unmarried cohabitation and parenthood in Britain and Europe. *Law & Policy, 26*, 33–55.

Leinarte, D. (2012). Cohabitation in imperial Russia: The case of Lithuania. *The History of the Family, 17*, 16–30.

Lewis, J. (2001). *The end of marriage? Individualism and intimate relations*. Cheltenham/ Northhampton: Edward Elgar.

May, V. (Ed.). (2011). *Sociology of personal life*. London: Palgrave Macmillan.

Nazio, T. (2008). *Cohabitation, family and society*. New York/London: Routledge.

Noack, T. (2001). Cohabitation in Norway: An accepted and gradually more regulated way of living. *International Journal of Law, Policy and the Family, 15*, 102–117.

Noack, T. (2010). *En stille revolusjon: Det moderne samboerskapet i Norge [A silent revolution: Modern cohabitation in Norway]* (Unpublished doctoral dissertation). Department of Sociology and Human Geography, University of Oslo.

Ramsoy, N. R. (1994). Non-marital cohabitation and change in norms: The case of Norway. *Acta Sociologica, 37*, 23–37.

Reneflot, A. (2010). *The drift away from marriage. Implications for children's family lives and future welfare* (Dissertation for the PhD degree) Department of Economics, Faculty of Social Sciences, University of Oslo.

Ruggles, S. (2012). The future of historical family demography. *Annual Review of Sociology, 38*, 423–441.

Scott, J. (1990). *A matter of record. Documentary sources in social research*. Cambridge: Polity Press.

Skevik, A. (2001). *Family ideology and social policy*. (Report No. 7) Oslo: Norwegian Social Research (NOVA).

Skevik, A. (2004). A Gilded cage? Help and control in early Norwegian Social Policy. *Journal of Family History, 29*, 211–224.

Smart, C. (2007). *Personal life. New directions in sociological thinking*. Cambridge: Polity.

Smock, P. J. (2000). Cohabitation in the United States: An appraisal of research themes, findings, and implications. *Annual Review of Sociology, 26*(1), 1–20.

Sogner, S. (Ed.). (2003). *I gode og onde dagar: Familieliv i Noreg frå reformasjonen til vår tid [In good an evil days: Family life in Norway from reformation till today]*. Oslo: Det norske samlaget.

Solli, A. (2004). *Fødslar utanfor ekteskap og sambuarskap mellom ugifte. Normer og åtferd i Noreg på 1800-talet [Extramarital births and cohabitation between unmarried persons. Norms and behaviour in Norway in the 18th century]* Lecture for the degree of Dr. Art, University of Bergen 27th of May 2004. Retrieved from https://bora-uib-no.pva.uib.no/

SSB [Statistics Norway]. (2012). *Samboere 2011 [Cohabitation 2011]* (published 31 May 2013). Retrieved from http://www.ssb.no/samboer

SSB [Statistics Norway]. (2013). *Fødte 2012 [Births 2012]* (published 18 April 2013). Retrieved from http://www.ssb.no/fodte

Sundt, E. (1968). *Om sæderlighetstilstanden i Norge 2 [On sexual morality in Norway]*. Oslo/ Gjøvik: Gyldendal Norsk Forlag.

Sverdrup, T. (1999). Ekteskapet – arbeidsfellesskap eller livsfellesskap? [Marriage – working relationship or life relationship]. *Tidsskrift for velferdsforskning, 2*, 102–116.

Syltevik, L. J. (2000). *Differensierte familieliv [Differenciated family lives]* (Report No. 1) Bergen: Senter for samfunnsforskning (SEFOS).

Syltevik, L. J. (2010). Sense and sensibility: Cohabitation in 'cohabitation-land'. *Sociological Review, 58*, 444–462.

The Norway Post. (2000, July 5). *Weekend feature: Royal cohabitation*. Retrieved from http://www. Norway post.no/index/php/news/62/20409

Therborn, G (2004). *Between sex and power: Family in the world, 1900–2000*. London/New York: Routledge.

Vollset, G. (2011). *Familiepolitikkens historie – 1970 til 2000 [The history of family policy – 1970 to 2000]* (Report No. 1) Oslo: Norsk institutt for forskning om oppvekst, velferd og aldring (NOVA).

Official documents

NOU 1976:19 *Stønad til enslige forsørgere m.v. [Support for single parents].*

NOU 1980:50 *Samliv uten vigsel [Living together without marriage].*

NOU 1988:12 *Husstandsfellesskap [Household community].*

NOU 1999:25 *Samboerne og samfunnet [Cohabitants and society].*

Ot. Prp. No. 5 (1971–72) *Om lov om endringer i den alminnelige borgerlige straffelov 22 mai 1902 Nr 10 [On changes in the general penal code No. 10].*

Ot. Prp. No. 52 (1990–91) *Om lov om rett til felles bolig og innbo når husstandsfellesskap opphører [On the right to a shared house and furniture when a household splits].*

Ot. Prp. No 82 (2003–2004) *Om lov om endringer I barneloven (felles foreldreansvar for samboende foreldre) [On changes in the Children's Act (shared parental responsibility for cohabiting parents)].*

Ot. Prp. No. 73 (2007–2008) *Om lov om endringer i arveloven (mv.) (arv og uskifte for samboere) [On changes in the Inheritance Act (with more) (Inheritance and undivision for cohabitants].*

Ot. Prp. No. 33 (2007–2008) *Om lov om endringer i ekteskapsloven, arveloven, adopsjonsloven, bioteknologiloven m.v. (felles ekteskapslov for hetereofile og homofile par) [(Common Act of Marriage for heterosexual and homosexual couples].*

Prop. No. 171 L (2012–2013) *Endringer i adopsjonsloven m.v. [Changes in the Act of Adoption].*

St. Meld. No. 117 (1972–73) *Barnefamilienes levekår [The living conditions of families with children].*

St. Meld. No. 25 (1981–85) *Om noen familiepolitiske spørsmål [On some family political questions].*

St. Meld. No. 50 (1984–85) *Om familiepolitikken [About the family policy].*

St. Meld. No. 29 (2002–2003) *Om familien – forpliktende samliv og foreldreskap [About the family – committed relationships and parenthood].*

Stigmatized cohabitation in the Latvian region of the eastern Baltic littoral: nineteenth and twentieth centuries

Andrejs Plakans and Ineta Lipša

The social history of coresidence arrangements in the Latvian region suggests that forms of cohabitation without marriage were present in the Latvian population since the eighteenth century when empirical evidence became available. Before the twentieth century, however, these forms remained marginal and seldom involved choice. The subject of severe criticism until the 1960s–1970s, such forms become more widespread thereafter as the Latvian population began to exhibit many key features of a second demographic revolution. Post-Soviet censuses now suggest that such coresidence patterns in the Latvian population approach the levels of those in most western European states, including the Scandinavian countries.

1. Introduction

A series of earlier publications based on microdata and focusing on the eighteenth and nineteenth centuries has already analyzed in some detail the coresidential patterns and other socio-demographic characteristics of the Latvian-speaking population of the Baltic provinces of the Russian Empire (Plakans, 1975; Plakans & Wetherell, 1992, 1995, 1998). In these centuries, virtually all Latvian-speakers – estimated in 1800 at about 873,000 persons – lived in the adjacent provinces of Livland and Courland (two of the so-called Baltic Provinces) as well as in the western districts of of Vitebsk province (Dunsdorfs, 1973, p. 282). At the beginning of the nineteenth century, the vast majority of them were enserfed peasants on landed estates owned primarily (in Livland and Courland) by members of the Baltic German minority (about 6.5% of the total population), and, in the Vitebsk districts, primarily by Russian, Polish, and polonized German landholders. The dominant form of rural settlement in Livland and Courland was the isolated farmstead, and in the western districts of Vitebsk differing kinds of farmstead clusters. In most localities, the proportion of farmsteads with complex families of the heads was relatively high, but these complex groupings coresided with married and unmaried male farmhands and unmarried female farmhands. If farmhands had families, these families were usually simple in structure. Mean *farmstead* size therefore tended to be high, in the range of 15–16 persons (Plakans, 1983, p.180).

Among the privileges landowners possessed were patronage rights (Ger. *Patronat*), which included the right to appoint pastors of the local congregations – Lutheran in Livland and Courland and Roman Catholic in the Vitebsk districts. As a consequence, most of the local clergymen, who were also the record-keepers for their congregants, had

had to learn the Latvian language used by members of their flocks. When Imperial Russia acquired the eastern Baltic littoral from Sweden in the early eighteenth century, Tsar Peter I ('the Great') had agreed that the political class of the Baltic provinces – the titled Baltic German aristocracy – would retain a substantial amount of autonomy in matters of local governance. As a consequence, until late in the nineteenth century, the historical records containing population microdata were prepared in the German language rather than in Russian, as might have been expected. The Latvian language began to appear in local records only in the second half of the nineteenth century, and then only sporaidically.

Counting from 1795 when the last fragment of Baltic territory passed to the Russian Empire as part of the last partition of the Polish–Lithuanian Commonwealth, the Latvian territories of the eastern Baltic littoral experienced six regime changes in the next two centuries: 1795 (Russian Empire), 1918 (first independence), 1940 (annexation to the USSR), 1941 (inclusion in the Third Reich), 1944–45 (re-occupation by USSR), 1991 (second independence). Each change in governing systems brought with it new ways of enumerating the general population, and though there was always a degree of continuity between the records of contiguous regimes, there are no demographic and social-structural variables for which there are continuous documentary records over the entire two centuries. Consequently, when in the late 1960s innovative approaches to quantitative social-structural history and in historical demography came to the fore in western historical scholarship, the social-structural data from Latvian territories that could be used for comparisons was by necessity fragmentary. During the decades when the Latvian territory was part of the USSR, detailed information about the population was in any case surrounded by secrecy, and published results of the Soviet censuses (as carried out in the Latvian SSR) remained very general. As far as information about periods of time in the distant past were concerned, historical demography has never developed as a distinct specialty among Latvian historians, and Soviet- period Latvian demographers generally focused on the post-1945 decades, occasionally glancing backward to the so-called interwar period of 'bourgeois dominance' and to the aggregate population figures of the 1897 Russian Imperial census. Western historical inquiry focusing on such questions as family and household structure, family formation, the demographic revolution, marriage age, fertility, mortality and related matters found little resonance in Latvian-language scholarship (an exception is Efremova, 1982); moreover, interest in such themes has remained minimal even in the two decades since the re-establishment of Latvian independence in 1991. The difficult task of extracting comparable information from archival sources for a time series for any social-structural and demographic variable remains to be started, though a few exceptions do exist to this general observation as far localities are concerned (Auns, 2004; 2006; 2007; 2009). The task of identifying the approximate beginning of long-term trends of any kind has therefore remained difficult, particularly so in the case of the social practices that produced different forms of the domestic group.

2. Coresidence and cohabitation: pre-modern era

As of this writing, coresidence in households in the Latvian-speaking territory (i.e. who lived with whom) is the only micro-social-structural variable about which there is fairly reliable information for the long term, but even this evidence remains fragmentary and localized. Moreover, information about household composition in the distant past does not offer systematic empirical data about the coresidence of *unmarried* persons (cohabitation) who might have been living together *as if* they were married. Most of these eighteenth- and nineteenth-century microdata about coresidence come from fiscal censuses called 'revisions of souls,' and the enumerators who prepared the revision had little interest in probing the subtleties of personal relationships within a coresidential unit. The relational language used in the soul revisions is restricted to terms reflecting the formal marriage bond (husband, wife), kinship (son, brother-in-law), employer–employee relations (head, farmhand, herder), and temporary coresidential arrangements (lodger, retiree). The aggregate counts obtained from the soul revisions for localities and larger administrative units were used to calculate payments of a head-tax to the Crown, and practices used in local enumerations varied. Social descriptions using the soul revisions in any case have dealt almost exclusively with rural areas, so that coresidence/cohabitation patterns in small towns or cities of the Latvian territory in the distant past remain almost entire unknown at this time.

One institution that did have an interest in the deeper probing of the personal relationships among coresidents of domestic groups was the Evangelical Lutheran Church of the Baltic region. The 'chronicles' kept by local clergy about events in their own parishes and the reports sent by them to the Consistory have been shown to be useful for information about irregular personal relationships and about how local clergy dealt with infractions of Church regulations concerning married life. Unfortunately, these archival collections have not been used by historians extensively, and as of this writing only one Latvian historian – Gvido Straube – has recognized their potential for on-the-ground social history and has begun to use them systematically (Straube, 2013). Fortunately, Straube's current research bears on the central topic of concern to us and his findings deserve a brief description. He investigated these ecclesiatical sources for the centuries before the twentieth for evidence about 'civil marriage,' i.e. cohabitation without formal marriage, and discovered repeated mention of punishments for irregular sexual and/or marital relationships. These violations of the 'rules' of everyday social life were common enough not to surprise the local clergy. Embedded in these Church-stigmatized activities there may have been longer-term arrangments among the involved individuals that could conceivably resemble what much later on would be termed 'cohabitation.'

Straube's interpretation of these incidents is that in the cases where a couple did coreside this was most likely because of the Church's own internal rule. Thus, for example, the Church required of communicants a minimum of demonstrable knowledge of its teachings contained in the catechism, prayers, reading, and hymns. Those who had not learned these things by the normal confirmation age (mid-teens) and, at the moment of wanting to be married still did not know them, could not be accepted into the congregation – a prerequiste for official marriage. One outcome was cohabitation until the required examination was passed. Another example concerns widow- or widowerhood and the desire of the surviving partner to be remarried before the official one year of mourning had expired. Straube has uncovered appeals – mostly unsucessful – to the Consistory for permission to shorten the mourning period for such 'unmarried' couples since there was already a child in the offing. How complicated such localized infractions of official marriage rules could become can be illustrated by one story dealing with 'illegitimate' children (here presented with detail not in the cited source):

> In 1767 it was shown that Anna, the daughter of a peasant in Dole, then aged about 26 years, had had a son with Indrikis from Bēči farmstead, the two having met frequently since Easter of 1763. The parents of the child did not deny their sexual relationship, and in fact Indrikis proudly admitted that he had fathered the child. Yet since the parents had not formed an official and Christian marriage and therfore had produced an 'illegitimate' child, each of them received punishment of approximately fifty kopeks and corporal punishment (to be delivered in front of the local church) – Indikis ten and Anna five strokes of the switch (rod) (Straube, 2013, pp. 70–71).

The account does not make absolutely clear how cohabitation (living together) in the modern sense was managed by the two young people: their everday lives, after all, unfolded in a very open social context (the farmstead or farmsteads where they lived) and therefore their coresidents must have been accepting of their relationship to some extent. Judging by the punishment meted out by the Church, however, outright flouting of custom and church regulations could result in relatively harsh sanctions. On the other hand, lack of remorse by the man in the story also suggests that existing 'rules' – customary or religious – were insufficient for fully controlling the behavior of sexually active young people, with the result that various forms of sexual congress outside of marriage were interpreted by some of the laity as not 'sinful,' even if they produced out-of-wedlock children.

Straube ended his findings with the following observation:

> Summarizing the discussion, we can say that the conclusion has to be that peasants disliked living in 'civil marriage,' and that most often such a situation developed through circumstances beyond their control. Frequently, the blame rested with the estate owners, who at times refused to give permission for 'their' peasants to marry for reasons that can hardly be called rational. In other cases, the blame rests with the overly conscientious clergy who sought to strictly obey all church rules and regulations. It is also true that some peasants did not view cohabitation without the blessing of the church as sinful. At times, 'civil marriage' was exploited by those who did not wish to burden themselves with the responsibilities of marriage and were disposed to change their female partners frequently. Thus one can say with considerable certainty that in the nineteenth century, and even in the eighteenth and seventeenth centuries, in Vidzeme (Livland) one can find instances of 'civil marriage' and that these were brought about by external forces. The rural inhabitants themselves did not engender such forms of coresidence as a norm of their everyday life (Straube, 2013, p.75).

The extent to which Straube's findings can be accepted as characteristic for the whole of the Latvian territory remains an open question. Vidzeme (Livland; Livonia) was only one of the adjacent provinces in which Latvians lived: Kurzeme (Kurland; Courland) was another, as were the western districts of Vitebsk, to the east of Vidzeme. Also remaining open is the question of whether Lutheranism dealt with these matters in the same fashion as did Roman Catholic congregations or, for than matter, other denominations of the Baltic region that even in the eighteenth and nineteenth century was already multi-confessional and multi-cultural. And Straube's painstaking research also highlights another important fact about the pre-twentieth century era, namely, that unless enumerators of these populations deliberately chose to ask respondents about non-marital cohabitation (and few did), one is unlikely to find hard information about it in the census-like surveys that these enumerators produced. An accurate mapping of the phenomenon for the whole territory therefore remains a distant and perhaps unreachable goal.

3. Out-of-wedlock birth as an indicator

As Straube's research indicates, in the Latvian territories of the nineteenth century out-of-wedlock births may or may not be a good indicator of the co-residential arrangements of the partners that produced them. It is quite true, however, that the Latvian provinces were hardly immune to sexual activity outside marriage. The available archival sources seldom chronicle such activity systematically, perhaps assuming that they were merely localized and relatively rare. Out-of-wedlock births are mentioned in the ecclesiastical records (parish registers) but other descriptive sources barely speak of them. Only in the second half of the century did contemporary Baltic researchers who were exploring the new domain of public health begin an effort to measure the extent of the problem. Thus, for example, such publications as the 1867 *Land und Leute der Mitauischen*

Oberhauptmanschaft by Baron Alfons von Heyking (the scientific secretary of the Kurland Statistical Committee) began to analyze 'births' in the birth register of Sessau parish in terms of 'legitimate' (Ger. *ehelich*) and 'illegitimate' (Ger. *unehelich*) children, reporting in several paragraphs that in the period from 1859 to 1865 of the 2075 children born in Sessau 4.6% were in the latter category (Heyking, 1867, pp. 18–19). These social statistics were meant to be descriptive and the Baron analyzed them sparingly, leaving the impression that he was only interested in out-of-wedlock births as an indicator of the existence of a social problem of which authorities should take note. Another similar kind of contemporary publication frequently contained the term *Biostatik* in the title and went a few steps farther in analysis. Such monographs were frequently dissertations, or studies based on dissertations, written for doctor-of-medicine degrees at the University of Dorpat in Livland, and as a genre of scholarship appear to have grasped the larger significance of such data. Thus, for example, Ewald Kaspar in 1883 published *Biostatik der Stadt Libau und ihrer Landgeminde in the Jahren 1834–1882*, in which he devoted a whole chapter to the 'legitimacy standing of children born alive' (Kaspar, 1883). Here statistics about 'legitimately' and 'illegitimately' born infants were presented as percentages of all births (not in absolute numbers, as is frequently the case with these early analyses) so that they could be compared with findings in other areas of the Baltic region as well as with those from German lands and other European countries. Kaspar was thus interested in diagnosing the extent of the 'problem' and not just reporting its presence. One interesting aspect of the Kaspar figures is the much lower illegitimacy rate for the rural (ethnically Latvian) congregation of the city of Libau (a city in western Courland) – 4.06% – in comparison with the urban congregations (German, Russian Orthodox) for which the percentages range from 13.5% to 12.3% (Kaspar, 1883, p. 24). Only the urban Jewish congregation in Libau had a rate lower than the Latvian – 0.93%.

Neither Heyking nor Kaspar pursued in their publications the familial circumstances that might have led to 'illegitimate' births nor did they explore the living arrangements of the partners that produced them. There was no reason to expect such deeper analysis, of course, given the fact that indigenous Baltic-area socio-demographic fact-gathering was clearly in its infancy, even in the second half of the nineteenth century. Any attempt to relate the clumsily presented and generally sparse illegitimacy statistics from particular localities to underlying marital or non-marital relationships would have needed a higher order of awareness than these proto-statisticians had at their disposal. Findings were too often reported not as simply social facts about a population group but as an indicator of the level of its 'moral education' (Ger. *sittlichen Bildungstand*, e.g. Jung-Stilling, 1874, p. 46). Moreover, the entire subject of 'coresidence' still remained somewhat mysterious to these gatherers of social statistics, as was evident from the discussions accompanying the first region-wide Baltic provincial census, which ocurred in 1881. Enumerators had to devise questions that would clearly delineate a *household*, distinguish the place of residence where a respondent was *registered* from that where he or she was actually residing, solve the problem of family members actually living in different places, and sort out unrelated people living together as lodgers and as families with servants. The question of 'family status' (Ger. *Familienstand*) was similarly problematic and the enumerators finally settled on providing only four possible variants – single, married, widowed or separated (Stieda, 1881, pp. 150–151; Wittschewsky, 1881; Plakans & Wetherell, 2004). Disagreements over basic definitions, the decentralization of the published results and their tabulation by different people in different provinces, and the lack of good models to follow rendered the census results difficult to interpret. By settling on a restrictive definition of 'family status,' moreover, family-like formations not sanctioned by custom, religion, and the law were effectively excluded from any social portraiture based on the census results. Extreme subjectivity in the understanding of what constituted a micro-social structure continued in the sole Imperial Russian census of 1897 and into those taken after the Russian Revolution. As Anderson observed:

> Who was considered a married person or a divorced person... varied among censuses. In 1897, enumerators were only supposed to record as married those were were legally (officially) married. In later censuses, people were to be recorded as married who considered themselves so, whether the marriage was registered or not (Anderson, 1986, p. 144).

4. Public media to World War I

The deeper interest in social phenomena during the nineteenth century in these semi-scholarly writings materialized also in the proliferation in the Latvian regions of periodical publications and newspapers, primarily in German and Latvian (Zelče, 2009). This was the beginning of the Latvian information age in print form, but it did not yet include the appearance of modern journalism as a profession. Writing for newspapers and periodicals tended to be an adjunct activity to a person's real livelihood. Also, the print media directly reflected the views and interests of specialized groupings such as the 'enlightened' clergy who positioned themselves as educators of the peasantry, the Baltic German so-called *Literatenstand* which struggled with the Baltic German landed aristocracy for power and influence, Latvian nationalists who saw as their target the entire Baltic German population, and, toward the end of the century, radicals of various kinds who sought between the lines of their writings to criticize Russian autocracy. This welter of print publications from the 1820s onward seldom simply reported events and analyzed situations: the writing in them was didactic, unapologetically opinionated, unsystematic, and heavily reliant on uncollaborated stories that for one reason or another had come to the writers' attention. Licenses to publish had to be sought from St. Petersburg, and the institution of the government censor was omnipresent. Even in the least combative of these publications there was already a taste for sensational stories, such as reports about the murder of an abandoned female farmworker by her lover, and, from local communities, stories about births outside wedlock (Anonymous, 1822, March 23; W-r., 1824, May 29; –e, 1850, March 23; S...c, 1850, March 23). Such elements of everyday social life were reported less to keep readers informed than to create the opportunity for moralizing conclusions about proper behavior. In this vein, newspapers reported the presence in the Latvian countryside of an evidently widespread practice of 'going to the girls' (Latv. *meitās iešana*, also known as 'night courting' or 'night running'), which consisted of a small group of young men organizing night visits to one or another farmstead where unmarried young women were known to be living, and spending with them the whole night or part of the night (Reinsone, 2009, p. 22–29; Bērziņš, 2009, p. 93; Lapiņš, 1936, p. 149; Gr., 1873, December 8; Kln., 1875, August 9; Krastin, 1867, July 30; Lindenberg, 1871, June 16; T. M., 1864, October 5; T. S., 1864, March 30; W. A.S. W., 1859, May 28). Such reports suggested that the adults of the targeted farmstead were complicit in the visits or at least tolerated them. Moralizers condemned the practice in no uncertain terms, even though it may have been a semi-ritualistic custom of long standing meant to allow some contact among young people. No serious efforts were launched to investigate how widespread the practice was and what its consequences may have been, with descriptions of the practice being placed under the rubric of 'immoral behavior.' There were suggestions that the practice symbolized the spread of 'urban immorality' to the countryside, insofar as the second half of the ninteenth century experienced a rapid expansion in the population of the largest cities of the Baltic provinces such as Riga, Tallinn (Ger. *Reval*), Jelgava (Ger. *Mitau*), and Liepāja (Ger. *Libau*). Latvian-language authors such as Jēkabs Apsītis in the 1880s did much in his stories to juxtapose the 'immoral city' with the 'moral countryside,' thus further popularizing this already widespread stereotype (Hausmanis, 1998/2001, I/III, p. 153). It is of some interest that in this ménage of stigmatized behaviors cohabitation without marriage (in the modern sense) is mentioned seldom, this fact paralleling its near-absence from the statistical tables of more 'scientific' writings such as census publications and 'serious' journals such as the *Baltische Monatschrift*. If mentioned at all or even hinted at, illegitimate births and cohabitation without marriage continued to be seen as issues pertaining to 'public health.' Generally speaking, both Baltic German and Latvian authors in the second half of the nineteenth century reflected the Victorian-era puritanical avoidance of direct public discussion of matters involving sexual relations. The general belief was widespread that the public exposition of the reasons that lay behind various forms of 'immoral behavior' would have the effect of encouraging more of it. Occasionally, newspapers stories hinted at the existence of a sub-surface world of illicit behaviors: in 1904, a local meeting of clergymen called by the pastor of Skujene, V. Kasparsons, discussed the issue of whether a pastor should permit young girls who were known to have 'fallen' (Latv. *kritušām jaunavām)* to wear the traditional myrtle wreath at their wedding, since the wreath symbolized virginity (Anonymous, 1904, January 14; Anonymous, 1904, January 15). Kasparsons argued that girls have to be allowed to decide for themselves, but the discussion suggested that a large number of clergy wanted to issue such denials.

Public discussion in the print media of 'immoral' behaviors increased exponentially during the late 1880s and 1890s, forced into greater openness by literary influences from western Europe that resulted in the Baltic setting in young authors deliberately using controversial subjects such as the status and rights of women, 'free love,' and 'free marriages' to provoke their seniors and their audiences. Thus in 1894 the young playwright Aspazija (pseudonym for Elza Rozenberga) caused something of a press sensation with her play entitled *Zaudētās tiesības* (Engl. *Lost Rights*) with its critical view of marriage; and in 1910 the popular clergyman and novelist Andrievs Niedra gave a conservatively phrased lecture on the consequences of male–female relationships outside traditional marriage (R., 1910a, February 10; R., 1910b, February 11; M., 1910, February 10). Public discussion of these themes continued at a high pitch until the eve of World War I, as, for example, in the controversy centering on the 1913 book *Iedzimtais grēks* (Engl. *Original Sin*) by Ivande Kaija, in which the author portrays gender relationships and women's experience within marriage and raises the possibility of unregistered cohabitation. Latvian literary historians later observed that 'the [public] discussion of this novel was conducted entirely in the social, ethical, and moral realms, and scarcely touched on the book's aesthetic qualities' (Hausmanis, 1998/2001, I/III, p. 310).

5. First period of independence (1918–1940)

Even though in 1920 the new Latvian state initiated quinquennial national censuses, the census categories used did not bring social statistics any closer to reliable microdata about the 'cohabitation' phenomenon than had pre-independence enumerations. The original census forms for individuals in 1935, for example, did require an entry in a column headed 'relation to family head' (Latv. *attiecība pret ģimenes galvu*), but it does not seem that enumerators ever took note of a 'relation' that was irregular. From the entries in use, analysts could infer marital status – unmarried, married, widowed, divorced – but not a long-term partnership outside of formal marriage. Similarly, the census language in the case of an out-of-wedlock child appears to have been indirect, and perhaps analysts had to rely on specialized surveys. Thus, for example, the annual publication of the National Statistical Bureau (Latv. *Valsts statistiskā pārvalde*) – the *Statistical Annual for Latvia* – for 1930, which contained some 353 detailed tables for the whole country, contained only two that signaled knowledge of birth out of wedlock (Latv. *ārlaulībā dzimušie bērni*) (Tables 13 and 15); both dealt with birth data, one with births and death crosstabulated with months of the year, the other with births crosstabulated with months and religion (Gada Grāmata, 1931, pp. 17,18–19). The interwar government statistical publications were in any case preoccupied with documenting other subjects of significance to the new state – the consequences of the huge population losses the Latvian territory had undergone during WWI, the economic development of industry and agriculture, the ethnic composition of the country. Many attractively produced government statistical publications aimed toward the outside world (usually with text and tables in both Latvian and French) did not mention out-of-wedlock births or any other social phenomena that might be understood by contemporaries as examples of social pathologies (e.g. Skujenieks, 1938). Especially after May 1934, when the Prime Minister, Kārlis Ulmanis, carried out his *coup d'etat* and established an authoritarian regime, 'the times,' as later observed a contemporary of these events, 'required writing only in superlatives' (Šilde, 1982, p. 326).

At the same time, the non-quantitative Latvian writing of the interwar years demonstrated repeatedly that public consciousness was aware of the existence of familial and personal relationships that fell outside traditional categories (Lipša, 2014, p. 380– 395). Continuing from pre-WWI years, the discussion of 'free love' remained a staple among social commentators and was normally accompanied by moral disapproval. Even so the language of these discussions suggested that unregistered cohabitation lay behind the phenomena being stigmatized. Publicists on the right wing of the political spectrum even went so far as to depict 'free love' as a Jewish plot to destroy the traditional family. At the same time, even among Latvian social democrats – the Social Democratic Workers' Party having become in Latvia one of the two dominant pre-1934 parliamentary parties – there was clearly an unease over the public's association of irregular sexual relations with the culture of the left. Writings about acceptable morality found resonance in governmental circles and this impulse expressed itself in the formation during the 1920s of government commissions for the prevention of immorality in popular literature (Lipša, 2012, p. 86–103; Lipša, 2013, p. 175–179). By the end of the 1920s, the language used in these controversies began to shift its vocabulary, importing and translating from western Europe such terms as 'trial marriage' and 'friendship marriage.' Critics of non-traditional marital arrangements went out of their way to point out how disadvantageous they were for the women involved, and sought to tie the alleged growth of 'immorality' to the human destruction of WWI that in younger age cohorts had produced sex ratios in which the number of women substantially exceeded that of men. Unfortunately, public attitudes and targeted behaviors were seldom quantified or, if quantified, drew on imprecise statistics, and therefore it is impossible to gauge whether public alarm – as reflected in media commentary – resulted from a growing popularity of irregular marital arrangments or from the need of an expanding media sector to have sensational subjects to write about. Discussions of one aspect of the 'problem' – out-of-wedlock births – could be grounded in some empirical evidence since the five-year censuses occasionally did include such information. But the interwar levels of 'illegitimacy' did not suggest a radical break with pre-WWI levels. Measures of the *national* level of illegitimacy placed the numbers at about 4.6% in the early 1920s and at about 9.7% in the mid-1930s, with the urban–rural differences coming close to achieving parity in 1939 (9.4% for rural, 10.1% for urban) ('Gada Grāmata', 1923, p. 8–9; 1924, p. 8–9; 1925, p. 8–9; 1926, p. 6–7; 1927, p. 6–7; 1928, p. 23; 1933, p. 15; 'Statistikas tabulas', 1940, p. 19). The increase of the rural level of illegitimacy from 7.5% in 1934 to 9.5% in 1938 coincided with the growth of the number of foreign itinerant farmhands (mainly from Lithuania, Poland and Estonia) from 28.2 thousand in 1934 to 46.3 thousand in 1938 (Aizsilnieks, 1968, p. 398, 520, 736). Opinion leaders were convinced that exactly itinerant farmhands had driven illegitamacy rates (Lipša, 2014, p. 393). At the same time, analyses of 'illegitimacy' in the longer term – in comparison, say, with nineteenth-century rates – were non-existent as were attempts to disentangle the interwar levels from the period effects of WWI and the economic turmoil of the early 1930s. For the most part, 'illegitimacy' was dealt with under the rubric of 'sexual ethics' and discussed in terms of what the government could do to minimize levels. Since the presence of out-of-wedlock children in the population was clear, and since many of them were uncared for, the problem brought into focus the questions of public funding for foundling, orphan, and children's homes and state supplementary payments to unwed mothers. Often the charge that the state (i.e. taxpayers) were being obliged to subsidize 'immorality' was predictably nearly always part of the discussion.

The large volume of critical comment on various form of 'immorality' during the interwar period makes it unlikely that the numbers for such behaviors were all unneccesarily inflated. A much more productive hypothesis would be that, as part of the various complex processes of modernization and cultural change, traditional marital norms that were still practiced widely and probably endorsed by vast majority of Latvians were being joined by other forms of cohabitation, perhaps, in these decades, still only on the margins of society. Numerical evidence to support or reject the hypothesis remains unavailable, especially such evidence as would connect the pre- and post-independence periods. It is unlikely that the founding of the new Latvian state in 1918 – a political event – would have radically altered long-term marital habits among Latvians, but evidence one way or another remains sparse at this writing.

6.   The Soviet period 1945–1991

From 1945 onward Latvia – now officially the Latvian SSR – was part of the Soviet Union, and therefore the main lines of population analysis in Latvia correlated with the conceptual equipment of Marxist-Leninist ideology, as formulated by the periodic congresses of the Communist Party of the Soviet Union (CPSU). The USSR had altogether four censuses in the post-WWII years – in 1959, 1970, 1979, 1989 – and the date of the first meant that the population of Latvia was being counted twenty-three years after the last national census of 1935. As earlier between 1897 (only Imperial census) and 1920 (first Latvian census), the interim decades contained a destructive world war (Latvia lost about a fifth of its population (Zvidrinš & Vanovska, 1992, p. 46), and in the post-WWII period also a major deportation (1949) of about 42,000 persons and the beginnings of a long-term shift in the ethnic composition of Latvian territory with the in-migration of Slavic-language populations from other parts of the USSR. As evidenced by the infrequent monographs of the Soviet period (Mežgailis & Zvidrinš, 1973; Mežgailis, 1985; Zvidrinš, 1989), published aggregate statistics about marital life continued to use the tripartite formula 'not married/married/widowed,' occasionally adding columns for 'divorced' and 'separated.' Although these descriptive monographs all refer to various kinds of non-census surveys and specialized 'sociological' inquiries, these were adduced to serve the dominant main subjects: total population growth/decline, fertility, mortality, migration, ethnic composition, labor force size. As a result, the Soviet-era censuses in Latvia did not bring analysis any closer to the subject of unregistered cohabitation, and even 'illegitimate' births are referred to only tangentially as part of the discussion of birth rates. Interestingly, the first direct mention of illegitimacy in such monographs occurred only after 1991 and the breakup of the Soviet Union (Zvidrinš & Vanovska, 1992, p. 42), where it is folded into a brief discussion of infant mortality rates. The observation that 'in Latvia as in other countries infant mortality was the highest among illegitimately born children' was used in this instance to characterize the situation 'in the second half of the 1920s' (i.e. in 'bourgeois' Latvia), and illegitimacy was not mentioned again as a aspect of social life for any later period. The general impression left is that the demographers of the Soviet period again skirted the subject of out-of-wedlock children, possibly because the Party's ideology associated the phenomenon with capitalist countries.

In Soviet-era publications in the Latvian SSR, circumlocutions concerning unorthodox family arrangements and the results of those arrangements (e.g. 'illegitimate' children) should come as no surprise, since there were large areas of everyday social reality toward which the Party exhibited avoidance behavior. Early western research by Geiger in the later 1960s on families and divorce in Soviet *Russia* observed that 'millions of Soviet couples have lived and are living in a state of unregistered or *de facto* marriage. No one knows, of course, exactly how many there are' (Geiger, 1968, p. 258–259). He surmised that this form of unregistered marriage (or cohabitation) was somehow tied to the high levels of 'illegitimte' childbirth. In sum, '*de facto* marriage has become so common that by sheer force of numbers and mutual sympathy it has won a measure of social acceptance, though there are still traces of a deprecatory attitude toward it' (Geiger, 1968, p. 261). How and whether the general situation in the Russian Socialist Republic was reflected in all the smaller Union republics remains uncertain at this juncture. But post-Soviet comparative research on this question for all three *Baltic* republics, using life-event data and cohort analysis, confirms Geiger's speculative observations and unequivocally states that unregistered cohabitation began to be a significant presence in Latvian family life *precisely* during the Soviet period:

> Starting with the cohorts born in the 1940s, who formed their first partnerships mainly in the 1960s and 1970s, the proportion [of direct marriages] began to decrease rapidly. In the 1944–53 birth cohort it dropped below 50 percent, which means that for the first time consensual unions had replaced direct marriage as the mainstream route to family building. In the following generations entry, into partnership through direct marriage gradually became an exception than a rule: in the 1969–73 cohort 11.2 percent of men and only 5.9 percent of women started their first conjugal union without preceding cohabitation (Katus, Puur, Põldma, & Sakkeus, 2007, p. 268).

The Party's stance toward unregistered liaisons and cohabitation when these phenomena were expanding was one of disapproval. For Party members to remain in good standing, 'socialist morality' dictated regular familial behavior. An individual's involvement in irregular family arrangments was likely to come to the attention of other members who were then obliged to carry the matter to the Party's primary-level organization – the 'cell' that guided personal behavior of Party members in each institution, factory, and any other large organization.[1] It was at this level that the 'problem' was identified and solutions to it sought, with the sanctions against individuals ranging from reprimands to expulsion. The charge used was 'lowered morality' (Latv. *morālais pagrimums*). The largely unresearched archived files of primary Party organizations are replete with individual complaints in the form of separate cases: a married person has abandoned family to live with another partner; a man refuses to marry the women with whom he is living and with whom he has had children; a person who changes one partner for another but in the end marries neither. The Party could order such persons to 'regularize his or her family relationships' so that change would eliminate a quasi-familial tie that did not fall into the category of an officially registered marriage. Though for most of the Soviet period complaints about unregistered liaisons remained below the level of official published statistics, occasionally these matters would surface in policy discussions. Thus, for example, in 1980 the Executive Committee of the Workers' Deputies Council of Riga City decided to improve the demographic profile of the capital city and in a policy statement directed lower Party committees and other agencies to work to reduce the level of irregular marital, familial, and sexual behaviors.[2] The wording of these documents made very clear that unregistered cohabitation was one of the forms of irregularity that the Party expected to be reduced if demographic improvement – i.e. moderate population growth – was to be the result. The Party was worried about the impact on the labor force of late marriages, small families, one-person households, and an excess of deaths over births. It is possible that future oral histories of persons who lived through this period might yet yield information about this phenomenon because currently available written and oral sources contain no usable information.

7. The contemporary situation

The 1989 Soviet census was the last one Latvia participated in as a Republic of the USSR. Subsequent national-level population counts took place in 2000 and 2011 in a newly independent Latvia that in most matters, including the gathering of social statistics, saw itself as 'returning to the west' and therefore embraced the idea of the free flow of information. The Soviet regime's phobias about population statistics and their availability did not continue into the post-1991 era, and published results have been formulated in terms of subjects of international interest, including 'cohabitation' that in the 2000 census is designated in Latvian 'unregistered marriage' and translated in English as 'cohabitation'; in the 2011 census the phenomenon is described in Latvian as 'family of cohabitation partners' (Latv. *kopdzīves partneru gimenes*) and translated into English as 'consensual union couple' (Census, 2000, pp. 207–208; Census, 2011, Tables 28–29, 31–32). Information culled from the two post-1991 censuses and numerous surveys and studies suggests that the population of Latvia was taking on several of the characteristics of what in western Europe has been called 'the second demographic revolution' (Lesthaeghe, 2010, p. 4–6). Single-person (the Census, 2011 uses the description 'one-person households') households grew from 24.9% of all households in the year 2000 to 34% in 2011, childless couples (married or unmarried) increased from 24% of all couples in 2000 to 26% in 2011, and one-child couples (married or unmarried) grew from 45% of all couples in 2000 to 47% in 2011. In regard to couples with or without children who were cohabiting without marrriage, the proportion more than doubled from 6% of all couples in 2000 to 13% in 2011. Of the unregistered cohabiting couples, 29% in 2000 had one child, but in 2011 35% had one child; of these same couples, 45% had no children in 2000 and 40% were without children in 2011. The 2011 census provides data for 275,265 persons in age cohort 15–24, with the cohabitation of 5% based on a registered marriage, but there are no data on the cohabitation that was based on personal decisions that did not involve marriage (Census, 2011, Table 10). At the same time, of all births, those out-of-wedlock rose from 12.5% in 1980, to 39.1 in 1999, to 40.3% in 2000 and to 44.6% in 2011 (Annual, 2011b). Marriage as such could not be considered stable, with divorces per 1000 marriages rising from 496 in 1991 to 770 in 1992 but decreasing from 772 in 2011 to 650 in 2012 (Annual, 2011a). At this writing, descriptive demography in Latvia continues to develop a 'portraiture' of the post-Soviet era population, but the findings of the 2011 census have not yet been fully absorbed. Confounding the creation of a reliable cross-sectional characterization in recent years has been the steady outflow – estimated in the aggregate at 250,000–300,000 persons – who have emigrated from the country in search of economic betterment (Zepa & Klava, 2011, pp. 70–91). In a total national population that now numbers around two million, a large and continuing departure of persons from the age cohorts aged 20–40 (the same cohorts that involve 'first-union formation' and childbearing) render calculations impermanent. It must be observed, however, that current research on this subject in Latvia generally has not been placed within the context of the theory association with the concept of a 'second demographic revolution.' The link between values and behaviors remains to be explored.

With respect to cohabitation, the published results of the 2000 census of Latvia made no effort to disguise the fact that of the 624,305 family units in the country, altogether 205,696 or 32.9% had as their base an unregistered marriage. The enumerators in 2000 defined the 'family' as 'two or more persons within a private or institutional household who are related as husband or wife, as cohabiting partners, or as parent and child.' (Census, 2000, p. 283). The definition 'consensual union couple' was used in the 2011 census, indicating that cohabitation without official marriage has been normalized as a census category. The published table on this form of coresidence classified couples into those whose cohabitation is 'registered' as a marriage and those whose cohabitation is based on partnership. The latter grouping – the 32.9% of all family units in 2000 – has grown to 46% in 2011 (13% of consensual union families and 33% lone parent families [Census, 2011, Table 32]); this leaves open the questions of how precisely they were formed, the relative ages of the cohabiting partners, and what kind of a union the partners themselves believe they have formed. With such questions, of course, we enter the differences between the 'data' that satisfy demographers and the 'evidence' social historians of the family would like to have, i.e. the differences between demography and social history. Some of these open questions could be answered by further cross-tabulation of census data, but the answers to others would need further inquiry (perhaps in-depth interviews) to establish their nature. The observation made by Straube about pre-modern Latvian peasants – that they appear not have 'engendered irregular forms of coresidence as a norm of their everyday lives' – can be reformulated as a question for the population of Latvia in 2011 as well, but the published census information does not provide us with an unambiguous answer. What proportion of these 'unregistered' couples had arrived to the decision to form such unions as a 'life-style' choice and what proportion was living as 'unregistered' because of unavoidable circumstance still remains illusive. What is fairly obvious from the descriptive discourse surrounding the quantitative information about them, however, is that the avoidance techniques in the presentation of data, so characteristic of earlier censuses, have disappeared, and the presence of the 'unregistered' couple in the population is now reported as just another socio-demographic fact with no moral connotations. This neutral style of presentation and analysis is clearly a step forward in obtaining clarity about different ways of living together. The habit of mind that understood non-traditional cohabitation forms as symptoms of impaired 'public health' appears now to have dissolved.

Unless and until the census microdata for all the pre-1991 periods of Latvian social history are unearthed and analyzed, however, we will have no usable time series about cohabitation and related matters that would enable us to place the post-1991 in the long-term context. The hypothesis that unregistered cohabitation after 1991 was a continuation of existing Soviet-era trends is plausible at this writing, particularly in light of the findings of Katus and his colleagues (2007). Looking farther backward, it is more than likely that cohabitation without 'official' marriage was primarily a twentieth-century phenomenon. Even if complaints about it can be found in pre-modern sources, religious and community pressures (at least in the rural areas where most Latvians lived) would no doubt have kept the phenomenon to a minimum. Such cohabitation gradually lost its social stigma in the generally loosening of 'traditional' moral rules after WWI, permitting alternative forms of living together especially in urban areas. The proportions of the population involved in such arrangement remains unknown, however. Even if the Communist Party in the Soviet period espoused a 'traditional' view of marriage and had more than adequate resources to coerce people into line, there is evidence that the Party's control over how people chose to live together was relatively weak and that its fiery strictures about 'socialist morality' remained mainly at the level of ideological discourse. The renewal of Latvian independence and the withdrawal of the state from heavy-handed and punitive social engineering created room for alternative forms of living together, as reflected in the post-1991 Latvian censuses.

Notes

1. The National Archives of Latvia, The State Archives of Latvia, Records of the Primary Party Organization's Office of the Militia Administration at the Ministry of Internal Affairs, 7265. fonds, 1. apraksts, 6. lieta, p. 5, The Record of the Meeting of the Primary Party Organization's Office of the Militia Administration at the Ministry of Internal Affairs on 7 January, 1952.
2. The National Archives of Latvia, the State Archives of Latvia, Records of the Central Commitee of the Communist Party of Latvia, PA-102. fonds, 39.apraksts, 8.lieta, pp. 34–35, The Plan on the Demographic Situation of the Riga City Commitee of the Communist Party of Latvia to the Resolution on 24 October, 1980.

Archival sources

The National Archives of Latvia, the State Archives of Latvia, Records of the Central Commitee of the Communist Party of Latvia, PA-102. fonds, 39.apraksts, 8.lieta, pp. 34–35, The Plan on the Demographic Situation of the Riga City Commitee of the Communist Party of Latvia to the Resolution on 24 October, 1980.

The National Archives of Latvia, The State Archives of Latvia, Records of the Primary Party Organization's Office of the Militia Administration at the Ministry of Internal Affairs, 7265. fonds, 1. apraksts, 6. lieta, p. 5, The Record of the Meeting of the Primary Party Organization's Office of the Militia Administration at the Ministry of Internal Affairs on 7 January, 1952.

References

Aizsilnieks, A. (1968). *Latvijas saimniecības vēsture, 1914–1945 [Economic history of Latvia, 1914-1945]*. Stokholma: Daugava.

Anderson, B. A. (1986). Marriage, family, and fertility data in Russian and Soviet censuses. In R. S. Clem (Ed.), *Research guide to the Russian and Soviet censuses* (pp. 131–154). Ithaca and London: Cornell University Press.

Annual. (2011a). Annual statistical data: Population and social processes. Table 1 ILG01. Marriages and Divorces. Retrieved from Central Statistical Bureau of Latvia website http://data.csb.gov.lv/Menu.aspx?selection=Sociala__Ikgad%C4%93jie%20statistikas%20dati__Iedz%C4%ABvot%C4%81ji__Iedz%C4%ABvot%C4%81ji%20D%20Nosl%C4%93gt%C4%81s%20un%20%C5%A1%C4%B7irt%C4%81s%20laul%C4%ABbas&tablelist = true&px_language = en&px_db = Sociala&rxid = 4df2a8c6-f511-4438-a311-f179f61faf7e

Annual. (2011b). Annual statistical data: Fertility. Table 4 IDG022. Marital births and extra-marital births in regions and cities under state jurisdiction by sex. Retrieved from Central Statistical Bureau of Latvia website http://data.csb.gov.lv/Menu.aspx?selection=Sociala__Ikgad%C4%93jie%20statistikas%20dati__Iedz%C4%ABvot%C4%81ji__Iedz%C4%ABvot%C4%81ji%20B%20Dzimst%C4%ABba&tablelist = true&px_language = en&px_db = Sociala&rxid = cdcb978c-22b0-416a-aacc-aa650d3e2ce0

Anonymous. (1822, March 23). Neškīstība dzemdina slepkavību [Impurity Breeds Murder]. *Latviešu Avīzes [The Latvian Newspaper]*, pp. 1-2.

Anonymous. (1904, January 14). Kāds svarīgs baznīcas un draudzes jautājums [An important issue of Church and Parish]. *Rīgas Avīzes [The Riga Newspaper]*, p. 1.

Anonymous. (1904, January 15). Kāds svarīgs baznīcas un draudzes jautājums [An important issue of Church and Parish]. *Rīgas Avīzes [The Riga Newspaper]*, pp. 1-2.

Auns, M. (2004). Ances muižas iedzīvotāji 1797. gadā [Inhabitants of Ance Manor in the year 1797]. *Latvijas Vēstures Institūta Žurnāls, 51*, 57–69.

Auns, M. (2006). Ēdoles muižas iedzīvotāji 1797. gadā [Inhabitants of Edole Manor in the year 1797]. *Latvijas Vēstures Institūta Žurnāls, 59*, 43–55.

Auns, M. (2007). Melnsila un Krustes ciems 18. gadsimta otrajā pusē [Villages of Melnsils and Kruste in the 2nd half of the 18th century]. *Latvijas Vēstures Institūta Žurnāls, 64*, 56–71.

Auns, M. (2009). Grobinas iedzīvotāji pēc Grobinas 16. gs. beigu – 18. gs. metriku grāmatu zinām [The inhabitants of grobina according to 16th–18th century data of church registers]. *Latvijas Vēstures Institūta Žurnāls, 73*, 64–70.

Bērziņš, J. (2009). *Latvijas rūpniecības strādnieku sociālais portrets 1900 – 1914 [A social portrait of Latvian industrial workers]*. Rīga: Latvijas vēstures institūta apgāds.

Census. (2000). *Latvijas 2000.g. tautas skaitīšanas rezultāti [The results of population census of Latvia 2000]*. Riga: Latvijas Republikas centrālā statistikas pārvalde [The Central Statistical Bureau of the Republic of Latvia].

Census. (2011). Population and Housing Census (2011, March 1). Retrieved from Central Statistical Bureau of Latvia website http://data.csb.gov.lv/Menu.aspx?selection=tautassk_11__2011.gada%20tautas%20skait%C4%AB%C5%A1anas%20gal%C4%ABgie%20rezult%C4%81ti&tablelist = true&px_language = en&px_db = tautassk_11&rxid = 992a0682-2c7d-4148-b242-7b48ff9fe0c2

Dunsdorfs, E. (1973). *Latvijas vēsture 1710-1800 [The history of Latvia 1710-1800]*. Stockholm: Daugava.

–e [Braše, G. S.]. (1850, March 23). Lasījam savās avīzēs [We read in our papers]. *Latviešu Avīzes [The Latvian Newspaper]*, p. 1.

Efremova, L. (1982). *Latyshskaia krest'ianskaia sem'ia v Latgale 1860-1939 [The Latvian peasant family in Latgale, 1860-1939]*. Rig? Zinatne.

Gada Grāmata. (1923). *Latvijas statistiskā gada grāmata, 1922 [The statistical annual for Latvia, 1922]*. Riga: Valsts statistiskā pārvalde [The State Statistical Bureau].

Gada Grāmata. (1924). *Latvijas statistiskā gada grāmata, 1923 [The statistical annual for Latvia, 1923]*. Riga: Valsts statistiskā pārvalde [The State Statistical Bureau].

Gada Grāmata. (1925). *Latvijas statistiskā gada grāmata, 1924 [The statistical annual for Latvia, 1924]*. Riga: Valsts statistiskā pārvalde [The State Statistical Bureau].

Gada Grāmata. (1926). *Latvijas statistiskā gada grāmata, 1925 [The statistical annual for Latvia, 1925]*. Riga: Valsts statistiskā pārvalde [The State Statistical Bureau].

Gada Grāmata. (1927). *Latvijas statistiskā gada grāmata, 1926 [The statistical annual for Latvia, 1926]*. Riga: Valsts statistiskā pārvalde [The State Statistical Bureau].

Gada Grāmata. (1928). *Latvijas statistiskā gada grāmata, 1927 [The statistical annual for Latvia, 1927]*. Riga: Valsts statistiskā pārvalde [The State Statistical Bureau].

Gada Grāmata. (1931). *Latvijas statistiskā gada grāmata, 1930 [The statistical annual for Latvia, 1930]*. Riga: Valsts statistiskā pārvalde [The State Statistical Bureau].

Gada Grāmata. (1933). *Latvijas statistiskā gada grāmata, 1932 [The statistical annual for Latvia, 1932]*. Riga: Valsts statistiskā pārvalde [The State Statistical Bureau].

Geiger, H. K. (1968). *The family in Soviet Russia*. Cambridge: Harvard University Press.

Gr. (1873, December 8). Vēl nebeidzās! [It hasn't stopped yet!]. *Mājas Viesis [The Home Visitor]*, pp. 388-390.

Hausmanis, V. (Ed.). (1998/2001). *Latviešu literatūras vēsture [The history of Latvian literature]* (Vol. vols. I/III. Riga: Zvaigzne ABC.

Heyking, A. (1867). *Land und Leute der Mitausichen Oberhauptmanschaft [The territory and the people in the district of Mitau]*. Mitau: Steffenhagen.

Jung-Stilling, F. (1874). *Riga in den Jahren 1866-1870 [Riga from 1866 to 1870]*. Riga, Moscau, Odessa: J. Deubner Verlag.

Kaspar, E. (1883). *Biostatik der Stadt Libau und ihrer Landgemeinde in the Jahren 1834-1882 [Demographical analysis of the city of libau and its district, 1834-1882]*. Dorpat: H. Laakman.

Katus, K., Puur, A., Põldma, A., & Sakkeus, L. (2007). First union formation in Estonia, Latvia and Lithuania: Patterns across countries and gender. *Demographic Research, 17*, 247–300.

Kln. (1875, August 9). Un neieved mūs kārdināšanā [And do not lead us into temptation]. *Mājas Viesis [The Home Visitor]*, p. 255.

Krastin, A. (1867, July 30). Prett puišu negodīgu nakts-vazāšanos [Against shameless night- running by young men]. *Cela Biedris [The Travel Companion]*, p. 56.

Lapinš, K. (1936). *Jaunības laiki. Atminas no Vidzemes vidienas ap gadsimtu mainu [Adolescence. Memories from Mid-Vidzeme around the turn of the century]*. Rīga: Valters un Rapa.

Lesthaeghe, R. (2010). The unfolding story of the second demographic transition. Population studies center research report 10-696 January 2010. Paper presented at the conference on 'Fertility in the History of the 20th Century –Trends, Theories, Public Discourses, and Policies', Akademia Leopoldina & Berlin-Brandenburgische Akademie, January 21-23, 2010.

Lindenberg, F. K. (1871, June 16). Zinna naktsvazankiem [News to the night runners]. *Baznīca un Skola [Latviešu Avīzes pielikums] [The Church and the School, Supplement of The Latvian Newspaper]*, pp. 2-3.

Lipša, I. (2012). *Izklaides kultūra Latvijā: Morāles komunikācijas aspekti (1918-1934) [Entertainment culture in Latvia: Aspects of moral communication 1918-1934]*. Riga: LU Akadēmiskais apgāds.

Lipša, I. (2013). 'Over-Latvianisation in heaven'. Attitudes toward contraception and abortion in Latvia, 1918-1940. In P. J. Weindling & B. M. Felder (Eds.), *Baltic eugenics. Bio-politics, race and nation in interwar estonia, Latvia and lithuania 1918-1940* (pp. 169–201). Amsterdam/ New York, NY: Rodopi.

Lipša, I. (2014). *Seksualitāte un sociālā kontrole Latvijā, 1914-1939 [Sexuality and social control in Latvia, 1914-1939]*. Riga: Zinātne.

M. (1910, February 10). Niedra par laulības problēmu [Niedra on the problem of marriage]. *Dzimtenes Vēstnesis [The Herald of the Motherland]*, p. 2.

Mežgailis, B. (1985). *Padomju Latvijas demogrāfija: Struktūra, procesi, problēmas [The demography of Soviet Latvia: Structure, processes, problems]*. Riga: Avots.

Mežgailis, B., & Zvidriņš, P. (1973). *Padomju Latvijas iedzīvotāji [The inhabitants of Soviet Latvia]*. Riga: Liesma.

Plakans, A. (1975). Peasant farmsteads and households in the Baltic littoral, 1797. *Comparative Studies in Society and History, 17*, 2–35.

Plakans, A. (1983). The familial contexts of early childhood in Baltic serf society. In R. Wall, J. Robin, & P. Laslett (Eds.), *Family forms in historical Europe* (pp. 167–206). Cambridge: Cambridge University Press.

Plakans, A., & Wetherell, C. (1992). Family and economy in an early-nineteenth-century Baltic serf estate. *Continuity and Change, 7*, 199–113.

Plakans, A., & Wetherell, C. (1995). Family and economy in an early-nineteenth century Baltic serf estate. In R. L. Rudolph (Ed.), *The European peasant family and society: Historical studies* (pp. 167–187). Liverpool: Liverpool University Press.

Plakans, A., & Wetherell, C. (1998). Intergenerational transfers of headships over the life course in an eastern european peasant community, 1782-1850. *The History of the Family: An International Quaterly, 3*, 334–349.

Plakans, A., & Wetherell, C. (2004). The 1881 census in the russian Baltic provinces: An inventory and an assessment. *The History of the Family: An International Quarterly, 9*, 47–61.

R. (1910a, February 10). Niedras priekšnesums par laulības problēmiem [Niedra's lecture on marriage issues]. *Rīgas Avīze [The Riga Newspaper]*, pp. 1-2.

R. (1910b, February 11). Niedras priekšnesums par laulības problēmiem [Niedra's lecture on marriage issues]. *Rīgas Avīze [The Riga Newspaper]*, p. 1.

Reinsone, S. (comp.) (2009). *Ādama stāsts. Mazsalaciešu dzīve, ieradumi un tikumi Ā. Purmala autobiogrāfijā 19. un 20. gs. Mijā [Adam's Story. The life, habits and mores of the inhabitants of*

Mazsalaca in the authobiography of A. Purmalis at the turn of the 19th and 20th centuries]. Rīga: Zinātne.

S...c. [Šulc, R.]. (1850, March 23). Jūs žēlojieties [You are complaining]. *Latviešu Avīzes [The Latvian Newspaper]*, pp. 1-2.

Skujenieks, M. (1938). *Latvijas statistikas atlass [The atlas of Latvian statistics].* Riga: Valsts statististikā pārvalde [The State Statistical Bureau].

Statistikas tabulas, 1940 [Tables of statistics]. (1940). Riga: Latvijas PSR Statistikas pārvalde [The Statistical Bureau of Latvian SSR].

Stieda, W. (1881). Zur bevorstehenden Volkszählung [About the upcoming census]. *Baltische Monatschrift, 28,* 141–158.

Straube, G. (2013). Civīllaulība' kā objektīva realitāte: Civīllaulības kā institūta pastāvēšanas nosacijumi Vidzemē 17.-19. gadsimtā [Cohabitation as an objective reality: 'Life in Sin' as One of the conditions of existence in 17th–19th century Vidzeme]. *Latvijas Vēstures Institūta Žurnāls, 89,* 60–79.

Šilde, A. (1982). *Pirmā republika [The first republic].* New York: Grāmatu Draugs.

T. M.. (1864, October 5). R. pie sestdienas vakara [R. on sunday evening]. *Mājas Viesis [The Home Visitor],* pp. 317-318.

T. S. [Silpaušs, T.]. (1864, March 30). Nakts skraidīšana. [Night courting]. *Mājas Viesis [The Home Visitor],* pp. 101-102.

W. A.S.W. [Wagners, W.A. S.]. (1859, May 28). Ne pievillaties, Dievs ne liekās apsmieties. [Don't fool yourselves, god will not be ridiculed]. *Baznīcas Zinas [Latviešu Avīzes pielikums] [The News of Church, Supplement of The Latvian Newspaper],* pp. 2-3.

W-r. [Wagner, F. W.]. (1824, May 29). No Nerretas 17 tā Mei. [On May 17 from Nereta]. *Latviešu Avīzes [The Latvian Newspaper],* pp. 1-2.

Wittschewsky, V. J. (1881). Die baltischen Volkszählung im Jahre 1881 [The Baltic census in the year 1881]. *Baltische Monatschrift, 28,* 407–440.

Zelče, V. (2009). *Latviešu avīžniecība: Laikraksti savā laikmetā un sabiedrībā [Latvian journalism: Newspapers in their time and social context].* Riga: Zinātne.

Zepa, B., & Klava, E. (Eds.). (2011). *Latvija: Pārskats par tautas attīstību [Latvia: Survey on human growth].* Riga: Sociālo un politisko pētijumu institūts.

Zvidrinš, P. (1989). *Demogrāfija [Demography].* Riga: Zvaigzne.

Zvidrinš, P., & Vanovska, I. (1992). *Latviešs: Statistiski demogrāfisks portretējums [The Latvians: A statistical-demographic portrait].* Riga: Zinātne.

'As if she was my own child': cohabitation, community, and the English criminal courts, 1855–1900

Ginger S. Frost

This essay uses evidence from 217 violence cases between cohabiting couples to investigate the reaction of neighbors to irregular relationships. Ostracism was rare as long as the couples did not flaunt their status, for a number of reasons. First, working-class families lived in tenements and row housing that promoted cooperation for survival. Second, women preferred to live near their kin, and families were less disapproving, as they knew the reason for the cohabitation. Third, neighbors often stepped in to fulfill familial roles if kin were absent, encouraging both sisterly and motherly bonds in particular. Fourth, both men and women intervened, though in different ways. Men's participation was especially facilitated by their use of public houses, which was a liminal space that permitted freer discussion of men's personal lives. Fourth, neighborhood values delineated the 'blame' for problem families carefully; both men and women could face disapproval for flouting gender norms. Overall, neighbors parsed the reasons for cohabitation, the harm done by the couple to others, and whether the couple was disruptive in other ways before accepting or rejecting cohabitants in their midst. Indeed, drunkenness and violence was more of a problem than sexual nonconformity in most of these cases.

1. Introduction

Cohabitation in nineteenth-century England was primarily the result of its strict laws on marriage and divorce. In other words, the vast majority of those who entered irregular relationships did so because they could not marry due to previous marriages or being too closely related. Unsurprisingly, then, whenever these couples became free to marry, they usually hurried to regularize their positions. Still, respect for marriage did not always equate with respect for the marriage *laws*. Many working-class people were well aware that England had one law for the rich and another for the poor, and feminists pointed out women's disabilities with increasing frequency. The Divorce Act of 1857, e.g., favored men and the middle and upper classes. Divorce was expensive and difficult, and men needed to prove only a single act of adultery, while women needed adultery and another ground, such as cruelty, bigamy, or desertion. The fact that the law favored well-off men left it open to criticism, especially by the 1890s, though only small changes in the law occurred before 1937 (Bland, 1995, pp. 133–34, 183–85; Caine, 1997, pp. 141–42, 155–56; Martin, 1911, p. 3; Phillips, 1988, pp. 412–22, 495–507).

In part because of these inequities, unmarried cohabitation, though not unknown in the middle and upper classes, was largely limited to the working class. When their marriages failed, poor spouses did not have the funds to divorce. Thus, after a separation, both husbands and wives who preferred not to live alone found new partners, either in cohabitation or bigamous unions. In addition, respectability was not as central to working-class home lives as in the middle classes, and even when poor couples accepted the tenets, they reworked its values to fit with their circumstances. Moreover, economic factors played a part in these decisions. For one thing, some poor professions also militated against permanent ties, such as sailors, soldiers, and tramping day workers. For another, the British poor law separated husbands and wives in the workhouses, so marriage conferred few benefits to those who were desperately poor. Cohabitants also avoided paying for weddings and interference from church and state. Without state statistics, historians can only estimate the number of cohabitants, as so many of them married illegally. They make up perhaps 10% of poor urban neighborhoods. Most of these couples could not marry legally or they would have done so, and they 'passed' as husband and wife when possible (Frost, 2008b, pp. 123–39; Gillis, 1985, pp. 231–59).

Historians have debated the social acceptability of cohabitation in the working class. Rebecca Probert argues that social historians have overstated the willingness of communities to tolerate marital nonconformity (notably, her analysis does not include couples who lived together because they could not marry). She is highly critical of the sources on cohabitation in the nineteenth century, which, she asserts, were too biased by their reform-minded agendas (Probert, 2012, pp. 52–63, 76–89). Probert is certainly right that all sources are problematic, but the main problem is not so much that the sources are all biased towards acceptance, but that they are contradictory and thus require careful parsing of values. Autobiographies record accounts of angry respectable women refusing their support to any 'home-wreckers' in their neighborhoods, while at the same time acknowledging calm acceptance of those 'living tally.' A good example of this was Robert Roberts in *The Classic Slum* (1971). In his section on the 'matriarchy' that ruled his Salford neighborhood, he wrote of the disgrace of illegitimacy, which set off 'a chain reaction of shame' amongst all those related to the unfortunate young woman. In the very next sentence, conversely, he claimed that those who lived together unmarried 'came in for little criticism,' though, of course, their children were also illegitimate (R. Roberts, 1971, p. 47). What is one to make of such juxtapositions? Similarly, historians of the Victorian working class found rigid morality in many working-class neighborhoods, with the matriarchs quite conservative in outlook. Yet most then detail exceptions to these rules, including irregular sexual relationships and illegitimate children taken into the maternal home (Chinn, 1988, pp. 145–46; Roberts, 1984, pp. 75–80). The many Royal Commissions on Marriage and Divorce in the Victorian period had disjunctions as well. Neighbors testified that they did not ostracize those living together due to the divorce laws, followed by different witnesses arguing that they ran adulterous couples out of their neighborhoods (Gillis, 1985, pp. 256–59).[1]

Such contradictory evidence showed the difficulties of analyzing local responses, given the wide variety of marital arrangements and regional norms in Victorian England. Were people sympathetic to those caught in legal limbo, but not to others? Was the working class indifferent to all marriage laws or only to some of them? If communities assessed blame, were women or men the more culpable? Did the difference in attitudes mirror the division between 'rough' and 'respectable' neighborhoods, or was it more complex? In general, I have argued that neighbors sympathized with those afflicted with impossible spouses and harsh laws, but they stopped short of condoning cohabitation in all cases, especially in adulterous unions. They also drew a difference between toleration of occasional lapses and continued 'libertine' or 'fast' behavior (Frost, 2008b, pp. 114–16;

133–35). Still, the complexities make judgments about nineteenth-century social conventions difficult to trace, especially given the agendas of the writers of these sources.

In order to examine these issues more closely, this paper will use the evidence of criminal courts. Of course, these records also have agendas and drawbacks. The information is incomplete, and both sides in the case have reason to conceal evidence. In addition, criminal cases involving these couples are heavily urban and cluster in crowded areas. Still, criminal courts offer some advantages. They do not rely primarily on middle-class observation of the poor, nor on the unusual family members who wrote autobiographies. They avoid the biases of those who argued for divorce law reform (or against) during Royal Commissions. Also, the adversarial nature of the English judicial system allowed both the prosecution and defense to state their cases, giving a broader range of views, and both sides could also challenge testimony in cross-examination. Most centrally, felony trials required neighbors as witnesses in all but the most straightforward cases. The depositions, in particular, give the reaction of all witnesses to the events soon after the crimes, before newspapers could sway public opinion one way or the other. They thus offer one way to gauge acceptance of cohabitation amongst the poor, using the words of the poor themselves.

The trials used in this paper come from a database of 217 violence cases amongst cohabitants between 1850 and 1914, of which 196 had enough information to analyze (Frost, 2008a, pp. 26–27). Of these, 93% were working-class families. Neighbors were the main witnesses in 74 cases, and intervened physically in 32 more. Thus, 54% of these cases had close neighborly involvement (Frost, 2008b, pp. 32–51, 134–35). This database has cases from every county in England and Wales, but urban cases predominate in the murder trials, comprising 68% of the cases. Of these, coal mining towns in the midlands and South Wales are disproportionately represented (25%), and London cases are a quarter of the total as well. This indicates that cohabitants living amongst their married neighbors were more frequent in industrial cities than in small towns or rural areas (of course, this is also partly a function of higher urban population). More specifically, of the 22 cases cited in this article, five were from London, five from Nottingham, and six from other industrial cities. Only six were from small towns or the countryside. Thus, the evidence largely applies to close urban neighborhoods, though such violence was not unknown in more rural areas.

Although the database uses cases from both the summary jurisdiction (or police or magistrate's) courts and the higher courts (assizes), the information on neighbors was much smaller in the police court cases. Magistrate court transcripts do not survive except in a handful of courts for limited years, and the newspaper coverage of such incidents was quite brief. Any indication of the roles and attitudes of neighbors in those trials, then, was minimal (Davis, 1984, pp. 309–335). As a result, this paper will rely on murder trials, since these generated more press accounts, were more likely to have surviving depositions, and had Home Office files. Though the degree of violence between the partners is exceptional in murder cases, the coverage makes clear that most of the victims and perpetrators lived enmeshed in typical urban working-class neighborhoods. When compared to other studies, the patterns of violence that emerge do not differ greatly from those based on summary jurisdictions (D'Cruze, 1999, pp. 39–55; Hammerton, 1992, pp. 34–67). Even those in the 'roughest' areas often had neighbors who were legally married and employed in respectable trades – colliers, craftsmen, domestic servants, publicans, traveling salesmen.

Change over time was limited; the period after 1850 was one of a stable economy and urbanization, with a steady decline in violent crime overall. My database has 25 cases in the 1850s, 42 in the 1860s, 58 in the 1870s, 37 in the 1880s, 40 in the 1890s, and five after 1900, so the average per decade was around 40 for most of the period under review. After the upheavals of the early nineteenth century, the mid- and late- Victorian working class established domestic patterns that remained relatively consistent for the rest of the century. These cases are numerous and had enough similarities to allow the historian to see patterns of behavior in the roles of neighbors in the lives of cohabiting couples, the gendered nature of their responses, and their assessment of the acceptability of such families. The point that emerges most clearly is that poor neighbors could not be choosy about their social interactions. Cohabiting couples mixed amongst the married ones indiscriminately, and the sources show few cases of ostracism. This was due to several factors, most notably the fact that row-housing and lodging tenements did not encourage much privacy; in fact, these constructions almost forced cooperation. Another reason was women's tendency to live near their sisters or mothers, a desire often marked by historians of the working class. Such ties meant that their neighbors were also their family members, and families were more tolerant of marital non-conformity than strangers.

Furthermore, neighbors occasionally shaded into familial roles, especially when an older woman lived near a younger, apparently friendless, woman. These older women were substitute mothers and behaved in protective ways to their charges rather than condemning them. In addition, neighborly intervention was not limited to women. Although female survival networks have received more coverage, men, too, needed help from their neighbors. Male neighbors also intervened more often than one might expect when violence broke out, though not in the same ways as women. The neighborhood pub, that center of working-class sociability, was one of the major forums for men's knowledge about family issues. Indeed, public houses overlapped with lodgings, bringing publicans and their families in as witnesses to troubled relationships. Such places did not have a strict divide between 'public' and 'private'; instead, arguments moved from pub to street to home with little interruption. This was only emphasized more when the pub also served as a lodging house, as was true in several cases.

Finally, groups of cohabitants could band together. When more than one cohabiting family existed in a limited area, tolerance was necessary for the neighborhood to function. At times, this was because the neighborhood was 'rough,' but such distinctions blurred more often than historians sometimes assume. As Shani D'Cruze put it, 'The distinction between "rough" and "respectable" was a highly unstable construct' (D'Cruze, 1998, p. 61). Every 'low' lodging house, full of part-time prostitutes or drunken tramps, was balanced by a cluster of cottages in respectable neighborhoods that nevertheless had more than one adulterous couple, known to all the neighbors. Thus, the working class delineated rather fine lines between types of cohabitation, responsible male and female behavior in these relationships, and their own notions of respectability. Over all, cohabitants lived amongst neighbors without much comment, as long as trouble did not erupt. Neighbors were far more likely to resent violence and drunkenness than marital nonconformity. Couples that made an issue of their unmarried status or flaunted their lack of respectability were more troubling, but rare. Most of these couples used the same last names, called each other husband and wife, and conformed to expected gender roles. As such, their marital status could be ignored until other issues drove it into the open.

2. Close confines and neighbors

Notions of privacy that were increasingly important in the middle classes were simply not applicable to the poor until at least the mid-twentieth century. Working-class families lived very close to each other, making necessary their constant interaction. The worst period was the 1840s, but things had not improved in many urban neighborhoods by the 1880s; those areas where slums were destroyed often simply increased crowding, since the buildings that replaced the slum homes were not affordable to workers. The countryside had less population density, but even there small cottages clustered in groups and lodgers were common. In towns and villages, at the best, a family might live in two rooms, connected with other row houses or tenements. At the worst, a lodging house had several rooms rented out to different families. In such situations, privacy was impossible and neighborly scrutiny – or at least interference from the landlady or landlord – the norm. Not only did the rooms share common halls and staircases, but the walls were paper thin (August, 2007, pp. 17–21, 97–100).

A case from 1866 in Preston, Lancashire, gave some idea of the closeness and intimacy of such housing. John Banks and Ann Gilligan lived together in a room connected to a pub run by a Mrs. Lawrenson and her cohabitant in Preston. Lawrenson clearly was not in a position to feel superior to her tenants, given her own marital status. In addition, her home was both connected to a place of business and a place of business in itself, blurring the distinction between public and private. Gilligan was the wife of an absent sailor, and the newspapers described her as a prostitute, though she was almost certainly only part-time (thus, she, too, was both public and private). She and Banks drank to excess, and when drunk, fought over money, as Banks was convinced she was 'stealing' from him, a typical source of friction in working-class marriage (Ayers & Lambertz, 1986, pp. 195–219; Clark, 2000, pp. 27–40; Conley, 1991, pp. 78–81; Ross, 1982, pp. 575–602). Their final fight began in the pub, moved to the street, and ended at their lodgings. Both male and female patrons and lodgers in and around the pub got involved in each setting. A local weaver (male) tried to protect Gilligan when the couple quarreled in the public house. Elizabeth Brown, who lived next door, interrupted Banks's violence on the street. She testified that she 'went up to him [Banks] and called him "a thundering bully." He then threatened her and she had to run away.' Once the couple went inside the lodgings, Lawrenson intervened several times, unable to ignore the noises across a thin wall. As a result, she saw Banks giving Gilligan his final beating (her bowel ruptured, leading to her death soon afterwards). The neighbors in what was clearly a rough neighborhood did not ignore the problem couple amongst them, in part because they could hardly have done so. And both men and women did not draw lines about public and private spaces, but instead confronted Banks in the pub, street, and within the couple's room.[2]

Tenements had more privacy than lodging houses, but they were still close confines. A case in 1874 involved a couple living in one of many small tenements connected on King's Road passage in Shrewsbury. The small dwellings along the road housed three to five families, all of whom could hear the quarrels and beatings between Henry Doricott and Emma Marston. The road ended in a pub owned by James Newton, whose premises were 30 yards from the Dorricott-Marston front door. In this case, as in many others, the pub marked a meeting place of both public and private matters and was at a crucial point in the street. The neighborhood was a mixed one, with some couples respectably married and employed, and others on the shady side of the law. Marston was a prostitute, while Dorricott had been arrested numerous times for petty crimes. Their neighbors, though, were married couples. Mary Burgoyne, a married woman, carried coals down the passage to earn money; not surprisingly, she overheard some of the last quarrels. Four other women who lived along the passage came to nurse Emma when Henry's last beating sent her to bed for several days; three of the four were married. Mary Ledbury, her closest neighbor, sat with her and inspected her wounds on Wednesday, and again came on Saturday.

Ledbury was with Emma when she died of septicemia from an infected wound in her thigh. Marston was clearly not respectable – she got drunk and could be violent herself – but the neighbors did not shun her, especially in her time of need. Most especially, the other women in the passage offered her nursing and food and sympathized with her plight, one they could hardly have missed, given the number of dwellings in the narrow passage.[3]

Other cases involved people living in row houses, whose construction required tenants to interact daily. Tenants in row houses shared a courtyard, a water pump, and privies. An example of a case of row housing was that of Agnes Oaks and John Wiggins who lived together in London in the mid 1860s. Their next-door neighbor was Mary Ann Wiltshire. She later explained that she had to pass their house every day to get water, and she could not help hearing their noisy conflicts. During one serious bout in the late summer, she was driven to intervene. She burst into the room to see John holding Agnes by her hair and kicking her. Wiltshire not only scolded Wiggins ('Oh! John, John what are you doing?'), but she pulled him off of Agnes, and informed him that 'You will be sorry for what you have done presently.' The proximity of their homes meant that Wiltshire become close enough to Oaks to discover the reasons for their arguments. She later told the court that Agnes was unhappy that John refused to marry her. Her threat to return to service if he did not 'do right by her' led to his retaliation. Mary Ann's testimony about the closeness of the houses was further supported by the fact that eight of her neighbors also heard the fight; privacy was simply not possible in this setting.[4]

In another case with row houses, from Nottingham, the couple, Elizabeth Williamson and Joseph Tucker, had lived together for eight or nine years by 1885. Four of their neighbors from their last home, on Trumpet-Street, testified at the trial. The next door neighbors were the Savages, married and with a 17-year-old son, who saw the immediate aftermath of Joseph's setting his lover on fire (Tucker claimed it was an accident, as both were drunk). Other neighbors hurried over to put out the flames and try to shame Joseph, whose cold response 'Let the – – – burn,' they all heard. As with the above case, the Savages saw the trouble beginning when they went out to the common source of water in the middle of a shared yard.[5] Both men and women knew the couple as quarrelsome drunks, but they had to find a way to live with them in such tight quarters. Five testified at the trial; they were all in respectable professions, e.g., a bleacher and a screw cutter. Three more came forward during Tucker's plea for a reprieve, two of whom were connected to Tucker in the shoe-making business.[6]

Cottage homes, seemingly more private than row houses or tenements, also afforded plenty of space for neighborly intervention. Frederick Andrews and Frances Short lived together in a group of cottages in Kensington Park Road in 1899 in London, when this address was a costermonger neighborhood. Frances, a widow, moved to the area two years earlier to be nearer to her daughter, but she chose not to marry Frederick, with whom she frequently quarreled. Her daughter, who was married, and the next-door neighbor, Mary Ann Sawyer, also married, were the main witnesses at the trial. Sawyer saw marks of violence on Short frequently, and she was suspicious when Andrews claimed Frances had gone for a visit to her daughter in March 1899. She explained to the court that if Andrews's story were true, she would have seen Frances leave, 'as she has to pass my place to go out, and I had not seen her . . .' As a result, she recruited a male neighbor, a Mr. Hardaway, and helped herself into the house when Andrews had left for the market. Frances's body was 'doubled up on the ground,' covered with a sack. Frederick had stabbed her 41 times and then covered her with flocking.[7] Despite being in a separate cottage, Andrews had little hope of keeping the murder a secret, given Sawyer's closeness, both spatially and emotionally, to her neighbor.

Similarly, the Birmingham neighborhood in a case in 1876 had houses and lodgings so connected that four neighbors saw some of the struggles and heard arguments between George Elwell and Mary Boswell. They had lived together for 12 years and had been in their present home for 18 months. Despite Elwell's desertion of his first wife, the neighbors did not shun them. Several of them testified to daily interactions, and on the night of Elwell's murder, Mrs Tain, a neighbor, offered Boswell houseroom at two separate times and eventually took in two of their children for the night. Later she protected Boswell from a mob convinced that Boswell had gotten away with Elwell's murder.[8] Poor communities could not afford complete privacy or isolation, nor would it have been advisable as a survival strategy. With only a small safety net, neighbors had to cooperate, share spaces, and help each other. Although women did this most often, since they were more concerned with domestic issues, all members of households had to work together to use privies, water sources, and courtyards. D'Cruze called these shared spaces 'public' because 'people were known and observed' by other residents there, one reason why conflicts there sparked neighborly interest (D'Cruze, 1998, pp. 47–62, quote from p. 59; E. Roberts, 1984, pp. 184–94; Ross, 1993, pp. 134–35, 150–51; Tebbutt, 1995, pp. 74–100).

As some of the above examples showed, another factor in acceptance of cohabiting couples was the practice for women to live near their female relatives. Carl Chinn argued that the relationship between mothers and daughters was the most important one in holding together poor working-class neighborhood in the late nineteenth century:

> More than the connections that existed between a husband and wife, parents and sons, or siblings, that between a mother and daughter was the most essential to the homogeneity of the extended family, to the interdependence of kin and hence to ... loyalty to the street of residence and pride in the neighborhood (Chinn, 1988, p. 23).

Though Chinn may overstate this case, women did show a preference to being near their 'mums' after marriage, for many reasons, including financial support, advice, and help with childbirth and rearing. Daughters also depended on their sisters and aunts; at times all clustered together. Families, then, overlapped with neighbors on a regular basis, and these relationships eased the acceptance of irregular unions (Chinn, 1988, pp. 25–29; Gillis, 1985, pp. 253–256).

In the 1890s, Sarah Oldham lived with a frame-work knitter, Edmund Kesteven, in Sutton-in-Ashfield, Nottinghamshire. Kesteven did not have close ties in the village, but Oldham did; her aunt and two of her sisters lived nearby. In fact, according to the depositions, Sarah owned her own home and the three surrounding it, and she had rented to her family, keeping them together. Both her sisters, Kesiah Dove and Harriett Clarke, were married, as was her aunt. (Sarah lived with Edmund unmarried because she was married to a man who had deserted her for America.) The sisters were in and out of each other's houses regularly and shopped together the morning of the crime, Christmas Eve, 1894. All Oldham's relatives knew the relationship between Sarah and Edmund was difficult, due to Kesteven's drunkenness and violent jealousy. Her sisters and brothers-in-law urged her to break with Kesteven because of his erratic behavior, however, not her problematic marital status. They did not appear to object to the union on moral grounds, and they must have known it could not be regularized, given that Sarah was the married partner.[9] Similarly, as mentioned above, Frances Short moved to be near her daughter, Priscilla Fielding, in Kensington Park Road in London, and her son later moved into her house. Fielding saw her mother frequently, she explained, because she 'lived quite close ...' In fact, after killing her, Andrews tried to excuse Frances's absence by saying she was visiting her daughter, a story that was entirely plausible, though, unfortunately for him, one did not convince Mrs. Sawyer.[10]

The closeness of female relatives mitigated the potential embarrassment if neighbors discovered the families' secrets. Even if some of the locals disapproved or shunned an adulterous couple, the woman could still rely on her mother or sisters for emotional and practical support. Many historians consider neighbors as a surrogate family, as they minded children for each other, offered small loans, and helped regulate behavior. How much neighbors could substitute for family is a subject for debate, but one that became truly academic when the neighbors literally *were* family (D'Cruze, 1998, pp. 47–50, 1999, p. 41; Roberts, 1984, pp. 183–201; Ross, 1985, pp. 39–59). Some men also wanted to be near kin, but women's relatives predominated. Not only did the woman have her natal kin, but, with siblings and children, she might also have in-laws of both genders to offer assistance and, if necessary, intervention when things turned violent. For instance, Oldham's two brothers-in-law and the fiancé of her niece were present when she staggered into her sister's home with her throat cut. One of her brothers-in-law, John Dove, roused Kesteven out of his home so his crime could be brought home to him.[11]

A final factor in neighborly acceptance was that, at times, cohabitants grouped together. Mayhew noticed this in his study of London in the 1860s, and the criminal cases show limited support for this (Mayhew, 1968, vol. II, p. 294). Lawrenson, the landlady of Banks and Gilligan, above, was one such example. She lived with a man who was not her husband, so could hardly pose as a disapproving landlady, refusing housing to unmarried couples. On the contrary, women like Lawrenson made their living by offering houseroom to part-time prostitutes and their mates. Wiggins and Oaks lived on lower North Street in Limehouse in London; John was a lighterman and needed to be near the canal. Amongst their immediate neighbors were William Dunn and Elizabeth Johnson, also living together outside of marriage. Elizabeth went by the name 'Dunn,' and both couples called each other 'husband' and 'wife,' but the local community knew their status. In this case, none of the many witnesses (on either side of the canal) expressed disapproval of the cohabiting couples in their midst. Indeed, Mary Ann Wiltshire, the landlady, saw Agnes as family, especially as Oak's mother was ill and her sister lived too far away to offer help.[12] Of course, they may well have preferred their neighbors to marry, but they did not consider the couples' status to be relevant to the violence that had occurred. Middle-class observers of the poor often elided sexual impurity, violence, drunkenness, and disease into a single category (D'Cruze, 1999, p. 44; Mearns, 1970, p. 61; Sims, 1883, pp. 24–26), but the working class did not, as they understood the complexities of marriage and family in their neighborhoods.

3. Neighbors and gender

Because in most of these cases the victims were women, women neighbors have predominated in these stories. Men were out to work for long hours and went to the public house or union meetings (both male spaces) after their work was done. Women tended to gossip and interact in their homes or to nurse each other as necessary. Sometimes couples were fortunate enough to have their own families near, but when they did not, neighbors filled the roles. The typical case was for two or three women neighbors of the same age to become close friends and to check on each other, as with Short and Sawyer, above. Women neighbors were crucial aids; many knew the background to the couples' problems because of long association (D'Cruze, 1998, pp. 71–72, 1999, p. 41). The main witness in Thomas Brown's trial for the murder of Sarah Caldwell was Charlotte Keeling, who interrupted their final argument twice and eventually fetched the police. She had known of their difficulties for months.[13] In the case of Johanna Nevin, three of her female neighbors testified at her inquest about her arguments with James Flynn. Her closest neighbor, Nancy Dronfield, intervened twice during the last argument and witnessed Flynn giving Nevin the fatal blow.[14]

These fairly equal, sisterly bonds were the commonest, but others also emerged between women. Older women, especially, were mother figures to younger women in trouble. Though judgmental landladies, barring the door to the unrespectable, were a Victorian stereotype, many of the landladies in these cases were kind-hearted. Mary Ann Wiltshire defended Agnes Oaks, her tenant, whom she saw as a victim of seduction by John Wiggins in the 1860s. She described her relationship with Agnes in the following terms: 'I spoke to her as if she was my own child.'[15] As we will see below, Margaret Peacock was equally protective of Sophia Jackson in the 1890s, to the point of facing down an angry, abusive ex-lover. Young women without their mothers were vulnerable to sexual scandal; they could not find respectable lodgings or work if they were tainted, and they had only one form of work available in that case – prostitution. Older women did not always approve of the young women's choices, but they showed compassion in trying to extricate them from the consequences of their decisions.

All the same, the predominance of women in the sources did not mean that men did not get involved. Often, both men and women handled different sides of a problematic family. A good example of this gendered division was the case of George Jalley and Sarah Smith, who had lived together in Maidstone, Kent for many years in the 1860s. The major female witness was Mary Ann Saunders who, with her husband, lived next door to the couple. She heard cries of 'murder!' on the day in question and immediately ran over. She explained, 'The partition between the houses is thin, and if there had been any quarrelling, I must have heard it.' She could not stop Jalley's kicking Smith two more times, but she did prevent his jumping on her, and she went to get her husband and another male neighbor she saw on the street. The men who testified were William Saunders, her husband, Thomas Pankhurst, the neighbor she recruited, and John Andrews, the keeper of the beer shop, who saw the couple spend most of their last day together in his pub. The men told the court about conversations in the pub and street (where Jalley confessed and expressed satisfaction that he had killed her). The women, in contrast, told of the precursors to the crime and spearheaded the efforts to prevent the murder. Both men and women, though, knew why Jalley killer her, since he believed she had been unfaithful. Mary Ann knew this because she heard the argument; Pankhurst knew because Jalley explained his motives during his confession. Both sexes were involved, but in different ways and at different times.[16]

These gender roles were particularly clear in the case of Richard Sabey and Sophia Jackson in 1893. Sabey had not informed Jackson that he had a mixed race wife he had brought back from India, and the two lived together in Liverpool when Sophia had his child (she later fell pregnant with another). The landlady, Mrs. Margaret Peacock, began as a neighbor; she kept the greengrocer's shop where Sophia bought vegetables. When Jackson complained that their lodgings were uncomfortable, Peacock and her husband offered them a room to rent. Peacock comes through strongly in the depositions and records as Sophia's most loyal friend, almost like another mother to her. Jackson trusted her enough to confide her secret – that she was not married to Sabey, though at that point Jackson assumed they would soon do so. Peacock showed she had earned Jackson's trust; she refused to evict her when she learned the truth, though her husband argued that they must. As Margaret told the court, 'she begged so hard that I could not refuse.' Peacock also agreed to speak on Jackson's character during any legal proceedings that might be necessary if Sabey did not support his children.[17]

Peacock's motherly concern became even more crucial to Jackson when the latter's relationship with Sabey fell apart. Saying he had to get his army pension, Richard disappeared for six weeks with no word. When he returned, Margaret, who kept his little family going, refused to shake his hand, asking 'whether he called himself a man to leave his wife and child starving while he went away.' Sabey then admitted that he had left his wife and child behind when he had eloped with Jackson and had been gaoled for desertion as a result. Because of the imprisonment, he said he had to return to his wife. Peacock, along with Louisa's family, then urged Jackson to sue Sabey for affiliation; Peacock explained later that 'I d[idn't] see why he should be free.' When Richard arrived to protest this action, Peacock refused to let him in the house though 'he abused me very much & used some very unbecoming language & called me horrible names.' As with Mrs. Wiltshire and Agnes Oaks, Peacock played the role of protective mother as long as Sophia was near her, though she could not entirely replace Jackson's family. At the affiliation hearing, Sabey was assessed 3s 6d a week for his child, and Sophia left to live with her married sister in another part of town (another example of the importance of sisters).[18]

Margaret Peacock was clearly a prime mover before the crime, acting as confidant, substitute mother, and friend. However, after Sabey murdered Jackson, far more men got involved. Male witnesses were all Liverpool residents who hunted down Sabey after the murder. They followed him to a pub where he insisted on getting a drink before turning himself in; they could then refute his claim to temporary insanity or drunkenness. In fact, when Richard hazarded that theory that Sophia had committed suicide in the immediate aftermath of the crime, his brother-in-law, Thomas Wright, said flatly, 'It's a lie, Dick.' Two other men testified that Sabey then admitted that he had killed her. This public action contrasts strongly with Peacock's constant support before the crime – indeed Mr. Peacock refused to testify and clearly did not want any part of the domestic squabbles and unpleasantness. But an attack meant men had to get involved, especially once the murderer tried to flee (D'Cruze, 1998, p. 59). Sophia's brother-in-law led the men, again showing the overlapping of family and neighbors for those in irregular unions. Given her ignorance of Richard's marriage, Sophia could be forgiven for her errors, and she was re-enveloped by her maternal kin, though in this case, they could not protect her.[19]

Men's roles were more than just in detection, though. Their tendency to talk in pubs meant that male neighbors, like the female ones, worked to prevent tragedies in their midst. Male action was probably over-represented in murder cases, given the extremity of the situation. Women were involved in daily interactions, while men dealt with domestic issues when they appeared to be headed to severe problems. Still, in a quarter of the cases with neighborly intervention, male neighbors tried to persuade the men in the relationships to avoid violence before the fact. When John Brooks contemplated killing Caroline Woodhead in 1877, William Godfrey, a carriage maker and old acquaintance, met him by chance in a coffee-house, where Brooks confessed his intentions. Godfrey urged him to give up drink and to turn to God rather than consider such an evil course. He also asked Brooks if he had a wife; when John admitted he did, 'he asked why he had another man's wife' then. John said 'he could not give her up...' In addition to this general advice, Godfrey offered to find him work with his old master, a Mr. Burton, practical help that he hoped would stop Brooks brooding and drinking. Godfrey was hardly to blame that Brooks ignored his advice; he had certainly taken several steps to help his old neighbor.[20]

Men also took the lead in the case of Francis Wane, who killed Amelia Blunt in 1864. They had lived together for three years, but he had broken up the home, and she became the housekeeper for James Warren and eventually got engaged to Warren's son (also named James). Wane, unable to bear losing her, cut her throat. Francis and Amelia lived in a small neighborhood of cottages in Essex, and almost all the witnesses had known Wane from his boyhood. Though an agricultural area, the cottages were 60–100 yards apart; Wane's brother's cottage was only 750 yards from the Warrens' cottage, an awkward situation at best. The people of the area well knew the history of the couple, but rather than ostracizing Blunt, they sided with the Warrens and supported James the Younger's desire to marry her. For example, the landlord of the pub, Charles Filch, argued for the Warrens against Wane when necessary:

> I was in my Bar and heard him swearing at Warren about her – I went in and said to Wane You are like a dog in the Manger – you wont [sic] live with the woman yourself and you wont [sic] let her live peaceably with any one else, then he swore at me and talked about punching my head. I told him to leave my House and he did so.

In addition to these long-time neighbors, Wane confessed his murderous plans to a peddler, Joseph Rogers, at another pub. Rogers, like Godfrey, tried to talk Wane out of his bad frame of mind, with no success.[21] These men tried to get Wane to recognize that his relationship was over. The closeness of the neighborhood – with everyone knowing their personal histories – probably militated against Wane being able to let Amelia go peacefully, but it also meant that most people in the area tried to stop his violence and testified against him after they failed.

Men's actions tended to be 'public' ones, but one can become too attached to this designation. After all, the men in the above case knew all about Wane's private life; they grew up with him, worked with him, drank with him. Indeed, the centrality of the pub to men's sociability meant that it became an important space for working out family problems. Pub discussions with male neighbors allowed men to comment on family matters that normally would not occupy their conversations; these discussions were liberally smoothed with drink. In addition, after arguments with their women, some men drank a great deal and talked more freely about their difficulties. In their turn, the neighbors then felt freer to comment on personal relationships, perhaps encouraged by the mix of openness and familiarity that a local pub offered. As many of the descriptions above attested, pubs were integral to neighborhoods, embedded within rows of tenements or homes or letting rooms. They were liminal spaces where private matters took a social aspect.

For instance, Joseph Tucker complained about Elizabeth Williamson, the women with whom he had lived for over 10 years, more than once in the local pub. Henry Emerson, who lived in the same row of houses as the couple, saw the two have a meal together in the public house, where Tucker was abusive to Elizabeth. After Williamson left, Emerson took the opportunity to berate Tucker for his brutality; he 'told the prisoner he would sooner leave her than ill use the woman as he did on the Saturday night previous,' to which Tucker replied, 'It was a bad job I did not kill her.' Emerson later provided key evidence at the trial.[22] Both male and female neighbors offered counsel to John Wiggins when he drowned his sorrows in the local beer shop. Martha Truss, the landlady, asked Wiggins why he was getting on 'so badly,' and he complained that Agnes Oaks had disappointed him. She advised him quite sensibly, 'I am very sorry to hear that; if you cannot be happy and comfortable together you had better part; you are not compelled to live with her if you are not married' –he said, "No, I am determined to get rid of her . . . "'[23] That Wiggins did not take Truss's excellent advice was unfortunate for all concerned, but at least she had the opportunity to try to stop him.

The difference between 'public' and 'private' was lessened even more when so many inns and lodging houses were either beer shops themselves or near to one. Neighbors gathered and rehashed their days, leaving room for confessions and advice. In some cases, the couples resided in inns that sold beer and liquor or lived so close that the innkeepers knew their business. The primarily masculine atmosphere and the alcohol consumption loosened tongues on men who otherwise would not have discussed their private lives or those of others. In all these ways, the pubs offered opportunities for advice and intervention.

4. Cohabitation and reputation

Both male and female neighbors also testified to reputations, a significant indicator of the acceptance or rejection of cohabitants in the working class. Histories of the working-class neighborhood stress the controlling aspects of gossip and women's networks, but also their roles in spreading information vital for families in trouble. Shani D'Cruze, e.g., discusses many behaviors that garnered disapproval; these included cohabitation, but also domestic violence, drunkenness, and promiscuity. Melanie Tebbutt also discusses the double-edged nature of much of the gossip, as the sense of belonging it brought also excluded some people (D'Cruze, 1998, pp. 59–61; Tebbutt, 1995, pp. 86–97). Due to the fact that my cases involve murders, both men and women tended to sympathize with the female victims, whatever their marital status; the extremity of their needs overrode any disapproval of their sex lives. In contrast, in the times before and after the crisis moments, neighbors came to careful judgments about the rights and wrongs of such unions. They based their assessments on the reasons for cohabitation, the degree of harm done to others by it, and the causes of the couples' difficulties.

Neighbors blamed women for the strife in the relationships for various reasons, mostly due to failing gender norms. The final argument of John Bishop and Mary Ann Ford in 1874 occurred late at night and annoyed all their neighbors. Those who testified included four women (three married women and one widow). The only man in the group, George Allen, a printer, was involved because his wife was ill. None of these witnesses had much good to say about Mary Ann, who was a raging alcoholic and used up Bishop's pay to fund her habit. Both men and women disapproved of her dissipation; her cohabitation was a minor issue in comparison. Mary Ann had clearly failed as a 'wife' from being an alcoholic and a spendthrift. They, then, pitied Bishop; none approved of his violence, but they could, at least, explain its context to the authorities.[24]

Women who were too masterful were also denied much neighborly support. When George Spurr murdered Hannah Hunt in 1883, the neighbors in her rural area of Nottinghamshire vilified her as 'Black Hannah,' a woman well able to look after herself, being 58 to Spurr's 33. Spurr had lived with her since he was 15 and had developed habits of drinking and poaching. As the owner of the property, Hunt was in charge, and when he drank too much she told him to leave. He included his shotgun in his packing, and while he lifted it off the wall, he shot her (he claimed it was an accident; she said he deliberately pointed the gun at her). Despite the fact that this was an agricultural area, many colliers lived nearby; five different ones testified they lived either 'next door' or a few doors away, and Hannah's daughter had a cottage only a hundred yards from her mother. The neighbors did not so much criticize Hannah for her extra-marital relationship as for her 'mastering' such a young man and using him ill. (Indeed, Mrs. Stevenson, her daughter, lived apart from her husband, so she evinced little disapproval of her mother's adultery.) Spurr's alcoholism, unlike Mary Ann's, did not lose him the sympathy of the locals, perhaps because they believed Hannah drove him to it.[25] Married women and men might disapprove of non-marital cohabitation, but they were more concerned with these women's breaches of gender roles, as neither followed expectations of a submissive, helpful wife.

In opposite cases, where the women were clearly victims of brutish or drunken men, the men's failure to fulfill their roles of protecting and providing caused both male and female neighbors to reprove them (Archer, 2000, pp. 41–54; D'Cruze, 1999, p. 41; McClelland, 1991, pp. 74–91; Tosh, 2005, pp. 63–71). Martha Peacock's remark asking Sabey how 'he called himself a man' when he had not provided for Jackson and her children was a telling turn of phrase.[26] Similarly, Francis Wane got all the blame for his dealings with Amelia Blunt, as he had refused to marry her and then objected when she made an engagement with another man. As the pub owner, Charles Filch told him, he was a dog in a manger who prevented her from making a respectable alliance; unsurprisingly, he got little sympathy from the community, despite having lived there all his life. Many of the violent men mentioned above got equally stinging rebukes from both men and women; Elizabeth Brown's description of John Banks as a 'thundering bully' for his treatment of Ann Gilligan was matched by Henry Emerson's scolding of Joseph Tucker for his treatment of Elizabeth Williamson in the pub.

Overall, the working class made interesting distinctions between types of cohabitation and proper male and female behavior in such families. Those who *could not* marry got more sympathy for their plights, especially if they had not broken up homes. Couples that acted 'the same as married' offered little threat to marriage, after all; drunkenness or violence were much bigger difficulties for the community. Those who were openly adulterous, leaving women without support or men without housekeepers, were more problematic, particularly when the first spouse had done no wrong. The reasons for the failure of the first relationships were key, a dynamic also seen in bigamy cases. Finally those deemed 'promiscuous' were outside the pale – including prostitutes, 'home-wreckers' and libertines (Frost, 2008b, pp. 72–95).

Still, not even all adulterous couples were equally culpable, as an example from mid-century showed. Frederick Hinson, a carpenter, lived in a cottage on the land of his employer in the Wood Green area of London in the 1860s. His partner was Maria Death, with whom he had one child, and they also kept one of his two children with his wife. Hinson thought of Death as his wife, and he reacted jealously when he suspected her of an intrigue with his neighbor, William Boyd. Boyd, a well-known libertine, was living with a young woman named Margaret Robinson. Three cottages in particular clustered together, but other houses grouped around them in broader circles. In the same neighborhood lived a surveyor (who testified), Hinson's father, also a carpenter, who lived within in five-minute walk, and a police constable, Edward Neale. Yet amongst this typical working-class area were two couples who lived outside of marriage, and two of those partners were having an affair. According to Isabella Heppel, Boyd's housekeeper, Boyd 'intended to turn Robinson away and to take Maria Death . . . he [also] told me that he had [already] had connexion with her.' Hinson, unable to bear the betrayal, shot Maria and then beat Boyd to death with the butt of the rifle after seeing them return after an excursion together.[27]

The distinctions working-class neighbors made between types of cohabitation showed through in the public reaction to the murders. Hinson, a carpenter, was a married man with two children when he seduced Maria, a governess. She did not know he was married when they began their courtship. When she became pregnant, she begged him to marry her, and he had to admit that he was already married. These circumstances made him seem dishonorable, but his later actions garnered him some credit. He negotiated a formal separation from his wife and set up house with Maria. They lived together eight years, and he sincerely loved her and was broken-hearted at her betrayal, though, of course, this does not excuse his violent reaction. Boyd, on the other hand, was a serial philanderer. He told Margaret Robinson he was a widower, left his two children in the care of her parents (who believed he had married their daughter), and then moved to London. While his 'in-laws' supported his children, he began an affair with Death. This kind of household was, then, distinct from that of Death and Hinson. To the modern reader (and the courts) the differences were not great – both men had broken up marriages and seduced previously virtuous young women – but to the locals, Boyd was much worse. Given the difficulties of divorce, neighbors tolerated adulterous cohabitation to a point, but a libertine behavior was another matter. According to the *Daily News*, 'Hinson's fate is generally pitied – too much it is to be feared – as if he were the hero of a romance; that of his illstarred [sic] mistress meets with partial sympathy, and the murder of Boyd is freely spoken of as a deed of retributive justice, rough and brutal though it might have been.'[28] Possibly, the neighbors accepted Hinson's own view that Maria was as good as his wife and, therefore, she should have been faithful. This did not convince the judge or jury, but Hinson, to his last breath, insisted that she was an adulteress as he had 'the right to regard her as his wife . . .'[29] Parsing the differences between these men was a complicated process for the local community.

An example like this, one which occurred at the height of Victorian morality, helps explain the contradictory nature of the evidence of the acceptance or rejection of cohabiting couples. Neighbors varied in their reactions based on their previous dealings and knowledge of the partners, their views of religion and the law, whether or not they were related to one of the partners, the reasons for the cohabitation, and other peculiar circumstances of each couple. No one explanation can encompass such a number of variables. Thus, some couples found limited acceptance in their home neighborhoods, while others sought places where they were not known and could 'pass' as married. Many men and women condemned irregular unions overall, but made exceptions for the 'hard cases' they knew. Others accepted unions in which the partners were discrete, but objected to those who flaunted them. At the least, the evidence of the English criminal courts indicates that broad generalizations about this issue risk oversimplification, pointing to the need to consider a wide range of sources before drawing conclusions.

5. Conclusion

The limited acceptance of neighbors discussed here did not mean that working-class families did not support marriage. Legal marriage was preferable for a number of reasons, especially for women, and would have been the first choice for the vast majority of the population. But England's marital regime, especially the strict rules and expense of divorce, meant that poor neighborhoods had to accommodate exceptions, even, in some cases, two or three families in a neighborhood. Boasting about marital nonconformity was unwise, but if the couple acted as if they were married, they were unlikely to be ostracized for cohabitation alone, particularly in industrial, urban centers. Neighbors were more annoyed by drinking, loud arguments, and violent behavior than by sex outside of marriage. The reasons were many. As these cases have shown, the poor lived very close together. Poorly-built housing meant that walls and partitions were thin, and overcrowding led many families to spend much of their time in the street or pub. Those living in row houses shared common privies and water butts. The difference between lodgings, street, and pub blurred as fights crossed borders middle-class families assumed were quite distinct. When so many people spent time in the street, avoiding overly crowded homes, 'public' and 'private' were less easy to identify. Thus, families had to cooperate together to survive, whether they approved of all their neighbors or not. Ostracism was often not a real option.

Poor couples also lived, when possible, near relatives, who were more tolerant of their personal choices or at least understood the reasons for them. Women wanted to be near their sisters and mothers, though men like Frederick Hinson also wanted kin close by (tellingly, he set up his irregular household within a five-minute walk of his father). Families might prefer their members to be respectably married, but they tacitly supported these unions when they were a fait accompli. Sarah Oldham, in fact, owned the buildings in her immediate vicinity; as the landlady, she surrounded herself with her kin. At times as well, neighbors became substitute family, either as close friends or in mother–daughter pairings. Martha Peacock defied her husband to care for her young lodger, urged Jackson to affiliate Sabey when he left her, stood up to his angry abuse when he got the summons, and then testified at the trial after he murdered her. Jackson's own mother could hardly have done more.

Another major issue these cases show is the influence of men on the process of policing unacceptable unions and actions. Men as well as women intervened to stop the worst abuses or to prevent life-threatening situations, just in different ways. Male neighbors counseled men against violence or to end disruptive unions; they also stepped in to protect women when necessary. When violence occurred, they helped arrest the perpetrators and refuted claims of insanity or drunkenness. Policing of femininity is well known to British historians, but these examples also show policing of proper masculinity by both men and women. Everyone, after all, had an interest in lessening the influence of disruptive households so that the crowded neighbors could live quietly. If the man's drinking or violence was the main problem, his failures as a man were the focus for those trying to maintain peace. Neighbors also had reasons to dispute the versions of relationships put forward by self-serving partners. The distinctions between 'libertines' like William Boyd and stable cohabitants like Frederick Hinson were delineated by both men and women in working-class neighborhoods.

The evidence of violence cases is limited, of course. It privileges less salubrious neighborhoods and urban areas. Attitudes towards cohabitation in the countryside were different, and the skilled working class considered legal marriage a marker of respectability. But the unskilled working class was the majority, and their attitudes encompassed more of the population. For this community, the reasons for the cohabitation were crucial, and openly adulterous couples might be seen as 'the same as married' if their unions were stable, they paid their bills, and they lived soberly. In short, for the poor, sexual purity was often a luxury a neighborhood could not afford.

Notes

1. *Royal Commission on Divorce and Matrimonial Causes* [Volumes 18–20 of the *Parliamentary Papers*], 1912, I: 383; II: 82.
2. *Times*, 28 July 1866, 12; *Lancaster Guardian*, 9 June 1866, 8; 28 July 1866, 3; *Morning Post*, 27 July 1866, 7; *Lancaster Gazette*, 28 July 1866, 3; *Preston Guardian*, 28 July 1866, 3.
3. *Shrewsbury Free Press*, 26 September 1874, 2; 27 March 1875, 2; see also the National Archives, Kew (hereafter NA), Home Office Records, HO 140/32, Calendar of Prisoners in the Lent Assizes, Shrewsbury, 18 March 1875. Dorricott had 11 previous convictions, though all but one, for stealing, were misdemeanors.
4. NA, Old Bailey Sessions Papers, PCOM, 1/92, 509–37; *Times*, 24 September 1867, 9; 26 September 1867, 9; 27 September 1867, 9; 16 October 1867, 11.
5. NA, HO 144/154/A40246; "Shocking Cruelty at Nottingham," *Yorkshire Gazette*, 16 May 1885, 5; *Nottingham Evening Post*, 11 May 1885, 3; 13 May 1885, 3. 16 May, 1885, 3; 21 May 1885, 3; *Nottinghamshire Gazette*, 17 July 1885, 3.
6. HO/144/154/A40246/7A.

7. NA, HO 144/276/A60972; Reg. v. Frederick James Andrews, Proceedings of the Old Bailey On-Line (hereafter POBO), 10 April 1899, Case #325; *Times*, 17 March 1899, 11; 18 March 1899, 13; 15 April 1899, 6; 4 May 1899, 6.
8. *Birmingham Daily Mail*, 6 March 1876, 3; 9 March 1876, 3; *Birmingham Daily Post*, 13 March 1876, 8.
9. HO 144/263/A56767; ASSI 13/25; *Nottingham Evening Post*, 5 March 1895, 3–4; 26 March 1895, 2.
10. *Times*, 16 March 1899, 10; 17 March 1899, 11; 18 March 1899, 3; 15 April 1899, 6; 4 May 1899, 6; POBO, 10 April 1899, Case #325.
11. HO 144/263/A56767/8; ASSI 13/25.
12. PCOM 1/92, 509–37; *Times*, 24 September 1867, 9; 26 September 1867, 9; 27 September 1867, 9; 16 October 1867, 11.
13. HO 144/85/A7411; *Nottingham and Midland Counties Daily Express*, 23 May 1881, 3; 24 May 1881, 3; *Times*, 23 May 1881, 12.
14. HO 45/9315/14967; *Manchester Weekly Times*, 20 April 1872, 7; 3 August 1872, 6; *Times*, 1 May 1872, 12.
15. PCOM 1/92, 511.
16. *Times*, 30 October, 1866, 9; 20 December 1866., 9; *South Eastern Gazette*, 5 November 1866, 2; *Tunbridge Wells Standard*, 2 November 1866, 3; 9 November 1866, 2; *Bury and Norwich Post*, 6 November 1866, 3; *The Standard*, 20 December 1866, 6.
17. NA, HO 144/249/A54992; ASSI 13/23; *Times*, 1 July 1893, 7; 9 July 1893, 9; *Northampton Daily Chronicle*, 29 June 1893, 4.
18. Quotes from the depositions, ASSI 13/23.
19. HO 144/249/A54992; ASSI 13/23.
20. NA, HO 45/9454/70865; *Times*, 18 December 1877, 7; 25 January 1878, 11; 8 February 1878, 5; *Nottingham Guardian*, 21 December 1877, 3; 25 January 1878, 7; 1 February 1878, 2.
21. NA, ASSI 36/11 Depositions, Frances Wane, 28 September 1864, 1 October 1864; *Morning Post*, 15 December 1864, 7; *Essex Standard and General Advertiser for the Eastern Counties*, 16 December 1864, 2; 28 December 1864, 2; *Times*, 15 December 1864, 10–11; 17 December 1864, 12.
22. NA, HO 144/154/A40246/3, Judge's Notes of the Trial, 13 July 1885.
23. NA, PCOM 1/92, 511–12; *Times*, 26 September 1867, 9.
24. *Times*, 29 October 1874, 11.
25. *Times*, 5 September 1883, 6; 10 November 1883, 11; *Nottingham and Midland Counties Daily Express*, 3 September 1883, 5; 4 September 1883, 5; *Morning Post*, 6 September 1883, 7; *Nottinghamshire Guardian*, 7 September 1883, 3; 21 September 1883, 3; 9 November 1883, 8. Spurr was found guilty of manslaughter and got twenty years' penal servitude.
26. HO 144/249/A54992/1.
27. Reg. v. Frederick Hinson, POBO, 22 November 1869, Case #35; *Times*, 28 October 1869, 9; 23 November 1869, 1; 25 November 1869, 9; 13 December 1869, 6; *Daily News*, 6 October 1869, 5; 7 October 1869, 4; 25 November 1869, 4; 14 December 1869, 2; *The Standard*, 12 October 1869, 6; *Morning Post*, 25 November 1869, 7; 13 December 1869, 7; *Birmingham Daily Post*, 13 December 1869, 8.
28. *Daily News*, 6 October 1869, 5.
29. *Birmingham Daily Post*, 13 December 1869, 8.

References

Archer, J. (2000). Men behaving badly? Masculinity and the uses of violence, 1850–1900. In S. D'Cruze (Ed.), *Everyday violence in Britain, 1850–1950* (pp. 41–54). New York: Longman.

August, A. (2007). *The British working class, 1832–1940*. Harlow: Pearson Longman.

Ayers, P., & Lambertz, J. (1986). Marriage relations, money, and domestic violence in working-class Liverpool, 1919–1939. In J. Lewis (Ed.), *Labour & love: Women's experience of home and family, 1850–1940* (pp. 195–219). Oxford: Basil Blackwell.

Bland, L. (1995). *Banishing the beast: Sexuality and the early feminists*. New York: The New Press.

Caine, B. (1997). *English feminism, 1780–1980*. Oxford: Oxford University Press.

Chinn, C. (1988). *They worked all their lives: Women of the urban poor, 1880–1939*. Manchester: Manchester University Press.

Clark, A. (2000). Domesticity and the problem of wife beating in nineteenth-century Britain: Working-class culture, law, and politics. In S. D'Cruze (Ed.), *Everyday violence in Britain, 1850–1950* (pp. 27–40). New York: Longman.

Conley, C. (1991). *The unwritten law: Criminal justice in Victorian Kent*. Oxford: Oxford University Press.

Davis, J. (1984). A poor man's system of justice: The London police courts in the second half of the nineteenth century. *The Historical Journal, 27*, 309–335.

D'Cruze, S. (1998). *Crimes of outrage: Sex, violence and victorian working women*. DeKalb, IL: Northern Illinois University Press.

D'Cruze, S. (1999). Sex, violence and local courts: Working-class respectability in a mid-nineteenth-century Lancashire town. *British Journal of Criminology, 39*, 39–55.

Frost, G. (2008). "He could not hold his passions": Domestic violence and cohabitation in England (1850–1905). *Crime, History, and Societies, 12*, 25–44.

Frost, G. (2008). *Living in sin: Cohabiting as husband and wife in nineteenth-century England*. Manchester: Manchester University Press.

Gillis, J. (1985). *For better, for worse: British marriages, 1600 to the present*. Oxford: Oxford University Press.

Hammerton, A. J. (1992). *Cruelty and companionship: Conflict in nineteenth-century married life*. London: Routledge.

Martin, A. (1911). *Working women and divorce*. London: David Nutt.

Mayhew, H. (1968). *London labour and the London poor*. Vol. II. New York: Dover.

McClelland, K. (1991). Masculinity and the 'representative artisan' in Britain, 1850–80. In M. Roper & J. Tosh (Eds.), *Manful assertions; masculinities in Britain since 1800* (pp. 74–91). London: Routledge.

Mearns, A. (1970). *The bitter cry of outcast London*. Leicester: Leicester University Press.

Phillips, R. (1988). *Putting asunder: A history of divorce in western society*. Cambridge: Cambridge University Press.

Probert, R. (2012). *The changing legal regulation of cohabitation: From fornicators to family, 1600–2010*. Cambridge: Cambridge University Press.

Roberts, E. (1984). *A woman's place: An oral history of working-class women, 1890–1940*. Oxford: Basil Blackwell.

Roberts, R. (1971). *The classic slum: Salford life in the first quarter of the century*. London: Penguin.

Ross, E. (1982). "Fierce questions and taunts": Married life in working-class London, 1870–1914. *Feminist Studies, 8*, 575–602.

Ross, E. (1985). "Not the sort that would sit on the doorstep": Respectability in pre-World War I London neighborhoods. *International Labor and Working-class History, 27*, 39–59.

Ross, E. (1993). *Love and toil: Motherhood in outcast London, 1870–1918*. Oxford: Oxford University Press.

Royal Commission on Divorce and Matrimonial Causes [Volumes 18–20 of the *Parliamentary Papers*]. (1912). London: His Majesty's Stationery Office.

Sims, G. (1883). *How the poor live and horrible London*. London: Chatto & Windus.

Tebbutt, M. (1995). *Women's talk? A social history of 'gossip' in working-class neighbourhoods, 1880–1960*. Aldershot: Scolar Press.

Tosh, J. (2005). *Manliness and masculinities in nineteenth-century Britain*. Harlow: Pearson Longman.

Education and transition from cohabitation to marriage in Lithuania

Aušra Maslauskaitė and Marė Baublytė

This article examines the role of individual educational resources in the transition from cohabitation to marriage in Lithuania over the past four decades that cover the communist and the transitional periods with various developmental stages of cohabitation. Two competing hypotheses were formulated based on cultural and structural approaches. The first hypothesis anticipated a stable negative effect of higher education, the second a positive gradient of education for the transition from cohabitation to marriage after the 1990s. Pooled data from two waves of the before Generations and Gender Survey is used to apply the descriptive and parametric event history analysis. The research results prove that the role of education in the transition from cohabitation to marriage is dynamic over time and across gender groups. The educational resources were not significant for the entry into marriage during the communist period that coincided with the initial stage of the diffusion of cohabitation in the society and this holds true for men's and women's matrimonial behavior. The transitional period marks the shift towards the positive educational gradient that is especially stable for the men. We conclude that the 'pattern of disadvantage' is pronounced in the contemporary Lithuanian society and this indicates the return to the socio-economically differentiated marital behavior.

1. Introduction

The increase in cohabitation which started in the late 1960s in Northern and Western Europe has been one of the most striking changes in the institution of the before family in the twentieth century. Although non-marital unions existed in the earlier historical periods (Kiernan, 2002), contemporary cohabitations play a substantially different role in the demographic and sociological development of the family. Changes in the family formation pattern are associated with the declining fertility and thus have far reaching consequences for the demographic structure of the population. Additionally, cohabitation is seen as one of the precursors for the destabilization of the institution of marriage and the overall increase in the risk of union dissolution/disruption (Amato & James, 2010; Liefbroer & Dourleijn, 2006). Moreover, it is debated whether non-marital union, due to its instability and lower relationship quality, is a favorable environment for childrearing (Kenney & McLanahan, 2006; Wu, 2000) and whether non-marital family ties have consequences for intergenerational family solidarity. Thus, considering the demographic and sociological consequences pertaining to cohabitation, research on the non-marital unions gains policy relevance.

However, even in the countries where the diffusion of non-marital unions started first, cohabitation did not become a substitute for marriage. In many cases it is not a life-long choice but merely a stage in the marital process (Andersson & Philipov, 2002; Ní Bhrolcháin & Beaujouan, 2013). Moreover, marriage sustains its social desirability and social value, even in such countries as Sweden, where cohabitation is widespread and socially acceptable (Bernhardt, 2004). The evidence on the temporary nature of cohabitation in the life course raises the question on the social forces that determine the progression from cohabitation to marriage. There is a growing body of research evidence from various developed countries that this process is socially differentiated in regard to individual social and economic characteristics (education, employment) (Kalmijn, 2011; Kalmijn & Luijkx, 2005; Kravdal, 1999; Oppenheimer, 2003) and that this differentiation is dynamic over time (Ní Bhrolcháin & Beaujouan, 2013) and its gradient depends on such contextual factors as the gender role segregation and the socio-economic outcomes of educational differences in the country (Kalmijn, 2013). Contrary to the growing evidence from the countries of North America, Western and Northern Europe, the research on Eastern Europe remains scarce although there are some studies on the role of the educational resources in the marital behavior in Russia, Ukraine and Romania (Gerber & Berman, 2010; Perelli-Harris, 2008; Perelli-Harris et al., 2010; Potârcă, Mills, & Lesnard, 2012).

In the current study we focus on the event of transition from cohabitation to marriage in Lithuania, an Eastern European country that within this region represents the case of relatively late adoption of the non-direct family formation pattern (Puur, Rahnu, Maslauskaite, Stankuniene, & Zakharov, 2012) and adherence to the familialistic values and traditional gender attitudes (Matysiak, 2011; Stankuniene & Maslauskaite, 2008). Together with other countries of the region, Lithuania shares large educational differences in employment (Heyns, 2005; MacIntosh, 2008). Our principal interest is the investigation of the effect of individuals' educational resources on the exit from cohabitation and entry into marriage. The analysis is guided by the following research question: what is the educational gradient in the transition from cohabitation to marriage across gender groups and across various partnership cohorts in the Lithuanian society?

Through answering this question we could assess several issues. First, we could identify the social groups that in the Lithuanian socio-economic setting stay in cohabitation longer and thus adopt the cohabitation as an alternative to marriage. Considering education one of the main precursors of individuals' economic and life-style outcomes, we could assess whether prolonged cohabitation is the choice of those with higher resources or those with lower. The answer to the question opens up the opportunity to theorize on the social mechanism of the family formation changes in the light of the two competing theoretical explanatory frameworks – the economic and the cultural. Second, looking at the effect of education on the transition from cohabitation to marriage in the dynamic perspective (across various partnership cohorts) we could assess the continuity or change of the role of educational resources in various socio-economic settings – both in the Soviet and the transitional society. Third, we hope that our case study from Eastern Europe could contribute to the broader socio-historic discussion on the return of the family to its historical complexity (Therborn, 2004, p. 314) and to the relevance of social class divisions in the marital behavior that were historically inherent to many societies (Kiernan, 2004; Mitterauer, 1983).

Family formation changes in Eastern and Central Europe attracted a lot of research interest during the past two decades (Bradatan & Kulscar, 2008; Gerber & Berman, 2010; Hoem & Kostova, 2008; Hoem, Kostova, Jasilioniene, & Mureşan, 2009; Perelli-Harris, 2008; Perelli-Harris et al., 2010; Philipov & Jasilioniene, 2008; Puur, Põldma, & Sakkeus, 2009; Speder, 2005; Stankuniene, Maslauskaite, Baublyte, Zakharov, & Régnier-Loilier, 2009). Nevertheless, we expect that the present study could complement the body of research in several ways. First of all, contrary to other existing studies, the focus of this research is not the union formation through cohabitation or marriage, but the transition out of cohabitation; thus we explore the issue that in regard to Eastern Europe attracted relatively little scientific interest until recently. Secondly, in this research, we rely on a more comprehensive dataset that provides an opportunity to run more precise empirical analysis of the dynamics of cohabitation in the life course. Thirdly, differently from the previous studies, we extend the observation time; thus our research covers the developments until the end of the first decade of the twenty-first century.

The paper is organized in five parts. After the introductory remarks we start with the development of the theoretical framework of the research. Afterwards, brief information on data and methodology is presented. The next part discusses the main results and we end the paper with the discussion on the empirical findings.

2. Theoretical background

Theoretical explanations of the family formation changes in the countries of Eastern and Central Europe that became visible and better empirically documented after the 1990s attracted a lot of scientific attention and basically replicated two predominant and competing explanatory frameworks employed in the Western scholarship. The demarcation line between the two frameworks in general follows the culture–structure divide and, in explaining family changes, prioritizes either cultural or structural, predominantly economic, factors. The first explanatory framework is the theory of the Second Demographic Transition (Lesthaeghe, 1983; Van de Kaa, 1987). The second one is 'the pattern of disadvantage' (Perelli-Harris & Gerber, 2011), 'uncertainty hypothesis' (Oppenheimer, 2003) or the 'crisis perspective', developed in relation to the family and fertility changes in Eastern and Central Europe (Macura, Mochizuki-Sternberg, & Garcia, 2002). In the following, we will briefly discuss both of them as they are substantial for the formulation of the working hypothesis of the paper.

2.1. Cultural framework

The framework of the Second Demographic Transition (SDT) (Lesthaeghe, 1983, 2010; Van de Kaa, 1987, 1994) which incidentally has almost a hegemonic status in European demography could be viewed as the demographic application of the general theory of modernization. SDT could be applied to the analysis of the changes in family formation on the contextual/macro and individual level. The modernization perspective and, accordingly, the SDT imply that institutional changes in education, employment, law, state, and religion generate value and behavioral change and this correspondingly transforms the institution of family. Thus, structural changes drive the ideational ones and these lead to new forms of family and fertility behavior. Rising female education and employment, the diminishing social role of religious institutions, post-WWII economic prosperity, the social rights movement, contraception, liberalization of sexual norms and other developments generated the normative expectations and new values attached to individual and family life in the countries of Northern and Western Europe in the 1960s and 1970s. Sometimes called the post-materialist values (Inglehart, 1990) of self-fulfillment, individual autonomy and self-realization interfere with the 'traditional' family formation model and 'the family' institution and thus motivate the innovative behavior patterns that result in the emergence of new forms of family life.

The SDT on the individual level implies that those with the 'more advanced' values are the forerunners of the family changes. Non-traditional values are a by-product of the individual enrolment in the system of higher education; thus, according to the SDT framework, it could be expected that individuals with higher educational attainment will be pioneers in the new family behavior. Consequently, they will be the first to arrange cohabitation and the first to reject marriage and live in cohabitation. On the macro level the logic of modernization theory implies that modernization is a global process, thus it is an irreversible and gradual process (Joas & Knöbl, 2009). This view is readily adopted by the proponents of the SDT regarding the diffusion of cohabitation as gradual and allowing to place the countries in the continuum of 'leaders' and 'laggers'.

The SDT has attracted many followers but also has generated a lot of criticism. First of all, the reality of the globalized world has led to some revisions of the general understanding of modernization and to reconsidering the universality of developmental paths, stages and outcomes of modernity. Secondly, and coming closer to the family, demographic developments in the last decades in some developed countries proved that the social groups that should be mostly affected by the SDT manifest most 'traditional' family behavior patterns. Those with higher educational attainment and stable employment have higher propensity to marry, form more stable unions, divorce less and have more children, thus they lead the way of life that represents 'more family' (Esping-Andersen & Billari, 2012).

Nevertheless, the SDT framework has been widely used and remains one of the most influential in articulating the family formation changes in the countries of Central and Eastern Europe before and after the 1990s. The theory is predominantly used in two ways: either more as an heuristic tool for the labeling of the empirical changes and thus adopting it only instrumentally and partially, or more as an analytical explanatory tool that presupposes a substantial similarity in character but not in timing of the social and cultural forces behind the family changes across the continent. Disregarding the reception, the general notion of changes as universal, gradual and varying in timing is sustained and consequently the countries are put in the line of 'leaders' and those 'lagging behind'.

There is a view that the SDT values were in place in several countries in this part of Europe even before the 1990s, but the institutional setting (housing policy, limited accesses to modern contraception, role of the extended family in securing consumer goods etc.) hampered the changes (Frejka, 2008; Gerber & Berman, 2010; Puur et al., 2012; Sobotka, 2004). The argument on the existence of the SDT values even before the 1990s is reinforced by the view that some structural preconditions were in place in the countries under the 'Iron Curtain'. During the Soviet period, in almost all countries high female employment rates with the dominant pattern of full time female employment were prevailing (Einhorn, 1993). In some countries women outnumbered men at the universities (Białecki & Heyns, 1993). Any role of religion in the public sphere had been almost eliminated and the role of religion in private life had been diminishing in several countries of Central and Eastern Europe (Tomka, 1991). Thus, it could be that the structural changes shaped a prerequisite setting for the upspring of the SDT values and dramatic changes in the institutional setting after the 1990s cleared the stage for the diffusion of the partnership behavior that corresponds to the SDT.

Cohabitation as an alternative to marriage is one of the key features of the SDT partnership behavior; thus, empirically testing the SDT hypothesis the duration of cohabitation could be seen as a more relevant indicator than the choice of the first partnership in cohabitation. Considering education, one of the main proxies for individualistic values and autonomy, we could expect that people with higher education were the first to initiate prolonged cohabitation in Lithuania and this association would be stable for the partnerships contracted at different periods during the 1980s and well into the 2000s.

2.2. *Economic framework*

The second explanatory framework puts the economic arguments at the forefront of the driving forces behind the family formation behavior. The view is based on the empirical evidence on the negative effect of low individual socio-economic resources measured in education, employment, incomes, and career maturity on the propensity to enter marriage after cohabitation or singlehood and this association is especially profound in men's partnership behavior (Bernardi & Nazio, 2005; Kalmijn, 2011, 2013; Kravdal, 1999; Liefbroer, 2005; Oppenheimer, 2003). A comparative study of several Western and Northern European countries revealed that for women low education in all countries is associated with a higher propensity of childbearing in cohabitation (Perelli-Harris et al., 2010). Similar results have been replicated for Russia and it has been proved that those with lower education stay in cohabitation longer (Potârcă et al., 2012) and that childbearing in cohabitation is more pronounced in the low education groups (Perelli-Harris & Gerber, 2011).

The link between individuals' socio-economic resources and marital behavior (postponement of marriage, transition into marriage or childbearing in cohabitation) is articulated pointing out the economic grounds of the family life and the structural constrains generated by the contemporary economy. The possession of relatively stable economic resources is needed and expected for setting up the household, for the childrearing and for the maintenance of the family life. Partners with higher and stable economic resources have better consumption opportunities and are less exposed to the economic risks that often translate to less social and personal risk. Additionally to the economic prerequisites for starting family relations, marriage normatively persists in being associated with family stability and status; it is still a personal aspiration (Kalmijn, 2007) and it embodies the successful transition into adult life and should be preceded by two other events: arriving at the status of 'good employment' and acquisition of a 'good home' (Cherlin, 2010). However, the achievement of these two life course prerequisites for marriage became more difficult during the era of globalized economy, post-industrialization and labor market insecurities of the new capitalism that started in the developed countries outside Eastern Europe during the 1980s. The new economic conditions were especially unfavorable for the youth with lower educational resources but general labor market uncertainty also affected the rest of the young generations in disadvantageous ways (Mills & Blossfeld, 2005). Job related uncertainty has led to the postponement of marriage and childbearing across the developed countries (Sobotka & Toulemon, 2008). Some authors argued that especially male employment uncertainties affected the delay of marriage and the rise of cohabitations (Oppenheimer, 2003), because 'men's failure to provide economically would be less of a problem for cohabitation than for marriage' (Kalmijn, 2011, p. 273).

Lithuania, together with other countries of Eastern and Central Europe, experienced an economic turmoil starting from the early 1990s. Several previous decades of secure employment and very low but relatively equally distributed economic living standards had been replaced by hyper-inflation, de-industrialization, unemployment, economic 'shock therapy' reforms and other developments associated with the transition to the capitalist economy. The massive restructuring of the economy during the 1990s especially affected men's employment opportunities because the severely shrinking industry could not supply enough jobs for low educated manually skilled men who dominated several Soviet male generations. The decline in economic well-being during the 1990s was so dramatic and strong that it fundamentally affected family related behavior of all social groups and according to many authors became the most relevant push factor in the initial stages of the transition towards the cohabitation based family formation model (Macura et al., 2002; Philipov & Jasilioniene, 2008; Rychtarikova, 2000; Stankuniene & Maslauskaite, 2008). The emerging fragile new service economy and spectacular economic growth for almost the whole decade of the 2000s brought to life social and economic divisions based on access to resources, and education started to gain a decisive role in defining social position and social economic prospects.

Thus, considering the economic explanatory framework and looking at the trends in other developed countries, we could expect that in Lithuanian society after the 1990s the educational resources would become relevant for the transition from cohabitation to marriage. Lower economic and social security, bleaker economic prospects associated with lower education would negatively affect the timing of transition and facilitate longer spells of cohabitation in the life course calendar.

3. Data and methods

We use pooled data sets of two waves of the before Generations and Gender Survey (GGS) carried out respectively in 2006 and 2009 in Lithuania. The GGS samples are large, nationally representative and include men and women aged 18–79 and living in non-institutional households (Simard & Franklin, 2005). The surveys recorded the complete partnership and fertility histories and dates of events in a monthly accuracy. Originally, the GGS was planned as the longitudinal panel three wave survey (UNECE, 2005), but this methodological requirement was not fulfilled in Lithuania due to the very large attrition rate during the first and the second wave (Stankūnienė, Maslauskaitė, & Baublytė, 2013). A large number of new respondents (5748) were included into the second wave of the GGS and thus the survey design was transformed from the longitudinal panel into the longitudinal cross-sectional survey.

In this analysis we use the pooled dataset that integrates the partnership histories from the first and the second waves of the GGS surveys. The pooled dataset has the advantage of recording more partnership histories and better opportunities to analyze the family formation behavior of the older generations that are less well represented in the single survey dataset. The sample size in the first wave was 10,036, in the second there were 8042 respondents. In the pooled dataset, there are 12,127 first partnerships; out of the total, 5780 are men's and 6347 women's partnerships. There are 3127 first partnerships that started as cohabitations, out of them, 1563 men's and 1564 women's. Considering the main aim of the study and in order to control for the union dissolution, the cohabitations that were dissolved were not included into the further analysis (223 men's cohabitations and 222 women's cohabitations).

Our main dependent variable was the transition from cohabitation to marriage. The population at risk was all women and men who entered the first partnership as cohabitation. The process time was measured in months elapsed since the entry into the first partnership that was cohabitation. The respondents were followed for the five years after the beginning of cohabitation and the right censoring was performed. The time axis was partitioned into five intervals each lasting up to 12 months. We applied the descriptive and parametric methods of event history analysis. A piecewise constant exponential models were used to examine the shift from cohabitation to marriage. Separate models were run for the male and female subpopulations and different calendar periods. The main control variable (time-varying) was education with four categories distinguished: high (ISCED 5–6), medium (ISCED 3–4), low (ISCED0–2) and in education. The variable was composed using the dates of birth and the dates of completion of highest achieved level of education. The other time varying covariate was the calendar period partitioned into five intervals 1970–1979, 1980–1989, 1990–1999, and 2000–2009. The other time-varying covariate was the parity-pregnancy status and it included three categories: childless and non-pregnant, childless and pregnant, and with children. Additionally we considered age at the first partnership, respondent's birth cohort and parental divorce till the respondent was up to 15 years old.

4. Results

4.1. Descriptive results

4.1.1. Development of cohabitation: general trends

Figure 1 shows the share of first partnerships that started as cohabitations and as marriages in the male (Figure 1(a)) and female (Figure 1(b)) subpopulations starting from the 1950s.

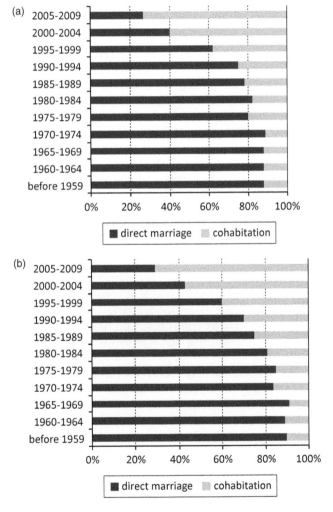

Figure 1.   First partnership as cohabitation and marriage by calendar period and gender. Note: GGS Lithuania (pooled dataset). (a) men; (b) women.

We observe the extensive change in the mode of union formation progressing from cohabitation as very selective behavior in the 1950s till the beginning of the 1970s, slow increase in cohabitation in the second half of the 1970s and stagnation for almost two decades all the way to 1994. Nevertheless during the period of 1975–1994, almost 20% of men and women started their family from cohabitation. The second half of the 1990s marks a fast proliferation of cohabitation for the 10 following years till 2004. During this decade, cohabitation became the dominant form of first partnership as at the end of this period more than half of first partnerships were cohabitations and direct marriage became very selective. Thus, in almost half a century, the Lithuanian family experienced the reverse of the family formation model although the most intense changes were squeezed into the decade embracing the turn of the century.

This brief overview of the general trends of family formation points to two relevant issues. First, cohabitation in Lithuania started to spread in the Socialist period though the process was slow and stagnated. Thus, the institution of marriage started to lose its hegemony during the Soviet period and it could be that this reflects changes in society's socio-normative moods, emergence of structural and cultural settings that stimulated the shift towards the cohabitation based family formation pattern. The slow pace of the process could be associated with the specific institutional factors that hampered the changes and that were discussed by various authors (Frejka, 2008; Gerber & Berman, 2010; Sobotka, 2004). Second, the turmoil of the beginning of the 1990s could not be directly associated with the revolutionary changes in the family formation. The first five transitional years that were marked by the most dramatic economic downfall did not substantially affect the established dominant family formation praxis and the extensive changes were postponed. Summing up and putting the Lithuanian trend in a comparative perspective we might conclude that it is similar to the one in Hungary, Russia and Romania where the shift towards the new family formation pattern started later, was slow for several decades and experienced significant acceleration at the turn of the last century (Puur et al., 2012).

4.1.2. Transition from cohabitation to marriage

The time of transition from cohabitation to marriage is a significant indicator of the evaluation of the developmental stage of the cohabitation in the society. The presence of cohabitation might not mark substantial changes if cohabitation is short-termed and is quickly transformed into marriage. And, on the contrary, if cohabitation becomes longer, it acquires the status of socio-normative family behavior. As the main aim of the study is the exit from cohabitation and entry into marriage, it is relevant to discuss the general trends in the timing of this transition.

Figure 2 shows the significant changes across the partnership cohorts in the transition from cohabitation to marriage. Three patterns of this transition could be distinguished and are manifest among both men (Figure 2(a)) and women (Figure 2(b)) although there are some gender specific fluctuations. The first pattern is specific for the cohabitations formed before the end of the Soviet period (till 1989) and features fast transition time and large extent of entries into marriage. The most intensive risk to experience the transition is concentrated in the first six months of cohabitation and at the end of the second year around 80% of all cohabitations have experienced marriage. The second pattern started to manifest itself in the cohabitations contracted in the periods of 1990–1994 and 1995–1999. This pattern significantly deviated from the model that was prevalent for almost three previous decades. The transition to marriage started to be postponed and this became

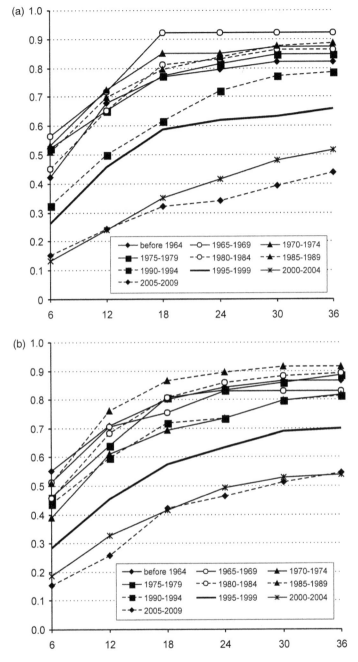

Figure 2. Conversion of cohabitation to marriage by time (in months) in cohabitation, calendar period and gender. Note: GGS Lithuania (pooled dataset). (a) men; (b) women.

first of all evident in the men's marital behavior in 1990–1994 (Figure 2(a)) and was replicated in the women's behavior in 1995–1999 (Figure 2(b)). Looking at the first half of the 1990s, it seems significant that even if the share of those who started partnerships from cohabitation remained almost stable, as it was discussed previously, the role of cohabitation in the life course and, first of all for men, started to change: the transition to marriage became more slow and the time spent in cohabitation had been expanded. In the second half of the 1990s the share of cohabitations that experienced marriage by the end of the second year decreased to around 60% for both men and women. The more pronounced turn towards the new pattern is observable in the first decade of the twenty-first century. In the 2000–2004 period only around 40% of cohabitations for both gender groups were transformed into marriage by the end of the second year of cohabitation. Thus, we observe a gradual postponement of entry into marriage from cohabitation by every successive partnership cohort and the turning point in this process is gender specific. For men it was synchronized with the sweeping social, economic and political changes of the beginning of the 1990s and for women it was delayed for a half of a decade. The gradual progression of the postponement of transition continued into the 2000s and this proves that cohabitation lost its role of a short prelude to marriage.

4.1.3. Multivariate results: social differentiation of transition to marriage

How has this shift towards the postponement of the transition progressed in various educational groups? Was it synchronic in all groups in various periods or could we distinguish groups that have had a higher risk of entry into marriage? In order to answer these questions and to eliminate the compositional effects, we employed the multivariate modelling analysis. As noted above, we used a piecewise constant exponential model with time constant and time-varying covariates. Time constant covariates were age at first partnership, parental divorce and birth cohort. Time-varying covariates were education, parity-pregnancy status and birth cohort. Considering the aim of the study, separate models were run for four calendar periods: 1970–1979, 1980–1989, 1990–1999 and 2000–2009. The standardized effects of education for the transition from cohabitation to marriage for men and women are presented in Table 1.

The results of the before multivariate analysis prove that the association between education and transition from cohabitation to marriage is dynamic over time and across gender groups. The earliest periods of observation that coincide with the two last Soviet decades portray the insignificance of educational resources for the transition from cohabitation to marriage. During the 1970s and 1980s, the relative risk to experience the transition was not significantly different if we compare high, medium groups and those in education to the low education groups controlled for various demographic and partnership

Table 1. Relative risk of transition from cohabitation to marriage by education, men and women, various calendar periods.

	Men				Women			
	1970–1979	1980–1989	1990–1999	2000–2009	1970–1979	1980–1989	1990–1999	2000–2009
Education								
Low (ref.)								
In education	1.24	1.57	1.88**	1.68**	0.57	0.94	1.70**	1.31
Medium	1.44	1.36	2.48***	2.11***	0.59	0.91	1.81**	1.64
High	1.04	1.44	2.59***	1.66**	0.55	0.99	3.32***	1.56
N (person months)	18966	28862	44436	79300	14516	30335	41994	50156

Note: controlled for parity pregnancy status, duration of cohabitation, age at first partnership, birth cohort, parental divorce. ***$p \leq 0.001$; **$p \leq 0.01$.

level factors. Although the association is not significant, the direction of gradient is gender specific: for men the gradient has a positive direction and for women a negative one.

The last decade of the twentieth century that was marked by revolutionary changes in political, economic and social conditions significantly transformed the role of education in the family formation process. For men, higher educational resources were associated with the increased risk to transform cohabitation to marriage compared to men with the low educational resources. Men with the highest education demonstrate the highest propensity to exit cohabitation and their chances were more than twice as high than those of men with low education. A similar effect size was characteristic for men with medium educational attainment. For women, the decade under discussion marked the reversal of the educational gradient in marital behavior as it became positive and replicated the one observed for the male subpopulation. Women with the highest education demonstrated the highest probability to transform their cohabitation into marriage if compared with the ones with the lowest education achieved. Thus, the last decade of the twentieth century marks the shift towards the positive educational gradient in marital behavior. We observe that the risk to convert cohabitation into marriage becomes significantly higher for the groups of the highest and the medium level of education and those still in education compared with the ones with the lowest educational attainment. The detrimental effect of lower educational resources on the chances to convert cohabitation into marriage is manifest for both gender groups, thus we observe the homogeneity of the educational gradient across gender.

However, this trend is discontinued in the first decade of the twenty-first century as we observe the different patterns of educational gradient for men and women. Men replicate the pattern of the positive educational gradient that was incidental in the previous decade. Cohabiting men with the highest education have more than 60% higher risk to enter marriage compared with cohabiting men with low education. The effect size is similar for those in education and even higher for those with the medium level of education. Contrary to men, the association between education and entry into marriage for cohabiting women becomes insignificant although the direction of the gradient is sustained.

Although the confounding factors are out of the scope of our main interest, we will very briefly report them. Model estimates are presented in Appendix 1. The study revealed that the most stable predictor of increased risk for the transition from cohabitation to marriage is women's pregnancy if compared with the state of being childless. The propensity to marry for cohabiting women and men significantly increases with the pregnancy and this trend is stable for all periods under observation. The risk of transition to marriage gradually decreases with every successive year in cohabitation if compared with the transition during the first year. Nonetheless, for the last decade, we observe that the decrease in effect sizes becomes less pronounced and this in general corresponds to the postponement of conversions discussed in the descriptive analysis.

5. Discussion and conclusions

The aim of this study was to explore the educational gradient in transition from cohabitation to marriage and its change over time in Lithuanian men's and women's subpopulations. We assume that the research on the transition from cohabitation to marriage is essential for the understanding of the broader changes of the institutions of marriage and family. The analysis was based on a pooled dataset of two waves of the before Generations and Gender Surveys (2006 and 2009) which secured sufficient number of observations for the precise analysis and the opportunity to trace back the partnership behavior for the four past decades. The theoretical underpinning of the research was shaped by two competitive explanatory frameworks: the theory of the Second Demographic Transition (Lesthaeghe, 2010; Van de Kaa, 1987) and the hypothesis of the 'pattern of disadvantage' (Oppenheimer, 2003; Perelli-Harris et al., 2010). As education is a resource that conditions individuals' life style, life chances, social and economic standing, we expected that, based on the first theoretical framework, educational gradient for the transition from cohabitation to marriage would be positive, disregarding of the degree of proliferation of cohabitation in the society and the role of cohabitation in the family formation process. According to this view, people with higher education would be more prone to postpone the transition from cohabitation to marriage because their behavior is motivated by non-traditional values and higher personal and social autonomy. Contrary to this, the second approach suggests that delayed transition is more common for the lower education groups because they do not possess the social and economic resources to enter the marriage that is associated with the long term personal, social and economic commitment.

Our analysis revealed that the role of education in the transition from cohabitation to marriage is dynamic over time, which in this study stretches across two essentially different societal conditions and encompasses diverse developmental stages of cohabitation. Educational resources were insignificant for the transformation of cohabitation to marriage during the two last Soviet decades that coincided with the initial stage of the diffusion of cohabitation in the Lithuanian society, when cohabitation was infrequent and played a role of a prelude to marriage. Thus, the exit from cohabitation to marriage was not conditioned by men's and women's education in the 1970s and 1980s in Soviet Lithuania, if controlled for various demographic and social factors. The two following decades mark a changing role of education in the marital behavior, with low education becoming disadvantageous for the transformation of cohabitation to marriage; cohabitants with higher education demonstrate higher propensity to enter marriage when compared with those with lowest education. This turn toward educationally differentiated partnership behavior progressed simultaneously with further development of cohabitation as it becomes the dominant pattern of family formation and loses its role as a short term partnership arrangement. Moreover, these developments happen in the context of sweeping political, social and economic transformations that the Lithuanian society experienced after 1990.

One possible explanation of the findings for the dynamic role of education for the entry into marriage after cohabitation may be related to the transformation of the role of education in the economy and in the structure of society in Lithuania during the last four decades. In the 1970s and 1980s, during the Soviet period, inequalities in the economic outcomes of education were small; moreover, education was not a significant asset in the centrally regulated economy where employment was safeguarded by the political system, wages were kept at a low level and everyday life was marked by the constant shortage of welfare goods for the majority of the society. Thus, it is quite plausible that within these contextual conditions the exit from cohabitation to marriage was determined not by education, as it played a minor role for the economic prospects of the family, but by other factors. One of them could have been the compliance with the social norms of marital family relations that had a strong pressure in the society where the diffusion of cohabitation was still in the initial stage. Thus, considering the Soviet decades, we found no proof either for the hypothesis derived from the SDT framework, or for the hypothesis of the pattern of disadvantage.

The shift towards the positive educational gradient observable in the two last decades after 1990 signifies the profound restructuring of the economy, the labor market and the reshaped role of education in securing individuals' employment, economic and social rewards, prospects and new societal setting for family building. In the service economy, higher educational resources safeguard better employment opportunities, social mobility and relative stability of the economic grounds of personal life and all this in turn affects the partnership behavior. Rising inequalities in Lithuania and across the region after 1990 (Heyns, 2005) brought to life class divisions in the family formation behavior and this trend corresponds to the hypothesis of the pattern of disadvantage. As cohabitation became widespread and socially acceptable and the social barriers to stay longer in non-marital union became lower, those at the bottom of society began to the largest extent delaying the transition from cohabitation to marriage because the limited economic resources hamper the entry into long term commitment of the partners.

It could be added that the effect of educational resources is especially stable for men as the positive educational gradient remains stable for the two decades after 1990. Since the beginning of the societal transformations, men with low education are in the most disadvantageous position to enter marriage after cohabitation as the effect of education for women becomes insignificant in the 2000s. The disadvantageous position of men with low education could be attributed to the gender expectations associated with the traditional gender culture of Lithuania (Matysiak, 2011) that sustains the gender asymmetry and attributes the breadwinner role to men.

Our study contributed to the understanding of the development of cohabitation in Lithuania and its social differentiation over time focusing on the event of exit from cohabitation to marriage, which safeguards a better opportunity to explore the process of family formation after cohabitation becomes the dominant pattern. The findings in general support the results of some previous studies that point to the pattern of disadvantage found in some other developed countries (Perelli-Harris et al., 2010). Unfortunately, our study was restricted to only one characteristic of individual socio-economic position which we see as a limitation of the study.

References

Amato, P. R., & James, S. (2010). Divorce in Europe and the United States: Commonalities and differences across nations. *Family Science*, *1*, 2–13. doi:10.1080/19424620903381583

Andersson, G., & Philipov, D. (2002). Life-table representations of family dynamics in Sweden, Hungary, and 14 other FFS countries. *Demographic Research*, *7*, 67–144. doi:10.4054

Bernardi, F., & Nazio, T. (2005). Globalization and the transition to adulthood in Italy. In H.-P. Blossfeld, E. Klijzing, M. Mills, & K. Kurz (Eds.), *Globalization, uncertainty and youth in society: The losers in a globalizing world* (pp. 359–385). Abingdon: Routledge.

Bernhardt, E. (2004). *Cohabitation or marriage? Preferred living arrangements in Sweden*. Vienna: Austrian Institute for Family Studies Publication.

Białecki, I., & Heyns, B. (1993). Educational attainment, the status of women and the private school movement in Poland. In V. M. Moghadam (Ed.), *Democratic reform and the position of women in transitional economies* (pp. 110–134). Oxford: Oxford University Press.

Bradatan, C., & Kulscar, L. (2008). Choosing between marriage and cohabitation: Women's first union patterns in Hungary. *Journal of Comparative Family Studies*, *39*, 491–507. http://www.jstor.org/stable/41604242

Cherlin, A. J. (2010). *The marriage go-round. The state of marriage and the family in America today*. New York, NY: Vintage Books.

Einhorn, B. (1993). *Cinderella goes to market: Citizenship, gender and women's movement in the "New Europe"*. London: Verso.

Esping-Andersen, G., & Billari, F. C. (2012). *Re-Theorizing Family Demographics*. Working paper.

Frejka, T. (2008). Overview chapter 5: Determinants of family formation and childbearing during the societal transition in Central and Eastern Europe. *Demographic Research*, *19*, 139–170. doi:10.4054

Gerber, T. P., & Berman, D. (2010). Entry to marriage and cohabitation in Russia, 1985–2000: Trends, correlates, and implications for the second demographic transition. *European Journal of Population*, *26*, 3–31. doi:10.107/s10680-009-9196-8

Heyns, B. (2005). Emerging inequalities in Central and Eastern Europe. *Annual Review of Sociology*, *31*, 163–197. doi:10.1146/annurev.soc.30.012703.110637

Hoem, J. M., & Kostova, D. (2008). Early traces of the second demographic transition in Bulgaria: A joint analysis of marital and non-marital union formation, 1960–2004. *Population Studies*, *62*, 259–271. doi:10.1080/00324720802313256

Hoem, J. M., Kostova, D., Jasilioniene, A., & Mureşan, C. (2009). Traces of the second demographic transition in four selected countries in Central and Eastern Europe: Union formation as a demographic manifestation. *European Journal of Population*, *25*, 239–255. doi:10.1007/s10680-009-9177-y

Inglehart, R. (1990). *Culture shift in advanced industrial society*. Princeton, NJ: Princeton University Press.

Joas, H., & Knöbl, W. (2009). *Social theory*. Cambridge: Cambridge University Press.

Kalmijn, M. (2007). Explaining cross-national differences in marriage, cohabitation, and divorce in Europe, 1990–2000. *Population Studies*, *61*, 243–263. doi:10.1080/00324720701571806

Kalmijn, M. (2011). The influence of men's income and employment on marriage and cohabitation: Testing Oppenheimer's theory in Europe. *European Journal of Population*, *27*, 269–293. doi:10.1007/s10680-011-9238-x

Kalmijn, M. (2013). The educational gradient in marriage: A comparison of 25 European countries. *Demography*, *50*, 1499–1520. doi:10.107/s13524-013-0229-x

Kalmijn, M., & Luijkx, R. (2005). Has the reciprocal relationship between employment and marriage changed for men? An analysis of the life histories of men born in The Netherlands between 1930 and 1970. *Population Studies*, *59*, 211–231. doi:10.1080/00324720500099587

Kenney, C. T., & McLanahan, S. (2006). Why are cohabiting relationships more violent than marriages? *Demography*, *43*, 127–140. http://link.springer.com/article/10.1353/dem.2006.0007

Kiernan, K. (2002). Cohabitation in Western Europe: Trends, issues, and implications. In A. Booth & A. C. Crouter (Eds.), *Just living together. Implications of cohabitation on families, children and social policy* (pp. 3–32). Mahwah, NJ: Lawrence Erlbaum Associates.

Kiernan, K. (2004). Unmarried cohabitation and parenthood: Here to stay? European perspectives. In D. P. Moynijan, T. M. Smeeding, & L. Rainwater (Eds.), *The future of the family* (pp. 66–95). New York, NY: Russell Sage Foundation.

Kravdal, Ø. (1999). Does marriage require a stronger economic underpinning than informal cohabitation? *Population Studies*, *53*, 63–80. doi:10.1080/00324720308067

Lesthaeghe, R. (1983). A century of demographic and cultural change in Western Europe: An exploration of underlying dimensions. *Population and Development Review*, *9*, 411–435. http://www.jstor.org/stable/1973316

Lesthaeghe, R. (2010). The unfolding story of the second demographic transition. *Population and Development Review*, *36*, 211–251. doi:10.1111/j.1728-4457.2010.00328.x

Liefbroer, A. (2005). Transition from youth to adulthood in the Netherlands. In H.-P. Blossfeld, E. Klijzing, M. Mills, & K. Kurz (Eds.), *Globalization, uncertainty and youth in society: The losers in a globalizing world* (pp. 80–104). Abingdon: Routledge.

Liefbroer, A. C., & Dourleijn, E. (2006). Unmarried cohabitation and union stability: Testing the role of diffusion using data from 16 European countries. *Demography*, *43*, 203–221. http://link.springer.com/article/10.1353/dem.2006.0018

MacIntosh, S. (2008). *Education and employment in OECD countries*. Paris: UNESCO.

Macura, M., Mochizuki-Sternberg, Y., & Garcia, J. L. (2002). Eastern and Western Europe's fertility and partnership patterns: Selected developments from 1987 to 1999. In M. Macura, G. Beets, E. Klijzing, & M. Corijn (Eds.), *Dynamics of fertility and partnership in Europe. Insights and lessons from comparative research* (Vol. 1, pp. 27–57). Geneva: United Nations.

Matysiak, A. (2011). *Interdependencies between fertility and women's labour supply*. Dordrecht: Springer.

Mills, M., & Blossfeld, H. -P. (2005). Globalization, uncertainty, and the early life course: A theoretical framework. In H.-P. Blossfeld, E. Klijzing, M. Mills, & K. Kurz (Eds.), *Globalization, uncertainty and youth in society: The losers in a globalizing world* (pp. 1–24). Abingdon: Routledge.

Mitterauer, M. (1983). *Ledige Mütter. Zur Geschichte illigitimer Geburten in Europa* [Single mothers. The history of illegitimate births in Europe]. München: Beck.

Ní Bhrolcháin, M., & Beaujouan, É. (2013). Education and cohabitation in Britain: A return to traditional patterns? *Population Council*, *39*, 441–458. doi:10.1111/j.1728-4457.2013.00611.x

Oppenheimer, V. K. (2003). Cohabiting and marriage during young men's career-development process. *Demography*, *40*, 127–149. http://link.springer.com/article/10.1353/dem.2003.0006

Perelli-Harris, B. (2008). Family formation in post-Soviet Ukraine: Changing effects of education in a period of rapid social change. *Social Forces*, *87*, 767–794. doi:10.1353/sof.0.0140

Perelli-Harris, B., & Gerber, T. P. (2011). Nonmarital childbearing in Russia: Second demographic transition or pattern of disadvantage? *Demography*, *48*, 317–342. doi:10.1007/s13524-010-0001-4

Perelli-Harris, B., Sigle-Rushton, W., Kreyenfeld, M., Lappegård, T., Keizer, R., & Berghammer, C. (2010). The educational gradient of childbearing within cohabitation in Europe. *Population and Development Review*, *36*, 775–801. doi:10.1111/j.1728-4457.2010.00357.x

Philipov, D., & Jasilioniene, A. (2008). Union formation and fertility in Bulgaria and Russia: A life table description of recent trends. *Demographic Research*, *19*, 2057–2114. doi:10.4054/DemRes.2008.19.62

Potârcă, G., Mills, M., & Lesnard, L. (2012). Family formation trajectories in Romania, the Russian Federation and France: Towards the second demographic transition? *European Journal of Population*, *29*, 69–101. doi:10.1007/s10680-012-9279-9

Puur, A., Põldma, A., & Sakkeus, L. (2009). Change and continuity in partnership and childbearing patterns: Early evidence from the Estonian GGS. In V. Stankuniene & D. Jasilionis (Eds.), *The Baltic countries: Population, family and family policy* (pp. 127–152). Vilnius: Institute for Social Research.

Puur, A., Rahnu, L., Maslauskaite, A., Stankuniene, V., & Zakharov, S. (2012). Transformation of partnership formation in Eastern Europe: The legacy of the past demographic divide. *Journal of Comparative Family Studies*, *3*, 389–411. http://www/jstor.org.stabel/41604526

Rychtarikova, J. (2000). Demographic transition or demographic shock in recent population development in Czech Republic? *Acta Universitatis Carolinae Geographica*, *35*, 89–103.

Simard, M., & Franklin, S. (2005). *GGS sample design guidelines*. Geneva: United Nations Economic Commission for Europe.

Sobotka, T. (2004). *Postponement of childbearing and low fertility in Europe*. Amsterdam: Thela Thesis.

Sobotka, T., & Toulemon, L. (2008). Overview chapter 4: Changing family and partnership behaviour. *Demographic Research*, *19*, 85–138. doi:10.4054/DemRes.2008.19.6

Speder, Z. (2005). The rise of cohabitations as first union and some neglected factors of recent demographic developments in Hungary. *Demografia. English Edition*, *48*, 77–103. http://demografia.hu/letoltes/kiadvanyok/Dem_angol/2005/Speder.pdf

Stankuniene, V., & Maslauskaite, A. (2008). Family transformations in the post-communist countries: Attitudes towards changes. In Ch. Höhn, D. Avramova, & I. Kotowska (Eds.), *People, population change and policies* (pp. 113–137). Berlin: Springer.

Stankūnienė, V., Maslauskaitė, A., & Baublytė, M. (2013). *Ar Lietuvos šeimos bus gausesnės?* [Are families to be larger in Lithuania?]. Vilnius: LSTC.

Stankuniene, V., Maslauskaite, A., Baublyte, M., Zakharov, S., & Régnier-Loilier, A. (2009). La transition vers de nouvelles formes d'union en France, en Lituanie at en Russia [The transition towards new partnership formation patterns in France, Lithuania, Russia]. *Revue d'études comparatives Est-Ouest*, *40*, 163–208. doi:10.4074/S0338059909003064

Therborn, G. (2004). *Between sex and power. Family in the World 1900–2000*. London: Routledge.

Tomka, M. (1991). Secularization or anomy? Interpreting religious change in communist societies. *Social Compass*, *38*, 93–102. doi:10.1177/003776891038001011

UNECE. (2005). *Generations and gender programme: Survey instruments*. New York, NY: United Nations Economic Commission for Europe.

Van de Kaa, D. (1987). The Europe's second demographic transition. *Population Bulletin*, *42*, 1–59. http://www.ncbi.nlm.nih.gov/pubmed/12268395

Van de Kaa, D. (1994). The second demographic transition revisited: Theories and expectations. In G. Beets, H. van den Brekel, R. Cliquet, G. Dooghe, & J. de Jong Gierveld (Eds.), *Population and the family in the low countries 1993: Late fertility and other current issues* (pp. 81–126). Lisse: Swets and Zeitlinger.

Wu, Z. (2000). *Cohabitation. An alternative form of family living*. Oxford: Oxford University Press.

Appendix 1. **Relative risk of transition from cohabitation to marriage, men and women, various calendar periods.**

	Men				Women			
	1970–1979	1980–1989	1990–1999	2000–2009	1970–1979	1980–1989	1990–1999	2000–2009
Parity pregnancy status (Partner) Childless, not pregnant (ref.)								
(Partner) Childless, pregnant	1.41	3.14***	3.14***	4.01**	2.54***	1.9**	5.7**	3.39**
(Partner) Mother	0.76	0.91	0.92	0.61**	1.01	1.03	0.78	0.7
Transition to marriage 1st year (ref.)								
2nd year	0.53**	0.62**	0.66***	0.66**	0.42***	0.52***	0.48***	0.64***
3rd year	0.16***	0.29***	0.30***	0.58**	0.43**	0.15***	0.37***	0.48***
4th year	0.3**	0.16***	0.32***	0.52**	0.14***	0.19***	0.19***	0.35***
5th year	0.19**	–	0.34***	0.48**	0.08**	0.04***	0.15***	0.43**
Age at first partnership								
15–16	–	0.67	0.38	2.56	0.67	0.45	1.04	0.6
17–18	0.49	0.45**	1.47	0.32***	1.59	0.9	1.31	0.42***
19–20	0.5**	0.81	0.83	0.64**	1.32	0.9	0.9	0.75
21–22	0.68	1.0	0.83	0.53***	1.15	0.74	1.06	0.85
23–24 (ref.)	1	1	1	1	1	1	1	1
25–26	0.93	0.87	0.69	0.45***	1.01	0.73	0.55**	0.71
27–28	0.46	0.77	0.36***	0.6**	1.53	0.98	0.76	0.43**
29–30	0.47	0.74	0.22***	0.59**	1.5	0.41	0.48	0.59
31–34	0.57	0.46	0.18***	0.15***	1.26	3.4**	0.69	0.19
35+	0.2**	0.34	0.19***	1.23	0.88	0.74	0.34	0.3
Parents family Divorced (ref.)								
Not divorced	1.14	0.66	1.0	0.89	1.54	1.05	1.23	1.04
Birth cohort								
1930–1934	5.74	–	–	–	0.54	–	–	–
1935–1939	3.75*	–	–	–	0.62	–	–	–
1940–1944	2.2	0.52	–	–	0.55	–	–	–
1945–1949	1.32	1.51			0.89	0.68	0.71	
1950–1954	1	1.35	1.77	–	1	0.51	1.89	–
1955–1959	1.83*	0.98	1.76	–	1.0	1.03	1.48	–
1960–1964	0.67	1	2.26	–	1.3	1	1.17	–
1965–1969	–	1.1	1.09	–	–	0.88	1.1	–
1970–1974	–	0.75	1	1.34	–	0.91	1	–
1975–1979	–	–	0.83	1.14	–	–	0.68	1.51**
1980–1984	–	–	0.46	1	–	–	0.45	1
1985–1989	–	–	–	0.95	–	–	–	0.85
1990+	–	–	–	1.21	–	–	–	1.52
N (person months)	18966	28862	44436	79300	14516	30335	41994	50156

Note: Controlled for education. ***$p \leq 0.001$; **$p \leq 0.01$.

The unmarried couple in post-communist Romania: a qualitative sociological approach

Anca Dohotariu

Over the last few decades, 'new' contemporary couple relationships have been at the heart of international research on the cultural meanings and reference values that organize life couple nowadays. What is the situation in Romania? After the fall of the communist regime, the rise and development of new forms of couple relationships (other than the legitimate nuclear family that was widely accepted during the former political regime) have become more and more visible. During the transition to a market economy and pluralistic democracy, the development of living together outside marriage and the progressive spread of democratic values, as well as the slow but deep redefinition of the institution of marriage, have been obvious. Yet there have been insufficient efforts in tracking and reporting these transformations. This article presents some results of the first qualitative sociological investigation dedicated to cohabiting unmarried couples in post-communist Romania. In order to have a greater understanding of cohabitation at a macro level, it first focuses on the way cohabitation is presented in the Romanian demographic literature. Second, the analysis is followed by a micro-level study based on qualitative field research conducted in Bucharest with young people living as part of cohabiting opposite-sex couples.

For more than 40 years, transformations of the contemporary couple have been at the heart of the international literature on family and private life. Western analysis focusing on the decline of marriage, the rise in divorce rates, the development of cohabitation in the case of same-sex or opposite-sex non-marital unions (Cherlin, 2004; Coontz, 2004; Déchaux, 2010; Manning & Cohen, 2012; Poortman & Mills, 2012), etc. underlines the difficulties in giving a short and clear definition of the '*couple*'. However, these analyses invite us to look in greater depth at the reference values, cultural meanings and ideals, as well as the social practices, that organize the couple and family life today. Married and unmarried couples are sometimes less different than one might think. In France, for instance, the institution of marriage has been profoundly redefined following the democratic values of individual freedom and gender equality, which emerged during the French Revolution but which were later diminished by the enactment of the Napoleonic Code in 1804 (Théry & Biet, 1989). Nowadays, the institution of marriage embodies new ideals of both commitment and freedom, which are no longer exclusive. Similarly to marriage, the social meanings of cohabitation have radically changed over time. While being a stigmatized social transgression or a way of contesting the legitimacy of marriage in the early twentieth century, cohabitation has become an ordinary choice of living together based on 'a redefinition of commitment as a purely private agreement' (Théry, 1998, p. 32), which may also be a locus of childbearing. Overall, the 'unmarried couple' covers a very large variety of situations: premarital unions, long-term cohabitation as an alternative to marriage, new relationships following a separation or divorce, and also free unions of elderly people after being widowed.

Beyond the French case, it is a general fact that cohabitation and marriage are interrelated, and their definitions change over time. In other words, the institution of marriage and the unmarried couple experience constantly slow and deep transformations, but their cultural meanings are always related to each other because both are based on the 'community of life' of the couple (Carbonnier, 2002, p. 468). What is the situation in Romania? After the fall of the communist regime, the rise and development of new forms of couple relationships (other than the legitimate nuclear family that was widely encouraged during the former political regime) have become more and more visible. During the transition to a market economy and pluralistic democracy, the development of living together outside marriage and the progressive spread of democratic values, as well as the slow but deep redefinition of the institution of marriage have been obvious. Yet there have been insufficient efforts in tracking and reporting these transformations.[1]

Given the heterogeneity of contemporary couples (with regard to gender, age, residence, socio-professional category, level of education, etc.), some initial decisions were required in order to define my research object clearly. First, one cannot limit unmarried couples to opposite-sex relationships. Opposite-sex cohabitation outside marriage has never been considered a crime, neither during the former political regime nor nowadays, as opposed to same-sex relationships.[2] Second, the seismic shift brought about by the fall of communism stands out as a chronological landmark in the study of unmarried couples in the current literature. However, any political turning point, as extreme as it might be, is almost never followed by a radical and swift change in the social structure. It would be too simplistic to attribute the spread of non-marital unions primarily to the democratic 'transition' (Burawoy & Verdery, 1999). Without giving it a conceptual value, which, moreover, constitutes an obstacle to understanding, I use 'transition' only as a reference point in the construction of my research object.

Focusing on contemporary unmarried opposite-sex couples in Romania, this research employs a sociological perspective, which emphasizes the institutional and symbolic nature of personal relationships. My main hypothesis is that Romania is witnessing significant changes at the level of cultural meanings, social practices and values concerning couples, especially among the younger generations. More precisely, these changes are inherent to the post-communist democratization process as a whole during the transition (Rotariu & Voineagu, 2012). In Romania, however, these transformations are still ongoing: the new cultural meanings of couple relationships, including free unions and marriage, have not entirely replaced pre-existing practices, and certain forms of resistance to these changes can be discerned in the society and current legislation. Therefore, I put forward another hypothesis, according to which free unions between young people in Bucharest have emerged and developed as a new phenomenon motivated by the newly found ideas of equality and freedom as democratic values. In summary, I believe that cohabitation as a social practice in Romania today is not similar to the living-together arrangements outside marriage during communist times. More precisely, it is an expression of the emergence of democratic values of freedom and gender equality, coexisting with a deep social attachment to the institution of marriage.

In order to gain a greater understanding of cohabitation at a macro level, I will first focus on how cohabitation is presented in the Romanian demographic literature. Second, this will be followed up by a micro-level study based on qualitative field research conducted in Bucharest with young people living as cohabiting opposite-sex couples.

1. Cohabitation in Romania through the lens of demography

John Hajnal (1965) identified the St Petersburg–Trieste line, which distinguishes between two types of European family formation: the early union formation in Central and Eastern Europe, which is different from the late transition to family life in Western Europe. This classic demographic division between East and West was adopted by many other scholars, who, after the fall of the former USSR, paid particular attention to the long-standing demographic trends in Eastern Europe. Alain Monnier (1991), for instance, shows that, while in the early twentieth century demographic behaviours were more heterogeneous in Eastern Europe compared to the West, between the end of the Second World War and the 1990s, they were profoundly reshaped in the sense of a real homogenization. More precisely, in the early 1990s, there was an important contrast between the East and West: in the West, there was no convergence or general stabilization of the demographic trends at that time. Marriage rates were, however, an exception. Even if they were obviously higher than in Western countries, they were quite diverse in the East from country to country. In Romania, for instance, marriage rates dropped until 1969, increased until 1979 and fell away again after that (Sardon, 1991, p. 552). Jean-Paul Sardon (2004) observes that in the 1960s, the decline in marriage rates was less significant in the East than in the West, and he explains this by the fact that the housing shortage in the East slowed down the development of cohabitation.

Today, the demographic literature no longer employs the former classic dichotomy between Eastern and Western Europe. A few decades after the fall of the former USSR, demographic trends in the East have become relatively homogeneous, yet still lagging behind Western European societies (Puur, Rahnu, Maslauskaite, Stankuniene, & Zakharov, 2012). More precisely, a comparison of marriage rates in the two regions of the continent shows that transformations in contemporary couple relationships began to be manifested later in the East than in the West. However, changes emerged before the fall of communism in the 1990s – around the 1980s in Hungary and Bulgaria, and 5 and 10 years later in Russia and Romania, respectively – which means that the spread of cohabitation began before the fall of communism (Hoem, Kostova, Jasilioniene, & Mureşan, 2009a). Without arguing for or against this hypothesis, I would simply underline that it is particularly important because it means that precautions must be taken when analysing the 'cut' of the 1990s in the larger context of Eastern Europe. Romania, however, seems to be an exceptional case:

'Romania is another exception from the general trend in the risks of entry into cohabitation, relative to that of marriage formation. Even if the process of first union formation largely follows the trends observed in the other three countries [Russia, Bulgaria and Hungary], marriage was the dominating type of first union throughout the entire period of observation. 1960–2004' (Hoem, Kostova, Jasilioniene, & Mureşan, 2009a, p. 246)

For instance, if we look at the divorce rates during the communist regime, we can observe that they decrease suddenly in 1967 and then increase after that date: in 1966, there were 25,804 divorces, in 1967 there were only 48, and in 1976 there were 35,945 or 1.63% (Mureşan, 1996, p. 824). After the fall of the communist regime, the divorce rates oscillate between 1.42% in 1990 (Analize demografice, 2001), 1.68% in 2011 and 1.47% in 2012 (Divorţialitatea, 2013). Before the 1990s, the demographic fluctuations were directly influenced by political decisions related to divorce and family life. The demographic data concerning divorce rates proves that, unlike other former communist regimes, in Romania the level of intrusion into people's private life was extreme (Doboş, Jinga, & Soare, 2010; Kligman, 1998). The 48 divorces registered in 1967, of which 33 were in urban areas and 15 in rural areas (Anuarul statistic al Republicii Socialiste România, 1974, p. 398), were the direct result of Government Decree no. 779 (1966, October 8), which imposed a variable tax of between 3000 and 6000 lei (Article 3), whereas the average monthly income in 1967 was 1210 lei before tax and 1107 lei after tax.[3] In addition, during the former communist regime, statistics were one of the major instruments of the pro-natalist population policy, hence they were politically censored and controlled. For instance, the Romanian Statistical Yearbook has been published almost every year since 1904 and comprises around 700 pages, with statistical tables relating to the economic and social dynamics of the country. However, during the communist regime, the Statistical Yearbook comprised less than 200 pages, with 188 pages in 1989 and only 127 pages in 1987 and 1988 (Anuarul statistic al Republicii Socialiste România, 1987, 1988, 1989).

It is very difficult to find quantitative data about cohabitation in Romania before the 1990s.[4] Studying the existing literature reveals that living together outside marriage existed during the former regime, but it was, rather, 'tactical cohabitation,'[5] which did not constitute a social fact: although it was not illegal, heterosexual cohabitation was far from being a legitimate societal way of acting (Kligman, 1998). These situations were the exception – only the marginalized or particular categories of people were likely to live together outside marriage at a time when cohabitation was stigmatized by the political discourse, as well as by society as a whole. Since the consequences of such behaviour were too costly, the social actor was not, in fact, very interested in it. Hence, cohabitation was not a way to 'fight' against the legitimacy of marriage, but rather a convenience strategy whenever there was no legal or social solution to legalize the union.

After the 1990s, the demographic literature presents Romania as being one of the slowest changing countries concerning cohabitation in the wider context of Central and Eastern Europe (Rotariu & Voineagu, 2012). At the same time, the Romanian literature on living together outside marriage is still not that developed. There have only been three national surveys (including the Generations and Gender Survey) conducted since 2002, and the last two censuses, which offer data about cohabiting couples. The 2002 census and the most recent 2011 census are the only censuses ever in Romania's history in which counting the number of cohabitants has been an explicit goal of the survey. More precisely, in 2002, the cohabitation rate was only 3.8%. In addition, 73% of the registered cohabitants were single, 17.9% were divorced, 7.1% were widowed and only 1.4% were married. Similarly, the demographers state that almost half of these people were between 20 and 34 years old. More importantly, 56.3% of the 'consensual unions' were registered in rural areas (Recensământul populaţiei şi al locuinţelor, 2002, 2003). Comparing the available data allows us to observe that, in 2011, there were 745,534 cohabitants among 20,121,641 Romanians, while in 2002 there were 828,122 cohabitants among 21,680,974 Romanians.[6] According to the National Institute of Statistics, in 2011, almost half the stable population was legally married. However, beyond these statistics, some observations have to be underlined. First, one of the major problems of the two censuses is that these surveys were supposed to count the number of 'consensual unions –' an expression which does not exist in common parlance. (How can one answer a question when one does not understand its meaning?) Second, a 'consensual union' is only supposed to be a union between a man and a woman, which shows that, for the Romanian demographers, the 'couple' as a concept (whether married or not) is, in fact, synonymous with 'opposite-sex couples.'

But how do Romanian demographers analyse these trends and how do they explain the low spread of cohabitation at the national level? Theoretically and also methodologically, the Romanian literature seems to be organized around a dichotomy: according to most Romanian demographers and sociologists, since the fall of communism the analysis of cohabitation has been polarized around either 'premodern behaviour' or 'postmodern behaviour'.

After the 1990s, the Romanian demographic landscape changed less dramatically than that of the West 20 or 30 years earlier. Yet these transformations are analysed through the lens of a major issue in the field: the destabilization of the demographic balance resulting from an aging society. At the same time, Romanian scholars seek to interpret and explain these (relatively) recent changes using the Western literature that has been developed around the old *'individual versus society'* dichotomy. More precisely, they pay very special attention to the theory of the 'emancipation of the self,' according to which we are transforming from the old 'model' of the 'bourgeois family (based not only on altruism, but also on gender inequality, amongst other things) to the new model of the 'postmodern family (based on the rise of individualism and gender equality).

However, some Romanian demographers do not agree with the theory of the Second Demographic Transition. Traian Rotariu, for instance, considers it to be too deterministic, arguing that, in Romania, the demographic trends change mostly after the fall of communism, while the system of social values remains unchanged. Therefore, Rotariu states that the high level of births outside marriage along with the spread of cohabitation is nothing other than 'proof' of the 'premodern' characteristics of demographic behaviours in Romania:

> the pattern of extramarital births in Romania is not part of the postmodern value system, but part of a premodern one, whereas most of the women who give birth out of wedlock are young girls, below age 20, who do not have at least the compulsory level of education, who come from very poor areas and from particular ethnic communities (rroma, especially). (Rotariu, 2009, p. 361)

However, while some demographers cast light on the inertia of an old Romanian system of values, others prefer to underline the way behaviours change. For example, Hoem et al. write:

> 'There is a general impression that there is very little non-marital cohabitation in Romania (e.g. Mureşan, 2008). This does not really square easily with other findings by Mureşan ... who has estimated that one-fifth of all Romanian women would have entered a consensual union by age 40 according to the data for 1980–89 and that as many as over one-third would do so according to the data for 1996–2005. In fact, cohabitation may not be as rare in the country as is often supposed. ... We show that over the years since 1960 there has been a steady growth in the incidence of cohabitation. This increase is quite surprising, since the rigidity of the Romanian political system before 1989 must have suppressed the individualization of family forms suggested by the narrative of the Second Demographic Transition... and generally prevented the change in values implied by the growth in non-marital union formation.' (Hoem, Kostova, Jasilioniene, & Mureşan, 2009b, pp. 33–34)

Unlike Rotariu, Mureşan agrees with the theory of the Second Demographic Transition as elaborated in the Western literature. Therefore she uses the old individual/society dichotomy in order to analyse the recent demographic trends in Romania, but she is among the first Romanian scholars to observe that family behaviours in Romania do not fit well into this model. Mureşan (2008) not only states that cohabitation started increasing in Eastern Europe *before* the fall of the communist bloc, but she also insists on the importance of its spread during the last few decades. However, she does not go further in developing the hypothesis of 'postmodern' cohabitation in Romania today.

2. Living together *à la roumaine*

The available statistics show that there are still few unmarried couples who cohabit in Romania: between 1996–2005, 30% of men and 35% of women younger than 40 cohabited with their first partner, compared to only 18% of men and 20% of women in a similar situation during 1980–1989 (Rotariu, Mureşan, Hărăguş, & Hărăguş, 2012, p. 128). In addition, the marriage rate decreases from 9.3% in 1990 (*Femeile şi bărbaţii*, 2006) to 5.1% in 2012 (*Nupţialitatea. Anul 2012*, 2013); the average age for a first marriage increases from 22 for women and 25 for men in 1990 (*Femeile şi bărbaţii*, 2006) to an average age of 28.2 for women and 31.6 for men in 2012 (*Nupţialitatea. Anul 2012*, 2013); and the number of births outside marriage increases from 15% (of the total number of births) in 1992 (*Tendinţe sociale*, 2007) to 30% in 2012 (*Tendinţe sociale*, 2013).

Nevertheless, the statistics do not tell the whole story. In everyday life in Bucharest, in the case of young people with a high level of education, living together outside marriage seems to be common behaviour. This contradiction between the statistics and participatory observation within urban areas invites us to go deeper into this issue. Therefore my qualitative field research aimed to find out who these young cohabitants are and how they describe living together outside marriage. In this respect, I conducted individual interviews in two phases. First, in, 2005–2006[7] I conducted 47 interviews with young cohabiting people living in Bucharest. In the interest of balance, I cut seven interviews with women in order to give an equal distribution of men and women for my analysis. Out of the 40 interviews, I interviewed just women in 10 cases, just men in another 10 cases, and the remaining 20 interviews were conducted with both partners. The length of cohabitation varied between one and five years in most cases, except for one (nine years). The women were aged between 22 and 38, and the men between 24 and 37. Two of the interviewees were pregnant and another had a child from a former marriage. They had never been married, except for one woman and one man, who had divorced once (the divorced man had a child from his previous marriage). The rest of the participants had no children. In addition, almost all of the interviewees (38/40) were financially independent from their parents.

Second, I conducted another 17 interviews eight years later (from January–November 2013). In seven cases I interviewed just women, in another eight cases just men, and the remaining two interviews were conducted with both cohabiting partners. The women were aged between 31 and 38, and the men between 30 and 35. In 10 cases, they had one child and in 6 cases two children. Two of the women were divorced and the rest, both the women and the men, had never been married. The 2013 sample is very heterogeneous if we look at the interviewees' occupational status: architects, life coaches, artists, information technology experts, journalists, non-governmental organization experts and a flight attendant instructor. Moreover, 9 out of the 17 participants were freelancers. All of these young adults lived in Bucharest and had a university degree.

Going beyond the narrow 'qualitative/quantitative dichotomy' (Newman & Benz, 1998), an important school of thought in the social sciences underlines that the 'relevance' of a subject is not provided by the number of interviews conducted, but by the repetition of similar situations or thematic answers. My samples (from 2005–2006 and 2013) have been constructed according to this methodological framework, consisting of individual in-depth interviews conducted through the method of qualitative homogenous through saturation sampling (Hennink, Hutter, & Bailey, 2011, pp. 111–112) and the snowball technique. These qualitative interviews (which are therefore non-representative) are semi-structured: the interviewees were invited to 'feel free' to talk about their private lives but, at the same time, a thematic guide was followed for the purpose of discourse analysis. The duration of the interviews varied from around one to two and a half hours.

This staggered research aims to gain an in-depth understanding of the cultural meanings and social practices related to cohabitation in the case of a certain social category. More precisely, the socio-demographic characteristics of my interviewees have to be highlighted: they were young people with a high level of education, living in the capital city of Romania, who were financially independent and, in most cases, working professionals. Without classifying them as an atypical elite category, their life stories are very significant for the new trends regarding private life, marriage and cohabitation in Romania today. For instance, in 2005–2006 I met very few young cohabiting parents (only two pregnant women and a very small number of families with children from previous relationships), whereas in 2013 I often met cohabiting parents. This fact is very suggestive and relevant for cohabitation in post-communist Romania as a research object.

2.1. Living together in Bucharest: an expression of changing social practices

One of the most noteworthy findings of my field research concerns a considerable disconnection between social norms and values, on the one hand, and everyday practices, on the other. Highly educated cohabiting young adults in Bucharest usually have conservative values with regard to couple and family life, but their everyday behaviour does not seem to correspond to these strongly held values. Considering the issue of domestic tasks, the interviews conducted in both 2005–2006 and 2013 point out that, in Romania, the cultural meaning of the traditional division of domesticlabor labour continues to persist. However, more and more men take care of their children and play an important role in their education, and more and more men involve themselves in domestic life. Yet these transformations, which are visible among certain social categories, are not the consequence of a 'battle' against 'unfair' gendered roles. More precisely, claiming *gender equality* is not explicit at all. This interview is a suggestive example, showing that the battle for gender equality is fought in the domestic sphere rather than day-to-day public discourse:

> We share the domestic tasks, though she takes care of the largest part of them ... That's the main reason why we get upset with each other – only from time to time, of course. Each of us pushes the other to do more, and, well, I think I'm not a bad person, and especially not a bad man. When I look around me, I see that my position is legitimate. Most of the men around me don't even spend half the time I spend with my family. Therefore I can't reproach myself. But we have to negotiate all the time, and sometimes it is not easy at all. (Interview with Mircea, age 35, 2013)

Analysed as a whole, my qualitative field research suggests that, in Bucharest today, couple relationships are changing visibly but slowly. While in Western societies demographers were completely surprised by the fast changes taking place in the 1960s and 1970s, in Romania, on the contrary, the redefinition of behaviours looks like a silent revolution. In other words, Romania also follows, in its specific way, the dynamics of democratic social behaviours, in spite of the legacy of its recent past.

The repetitive nature of an implicit reference to the 'norm' in my interviewees' narratives can be interpreted as proof of this legacy. More precisely, within both samples, from 2005–2006 and 2013, nothing is more common than the phrase 'it's *normal* to live together'. In many narratives, the reference to the 'norm' is explicit, whereas in others it is implicit. This reveals the mundane nature of cohabitation, even if it is not a commonplace occurrence. In other words, this suggests that the young cohabiting people who were interviewed are living in a democratic society, following a recent seismic political, economic and societal shift. The traces of the recent past are visible through the need of the interviewees to highlight the 'normality' of cohabitation at the level of everyday life. Before 1990, living together outside marriage did not fit into the communist 'norms', therefore cohabitation was seen as deviant behaviour – as 'abnormal'. After the fall of communism, young people have contradicted the old ideology, therefore they stress that living together outside marriage is absolutely 'normal –' it is 'nothing extraordinary'. In addition, in the 2013 sample, another reference occurs: unlike those interviewed in 2005–2006, young cohabiting parents declared that it was not only 'normal,' but also 'natural' to live together outside marriage. This may be understood as an implicit reference to the contractual nature of couple relationships. Whether they are married or not, cohabiting young people feel free to constantly reinvent and renegotiate their relationship, regardless of their sex, their age, the number of children they have or other demographic characteristics.

2.2. The couple, cohabitation and commitment

Bearing in mind that it is difficult to define the concept of '*couple*' clearly, the interviewees were asked how their lives together began. In this respect, in both samples, couples were formed in several ways: step by step, after their first sexual encounter, by cohabitation or by declaring their relationship to be 'official'. Sometimes partners consider themselves to be a couple once their social group is aware of their connection, even without living together and regardless of a sexual relationship. However, in most cases the idea of 'being together' (i.e. forming a 'couple') is connected to the fact of also having a sexual relationship. This shows that Romanian young people do not separate (yet) their sexuality and their 'love' affairs, which suggests that, unlike in some Western countries (Kaufmann, 1993), in Romania there is still an interconnection between sexuality and a certain ideology of love.

'The couple', 'cohabitation' and 'commitment' are three different categories that are nonetheless connected. For instance, if we look at progressive cohabitation, which is best exemplified by the well-known story of the toothbrush, the forming of a couple is often defined by cohabitation. Entering the routine of sharing a living space is a sign that a couple relationship has been established. In this respect, I observed that there are different ways to begin cohabitation. First, there is *cohabitation following a decision*, where I would also include *cohabitation by necessity*, which is established for financial reasons. In this case, couples may simply decide to start sharing their living space or live in a shared house (especially students) or multigenerational cohabitation (with their parents, mostly for financial reasons). While multigenerational cohabitation can be temporary as well as a rational choice for an undetermined period of time, cohabitation in the case of a shared house is, rather, temporary and specific for the younger interviewees. Second, most of the couples choose gradual cohabitation, which allows for a certain amount of negotiation as the couple evolves. For example, Ioana talks about her gradual decision to cohabit, which is, in fact, the subject of an unspoken progressive negotiation:

> We met and … we had many things to talk about. This reminds me about a funny story of one old actress who had been married for more than 40 years. One of her colleagues phones her, and she answers, 'We're fine, thank you, we were having a coffee and talking'. And the colleague answers back, 'Again!? What are you still talking about, after so many years of being together!??' [laughing]. Well, that's essential for me. We have many things to talk about. We met, and he came to my place and stayed overnight, again and again, and we hadn't even realized that basically we were living together.' (Interview with Ioana, age 39, 2013)

However, in many cases, cohabitation occurs following a joint decision or for a 'specific' reason (such as a pregnancy):

> We had been together for three months and later on we broke up. And after that we got back together again, and once again we wanted to break up, just before finding out that she was pregnant. Of course, we decided to make up once again, though in fact we hadn't any real reason to split. Everything went well, so she moved into my place. (Interview with Sandu, age 32, 2013)

Spending the night together now and then (sometimes at her place, sometimes at his) allows some of the interviewees to call themselves a 'couple'. Nevertheless, in these cases, the relationship is definitely not cohabitation, but rather 'living apart together' (Duncan & Phillips, 2010). Beyond these situations, it is, however, difficult to establish the exact beginning of cohabitation. Furthermore, cohabitation means living together, which includes sharing a living space and also a sexual relationship, but does not necessarily involve *commitment*: shared or not, one can be committed but the other does not have to be. From the beginning of my field research, I realized that commitment (a transversal issue which runs through the whole discourse) is fundamental in observing that, beyond all the differences that might distinguish one couple from another, there are two main ways of living together. Interview analysis reveals that there are couples who have long-term commitments (children, their own apartment/house, family 'introductions', etc.) and those who do not. More importantly, the length of cohabitation has nothing to do with this: it is the interviewees themselves, and no one else, who decide whether they commit to each other or not. At the same time, however, being committed cannot 'guarantee' a long-term relationship.

Basically, 'cohabitation in the now' can extend indefinitely. Moreover, it can be a prelude to a stronger commitment, as well as a relationship lived primarily for the experience. The main difference between 'cohabitation in the now' and 'commitment' is related to the way it ends. The ending of the former usually does not entail the emotional distress of the ending of the latter. In order to categorize each couple, I asked questions about any possible 'long-term commitments'. Usually, couples who have such plans talk about their intention to have children, to marry, to make a substantial investment (in an apartment), etc. While in 2005–2006 I encountered both cohabitation 'in the now' and long-term relationships, in 2013 I encountered only committed unmarried young people. According to both samples, the decision to have a child is seen as 'proof' of commitment, which suggests the deep connection between the couple relationship and parenthood.

Five of the 40 subjects interviewed in 2005–2006 have concrete wedding plans; 29 intend to marry 'one day' (some to their current partner and others maybe to somebody else); nine are undecided; and only two declare that they would never institutionalize their couple relationship. In 2013, two interviewees have concrete wedding plans; another three are 'sure' that they want to marry; and the rest do not reject the idea of marrying 'one day', but have no concrete plans to do so. In addition, in 2005–2006 many of the interviewees declare that marriage is more for 'other' people (family, friends, etc.) and less for the couple, while only one subject says that 'marriage is a *commitment* which concerns the couple first and foremost' (Interview with Dragoş, age 29, 2005–2006). In 2013, the cultural meanings related to marriage seem to be unchanged. For instance, one interviewee declares that he would have been married if he lived in his hometown, near to his parents and extended family. Another chooses not to marry after the suffering caused by the abrupt end of a previous relationship. In addition, another interviewee says that once she became a parent, marriage did not seem to be that important. All these situations suggest that, in Bucharest today, marriage is not (yet) a matter of personal conscience. On the contrary, in the specific case of my interviewees, marriage continues to be a referential social norm.

Whether inherited or not, cohabiting young people's attachment to a religious marriage is obvious. In 2005–2006, 33 of the 40 subjects (16 men and 17 women) declare that, in their situation, a civil marriage would definitely be accompanied by a religious ceremony. In 2013, in only 4 out of the 16 cases do they absolutely reject the idea of having a religious marriage. Altogether, the situations encountered are very diverse: sometimes a religious marriage is seen as a 'fundamental ceremony', even more important than a civil marriage itself. At other times, the interviewees are totally uninterested in the subject of a religious marriage. But aside from these two extremes, the two samples reveal three possible situations: young people prefer to marry in a church sometimes for religious reasons, sometimes for family reasons and sometimes for the beauty of the ceremony.

Finally, the most important change revealed by the comparison between the 2005–2006 sample and the one from 2013 is that, in 2005–2006, most of the subjects underline that 'marriage is when you decide to have a child together'. Within the sample from 2005–2006, only 4 out of 30 couples had children outside marriage, compared to the 2013 sample, in which all of the interviewees had children. However, neither of the two samples reveals a clear rejection of the institution of marriage. At the same time, discourse analysis points out the discrepancy between the interviewees' attachment to the ideal of marriage and their actual marital status.

Analysed as a whole, my qualitative field research reveals a deep connection between the couple relationship and parenthood, whereas in Western societies they are clearly dissociated. On the one hand, at the level of cultural meanings, parenthood is undesirable outside of marriage. On the other hand, in everyday life, there are no differences between the way in which children born within a marriage or outside of wedlock are treated. This observation from almost eight years earlier still persists in 2013, when young people still value the idea of marriage but do not marry and, furthermore, having children is not 'the' primary reason to proceed quickly to a civil ceremony.

In addition, in 2005–2006 only one of the 47 interviewees declares that baptizing children is not necessary, while the rest argue that, in principle, they prefer the idea of baptizing their children shortly after birth. Unlike the previous sample, in 2013, there are two cases where a child has not been baptized at all, and another three where a child has been baptized after one year, which reveals emerging new social attitudes among educated young people living in Bucharest regarding previously accepted traditional practices. One of the interviewees who did not baptize his child comments:

> Being as cynical as possible … Why would I let a stranger dunk my baby into a vat of water while he's singing stupid things and feeding my baby wine!? Seriously now … I've been baptized myself, but I think it a ridiculous gesture. Moreover, I strongly believe in people's freedom to choose their religion. Of course, that's not entirely true: I know that my son's choice will depend on the education I will give him. (Interview with Andru, age 30, 2013)

This suggests that when religion becomes a matter of personal conscience, so does marriage. However, the attachment of my subjects to the issue of religion has nothing to do with the issue of religious practices and beliefs, but it reveals their attachment to the traditions and values held by their extended family. Hence, at least for the moment, marriage continues to be a valued social norm that coexists with different situations of cohabitation.

3. Conclusion

Cohabitation in post-communist Romania seems to be a lot more than a superficial effect of the post-totalitarian period. On the contrary, it is an expression of the redefinition of contemporary couple relationships. My field research in Bucharest shows strong evidence of this transformation, which can be attributed to the evolution of everyday cohabiting practices. Despite societal resistance to change, and the degree of commitment, these cohabiting practices in Romania today reflect a real spread of the democratic values of freedom and gender equality.

Romanian society during the totalitarian regime was thought of as a collection of workers who were powerless, lacking the freedom of opinion and choice, and somehow asexual in their workplace (Vasilescu, 2003). These workers were supposed to exist in a complete position of subordination to the unique political party. Since the 1990s, every way of expressing personal freedom has been very much valued: we now have the constitutional right to have an 'intimate family and private life'. In other words, the family is thought of as a 'private' matter by definition. Any attempt by the state to interfere in family matters is suspected as an attack on the freedom that was regained after the fall of the communist regime. After 1989, people became free from the totalitarian 'obligations of citizenship,' therefore they value their new democratic freedoms highly, including their identity, individuality and family life (Pasti, 2003). We are witnessing a paradox. On the one hand, there is a desire to reject the intrusion of the state in private and family life in some respects (with regard to abortion, contraception, etc.). On the other hand, state paternalism is not questioned and is increasing in strength: in the initial stages of the re-emergence of a democratic civic culture, people continue to demand the 'protection' of the state. At the same time, this desire to be 'protected' by the state is accompanied by persisting cultural meanings of family life that are at odds with the changing social practices of young people with a high level of education living in Bucharest. The interviewees did not express any proactive rejection of the idea of marriage, which, on the contrary, remains a common norm that is widely shared. More precisely, since the 1990s a sort of local *familialism* has developed, in the sense of a deep attachment to the family as a network of social belonging, which is more highly valued than mere citizenship. Local *familialism* can be seen in all kinds of discourses: from public political and media discourses (Băluță, 2013) to private common discourses. This explains why marriage is not a matter of individual conscience, but a referential social norm which still persists, even in the case of young people with a high level of education cohabiting in Bucharest.

Last but not least, this field research should be developed further in order to overcome some issues related to both the theoretical approach that was employed and the way the qualitative samples were constructed. First, although there is important quantitative research on cohabitation in Romania, there are very few qualitative analyses, which is one of the limits and also challenges I had to address. Hence, developing qualitative (eventually comparative) literature on living together outside marriage in Eastern Europe would contribute to a deeper understanding of cohabitation's specificities in post-communist societies. In addition, analysing the dynamics of the civil and social rights of cohabiting couples would allow for a better understanding of the social and political stakes that govern living together outside marriage. Second, including a wider range of cohabiting couples (for example, same-sex couples, young cohabiting people with a lower level of education, young couples living in rural areas, etc.) could increase the scope of the analysis. Nevertheless, all of these limitations constitute important opportunities for future inquiry into couple relationships and cohabitation in democratic societies.

Funding

This article was supported by the Sectoral Operational Program Human Resources Development, financed by the European Social Fund and the Romanian Government [contract number POSDRU/159/1.5/S/133675].

Disclosure statement

No potential conflict of interest was reported by the author.

Notes

1. Although Romanian analyses focusing on the current context rarely take into consideration the long-term historical, political and social aspects that contribute to the redefinition of living together, a historical overview is fundamental in order to understand the complex dynamics of contemporary marriage and family life. The existing historical Romanian research is very useful for understanding Romanian social history as well as the sociogenesis of the family institution and private life in Walachia, Moldavia and Transylvania between the seventeenth and twentieth centuries (see, for example, Băluță, 2008; Bolovan, Covaci, Deteşan, Eppel, & Holom, 2009; Deteşan, 2012; Dumănescu, 2012; Scurtu, 2001). However, the Western historiography of marriage and of the unmarried couple and the Romanian literature remain incomparable in terms of the sources available, academic importance and the resources allocated to these subjects.
2. After the fall of the communist regime, same-sex relationships became legal, although they were not legally recognized. Article 200 of the former Criminal Code, criminalizing same-sex relationships, was superseded in 2001 by Governmental Decision OUG no. 89/21.06.2001.
3. This information is available on the National Institute of Statistics' website at: http://www.insse. ro/cms/ro/content/castiguri-salariale-din-1938-serie-anuala.
4. The Generations and Gender Surveys surveys provide quantitative data about cohabitation before the 1990s. However, I have found no data about living together outside marriage elaborated during the communist regime that was driven by a nationalistic family ideology with a strong pro-natalist character. For more details about the roots of nationalistic family ideologies, see Leinarte (2006).
5. 'Tactical cohabitation' is used in the meaning of Michel de Certeau (1990, pp. xliv–xlvii).
6. For the 2011 census results, see http://www.recensamantromania.ro/rezultate-2/.
7. The 47 interviews were conducted as part of my PhD thesis in Sociology (Dohotariu, 2010).

References

Analize demografice [Demographic analysis]. (2001). Bucharest: National Institute of Statistics.
Anuarul statistic al Republicii Socialiste România [Statistical yearbook of the Socialist Republic of Romania]. (1974). Bucharest: Direcția Centrală de Statistică.
Anuarul statistic al Republicii Socialiste România [Statistical yearbook of the Socialist Republic of Romania]. (1987). Bucharest: Direcția Centrală de Statistică.
Anuarul statistic al Republicii Socialiste România [Statistical yearbook of the Socialist Republic of Romania]. (1988). Bucharest Direcția Centrală de Statistică.
Anuarul statistic al Republicii Socialiste România [Statistical yearbook of the Socialist Republic of Romania]. (1989). Bucharest: Direcția Centrală de Statistică.
Băluță, I. (2008). *La bourgeoisie respectable. Réflexion sur la construction d'une nouvelle identité feminine dans la seconde moitié du XIXe siècle roumain* [The respectable bourgeoisie. An analysis of the construction of a new feminine identity in the second half of the nineteenth century in Romania]. Bucureşti: Editura Universității din Bucureşti.
Băluță, I. (2013). Désimplication volontaire des femmes/monopole des hommes: féminité et masculinité à l'aune du politique dans la Roumanie actuelle [Women's involvement / men's monopoly: femininity and masculinity within the political life in contemporary Romania]. Chapter 11. In M. Gateau, M. Navarre, & F. Schepens (Eds.), *Quoi de neuf depuis la parité? Du genre dans la construction des rôles politiques* [What's new since the parity? Gender in the construction of political roles] (pp. 163–178). Dijon: Éditions Universitaires de Dijon.
Bolovan, I., Covaci, D., Deteşan, D., Eppel, M., & Holom, C. (2009). *Legislația ecleziastică şi laică privind familia românească din Transilvania în a doua jumătate a secolului al XIX-lea*

[Ecclesiastical and secular legislation concerning Romanian family in Transylvania in the second half of the 19th century]. Cluj-Napoca: Imprimeria Ardealul.

Burawoy, M., & Verdery, K. (1999). *Uncertain transition. Ethnographies of change in the postsocialist world*. New York, NY: Rowman & Littlefield Publishers.

Carbonnier, J. (2002). *Droit civil. La famille, l'enfant, le couple* [Civil law. The family, the child, the couple]. Paris: Presses Universitaires de France.

Certeau, M. (de). (1990). *L'invention du quotidien, 1. Arts de faire* [The invention of the everyday life]. Paris: Gallimard.

Cherlin, A. J. (2004). The deinstitutionalization of American marriage. *Journal of Marriage and Family, 66*, 848–861. 10.1111/j.0022-2445.2004.00058.x

Coontz, S. (2004). The world historical transformation of marriage. *Journal of Marriage and Family, 66*, 974–979. 10.1111/j.0022-2445.2004.00067.x

Deteşan, D. (2012). Matrimonial Behaviours of the Transylvanian Romanian Rural Elite (Second half of the 19th century). *Transylvanian Review, XXI*, 327–339.

Déchaux, J. -H. (2010). Ce que 'l'individualisme' ne permet pas de comprendre: le cas de la famille [What the 'individualism' doesn't allow to understand: the family case]. *Esprit, 365*, 94–111.

Divorţialitatea [Divortiality]. (2013). Bucharest: National Institute of Statistics.

Doboş, C. (coord.)., Jinga, L., & Soare, F. (2010). *Politica pronatalistă a regimului Ceauşescu. O perspectivă comparativă* [The pronatalist policy of ceausescu's regime. A comparative approach]. Iaşi: Polirom.

Dohotariu, A. (2010). *Le couple non marié en Roumanie et en France: une approche de sociologie comparée* [The unmarried couple in Romania and in France. A sociological comparative approach]. PhD thesis defended at EHESS Marseille, under the direction of Irène Théry and Cristian Preda (joint supervision).

Dumănescu, L. (2012). *Familia românească în communism* [The Romanian family during communist times]. Cluj-Napoca: Presa Universitară Clujeană.

Duncan, S., & Phillips, M. (2010). People who live apart together (LATS) – how different are they? *The Sociological Review, 58*, 112–134. 10.1111/j.1467-954X.2009.01874.x

Femeileşi bărbaţii. parteneriat de muncă şi de viaţă [Women and men. working and living partnership] (2006). Bucharest: National Institute of Statistics.

Governmental decision OUG no. 89/21.06.2001. Official Journal, 338 (2001, June 26). Retrieved from http://www.cdep.ro/pls/legis/legis_pck.htp_act_text?idt=28350

Government decree no. 779 (1966, October 8). Official Gazette, 64/8. Retrieved from http://www.cdep.ro/pls/legis/legis_pck.htp_act?ida=37069

Hajnal, J. (1965). European marriage pattern in historical perspective. In D. V. Glass & D. E. C. Eversley (Eds.), *Population in history: Essays in historical demography*. London: Edward Arnold.

Hennink, M., Hutter, I., & Bailey, A. (2011). *Qualitative research methods*. London: Sage.

Hoem, J. M., Kostova, D., Jasilioniene, A., & Mureşan, C. (2009a). Traces of the Second Demographic Transition in four selected countries in Central and Eastern Europe: Union formation as a demographic manifestation. *European Journal of Population / Revue Européenne De Démographie, 25*, 239–255. 10.1007/s10680-009-9177-y

Hoem, J. M., Kostova, D., Jasilioniene, A., & Mureşan, C. (2009b). The structure of recent first-union formation in Romania. *Romanian Journal of Population Studies, III*, 33–44.

Kaufmann, J. -C. (1993). *Sociologie du couple* [Sociology of the couple]. Paris: Presses Universitaires de France.

Kligman, G. (1998). *The politics of duplicity. Controlling reproduction in Ceausescu's Romania*. Los Angeles: University of California Press.

Leinarte, D. (2006). Nationalism and family ideology: The case of Lithuania at the turn of the 20th century. *The History of the Family, 11*, 81–92. 10.1016/j.hisfam.2006.06.002

Manning, W. D., & Cohen, J. A. (2012). Premarital cohabitation and marital dissolution: An examination of recent marriages. *Journal of Marriage and Family, 74*, 377–387. 10.1111/j.1741-3737.2012.00960.x

Monnier, A. (1991). L'Europe de l'Est, différente et diverse. *Population (French Edition), 46*, 443–461. 10.2307/1533402

Mureşan, C. (1996). *L'évolution démographique en Roumanie: tendances passées (1948–1994) et perspectives d'avenir (1995–2030)* [Demographic evolution in Romania. Passed tendencies (1948–1994) and future prospective (1995–2030)] *51*, 813–844.

Mureşan, C. (2008). Cohabitation, an alternative for marriage in contemporary Romania: A life-table description. *Demografia. English Edition, 51*, 36–65.

Newman, I., & Benz, C. R. (1998). *Qualitative-quantitative research methodology: Exploring the interactive continuum.* Carbondale: University of Illinois Press.

Nupţialitatea. Anul 2012 [Nuptiality in 2012]. (2013). Bucharest: National Institute of Statistics.

Pasti, V. (2003). *Ultima inegalitate. Relaţiile de gen în România* [The last inequality. Gender relationships in Romania]. Iaşi: Polirom.

Poortman, A. -R., & Mills, M. (2012). Investments in marriage and cohabitation: The role of legal and interpersonal commitment. *Journal of Marriage and Family, 74*, 357–376. 10.1111/j.1741-3737.2011.00954.x

Puur, A., Rahnu, L., Maslauskaite, A., Stankuniene, V., & Zakharov, S. (2012). Transformation of partnership formation in Eastern Europe: The legacy of the past demographic Divide. *Journal of Comparative Family Studies, 43*(3), 389–418.

Recensământul populaţiei şi al locuinţelor, 2002: fotografia principalelor rezultate [Census of population and housing 2002: the preliminary results]. (2003). Bucharest: National Institute of Statistics.

Rotariu, T. (2009). Marital and extramarital fertility in latter-day Romania. In A. Fauve-Chamoux & I. (coord.). Bolovan (Eds.), *Families in Europe between the 19th and the 2nd centuries, from the traditional model to the contemporary PACS* (pp. 361–380). Cluj-Napoca: Cluj University Press.

Rotariu, T., Mureşan, C., Hărăguş, M., & Hărăguş, P. T. (2012). Căsătoria şi reproducerea populaţiei [Marriage and population's reproduction]. In T. Rotariu & V. (coord.). Voineagu (Eds.), *Inerţie şi schimbare. Dimensiuni sociale ale tranziţiei în România* [Inertia and change. Social dimensions of the transition in Romania] (pp. 125–159). Iaşi: Polirom.

Rotariu, T., & Voineagu, V. (2012). *Inerţie şi schimbare. Dimensiuni sociale ale tranziţiei în România* [Inertia and Change. Social Dimensions of the Transition in Romania]. Iaşi: Polirom.

Sardon, J. -P. (1991). Mariage et divorce en Europe de l'Est. *Population (French Edition), 46*, 547–598. 10.2307/1533407

Sardon, J. -P. (2004). Recent demographic trends in the developed countries. *Population (English Edition), 59*, 263–314. 10.3917/pope.402.0263

Scurtu, I. (2001). *Viaţa cotidiană a Românilor în perioada interbelică* [Daily life of Romanians during the interwar period]. Bucureşti: RAO.

Tendinţe sociale [Social trends]. (2007). Bucharest: National Institute of Statistics.

Tendinţe sociale [Social trends]. (2013). Bucharest: National Institute of Statistics.

Théry, I. (1998). *Couple, filiation et parenté aujourd'hui. Le droit face aux mutations de la famille et de la vie privée* [Couple, filiation and family relationships nowadays. The legal provisions concerning the transformations of the family and of the private life]. Paris: : Éditions Odile Jacob/La Documentation française.

Théry, I., & Biet, C. (1989). *La famille, la loi, l'État de la Révolution au Code civil* [The family, the law and the state, from the revolution to the civil code]. Paris: : Éditions du Centre Georges Pompidou/Imprimerie Nationale – Éditions.

Vasilescu, P. (2003). *Regimuri matrimoniale. Parte generală* [Matrimonial Regimes]. Bucureşti: Rosetti.

Spatial variation in non-marital fertility across Europe in the twentieth and twenty-first centuries: recent trends, persistence of the past, and potential future pathways

Sebastian Klüsener

This article investigates spatiotemporal variation in non-marital fertility across Europe over the last 100 years. In the first 50 years of this period, non-marital fertility was generally declining, reaching very low levels in the mid-twentieth century. But starting in the 1960s, non-marital fertility increased strongly. The main aim of this paper is to investigate to what degree the persistence of the past might be relevant for understanding spatial aspects of the recent rise. A secondary aim is to explore how spatial non-marital fertility variation is likely to develop in the future, both between and within countries. The outcomes support the view that historical patterns are relevant for understanding current non-marital fertility variation in most parts of Europe. However, the persistence of the past varies spatially, and seems to fade over time. The analysis of current trends in spatial variation between countries suggests that an east–west dichotomy is currently emerging: i.e., countries that are not in the European Union and that have Orthodox Christian or Muslim traditions exhibit higher propensities to remain at or to revert to comparatively low levels of non-marital fertility. Within Northwestern Europe, suburban belts around big cities appear to be the last strongholds of marital fertility.

1. Introduction

A present-day observer might be astounded by the amount of attention the topic of births outside marriage has been given – and is still being given – by researchers and statistical offices (Kiernan, 2004; Kok, 2009; Laslett, 1980; Perelli-Harris et al., 2010). In many European countries, non-marital births have become the norm, with more than 50% of all new-born children being born to non-married women. But just 50 years ago, during the Golden Age of Marriage, a non-marital birth was a rare event associated with a range of potentially negative social and legal implications for the new-born child. Today, most non-married mothers are in a stable relationship (Perelli-Harris et al., 2012), and have the option of getting married prior to childbirth. Thus, the recent increase in non-marital fertility seems to reflect the reality that the social norm that marriage should precede childbirth – which was considered very important by past populations (Kok & Leinarte, 2015; Laslett, 1980) – has far less relevance for current populations. However, studies that have looked at present-day spatial variation in non-marital fertility across Europe have found a substantial degree of variation, mostly between but also sometimes within countries (e.g., Klüsener, Perelli-Harris, & Sánchez Gassen, 2013). Whereas in large parts of Northern Europe marital childbearing has become the exception, there are still countries in Southeastern Europe, such as Greece and Albania, where a non-marital childbirth is still a rather rare event.

The results of existing research indicate that the observed spatial variation in non-marital fertility may be attributed in part to the *persistence of the past*, as these patterns can be traced back over long periods of time (e.g., Klüsener & Goldstein, 2014; Kok, 2009). In some countries the spatiotemporal pattern of the recent increases in non-marital fertility closely resembles the spatiotemporal pattern observed in the fertility decline during the demographic transition (see, e.g., Lesthaeghe & Neels, 2002, on Belgium and France). These findings suggest that some regional populations might be more receptive to new family formation trends than others, and that these differences could persist over time.

My main aim in this article is to investigate the extent to which past patterns are relevant for understanding spatial aspects of the current rise of non-marital fertility across Europe. In examining this question, I use spatially sensitive descriptive analysis techniques to compare spatial variation patterns at different points in time over the last 100 years (1910, 1960, 1975, 1990, 2007). In the first 50 years of this period, non-marital fertility was generally declining, and reached very low levels in the 1950s and 1960s. In the 50 years that followed, non-marital fertility increased sharply in most of Europe. Indeed, in many regions non-marital fertility has risen to levels that are unprecedented in the period since modern vital registration was first introduced (Klüsener et al., 2013; Kok, 2009; see also Appendix 1). A secondary aim is to explore the question of what kind of regional variation in non-marital fertility might establish itself across Europe and within European countries after the current transition to higher non-marital fertility levels has come to an end. The focus of my analysis of the future of within-country variation will be on Denmark, the first European country to have completed an s-shaped transition from low to relatively high non-marital fertility levels, with the increase in the non-marital fertility ratio levelling off at around 50% in the late 1980s. Thus, relative to countries that are still undergoing the transition, Denmark may be expected to have a rather mature spatial non-marital fertility pattern that is less affected by the spatially dependent social diffusion processes that tend to occur during the transition.[1,2] As a result, the analysis of the Danish case may be expected to provide insights into the kinds of spatial variation patterns which might emerge in other countries after they have completed the transition.

2. Theoretical considerations

Whether a pregnancy results in a marital or non-marital birth can be related to both the individual-level attributes of the parents and the contextual conditions in which individuals and social groups are embedded (Cutright, 1971; Kok & Leinarte, 2015; Lesthaeghe & Neels, 2002; Shorter, Knodel, & van de Walle, 1971). The contextual conditions include, for example, the existing social norms regarding what constitutes a proper family, the economic circumstances, and the policies and laws of the country or region in which the birth takes place. The legal context is also important for the registration of a non-marital birth, as the law defines what constitutes a formal marriage. This definition allows statistical offices to determine based on the information that is available on a given birth event whether the child has been born within or outside marriage. According to Kok and Leinarte (2015), spatial and temporal variation in the share of births that occur outside marriage can be affected by both the degree to which mothers and couples consider it desirable or acceptable for themselves and for their family to have a childbirth that is registered as either marital or non-marital, and the degree to which it is feasible for mothers and couples to marry prior to the birth of a child or to prevent a non-marital birth by induced abortion (see also Cutright, 1971).

As my goal in this paper is to provide a general overview of the spatiotemporal aspects of non-marital fertility trends across Europe over the last 100 years, the analysis that follows cannot address in detail the question of how the relative importance of specific individual and contextual determinants has varied across space and time. Yet when interpreting the findings, it is important to be aware that a non-marital birth may reflect very different motivations and circumstances.

Particularly in the past, a non-marital birth often occurred because the mother did not have the option of marrying. For example, the mother may not have been in a stable relationship, or she and her partner may have been denied the right to marry due to a lack of resources (see, e.g., Knodel, 1967; Kok, 2009). Today, job insecurity might lead cohabiting couples to postpone marriage until they have found more secure employment. Thus, it may be assumed that non-marital fertility will increase sharply during periods of economic crisis, and evidence that this is the case has been presented for both historical (Abrahamson, 2000) and more recent contexts (Perelli-Harris & Gerber, 2011). In line with the assumption that non-marital fertility is associated with a pattern of disadvantage, many studies based on individual-level data – including some recent analyses of present-day patterns – have shown a negative social status gradient in the likelihood of a birth occurring outside marriage (e.g., Perelli-Harris et al., 2010).

The analysis of non-marital fertility is, however, complicated by the fact that, particularly as societies modernise, rising non-marital fertility may also reflect an expansion of positive freedoms (Berlin, 1958; Lesthaeghe, 2010). If, for example, women become more economically independent as a result of improved access to the labour market, they may also become less dependent on kin relations and the institution of marriage to secure their own livelihood and the livelihoods of their offspring (McLaughlin & Glendinning, 1994). Secularisation trends also provide individuals with more freedom to choose family formation strategies that are not in line with those advocated by religious institutions. At least historically, all major religious institutions in Europe have taught that procreation should occur within marriage (see also Kok & Leinarte, 2015).

Elevated non-marital fertility levels can also result from marriage being seen as less desirable in specific regions. In Iceland and in parts of Sweden (Trost, 1978), for example, there is a long tradition of cohabitation by non-married couples. Couples who live in these regions may find it easier to choose cohabitation than couples who live in regions that lack such a tradition. Moreover, in some contexts there might be discrepancies between legal marriage as defined by the state authorities, and the types of unions the people or a specific sub-population classify as marriage. Thus, in some societies certain couples might be seen as being married, even though their union is not registered with the state authorities (see also Kok & Leinarte, 2015). In Austrian Galicia, for example, a large share of the Jewish population did not register their religious marriages with the state authorities, primarily because they wanted to avoid giving their information to the government or having to pay fees (Lowenstein, 1994). As a result, a large share of Jewish births in that region was registered as non-marital.[3] A similar tendency to avoid registering unions with the state authorities can be observed in present-day Kosovo (see below).

When considering how spatial non-marital fertility patterns prior to the Golden Age of Marriage might help us to better understand the spatial patterns of the recent rise, the general non-marital fertility trends in Europe experienced over the past several centuries should be taken into account (see also Appendix 1). While rates of non-marital fertility appear to have been very low in early modern Europe until the early eighteenth century, these rates increased in the eighteenth and nineteenth centuries (Shorter et al., 1971). Thereafter, most European countries experienced a decrease in non-marital fertility that culminated in the Golden Age of Marriage. While these reductions started in a few countries in the nineteenth century, in the majority of the countries substantial declines did not occur until the period after World War I.

The decline in non-marital fertility in the first half of the twentieth century has been attributed to a number of factors. First, improved access to contraception made it easier for non-married women to avoid unwanted pregnancies (Shorter et al., 1971). In addition, expanding welfare states took steps to limit childbearing outside marriage, as these children were at high risk of requiring welfare support. Especially after the world economic crisis of 1929, many European countries attempted to limit unemployment by basing their labour market and social policies on a male breadwinner model. It appears that in this period many women accepted their labour market marginalisation, as the male breadwinner family was the most frequently chosen family form in the mid-twentieth century (Ruggles, 2015, on the US). In such family arrangements women were very dependent on their husbands, and were therefore likely to see marriage as an attractive strategy for securing financial support for themselves and their offspring. This changed again when the generations born after 1945 reached adulthood, as the women of these generations were less willing to limit their participation in the labour market.

If we follow this line of argumentation, we might make the claim that the very low non-marital fertility levels of the mid-twentieth century were rather exceptional. During this period, almost all European regions had low non-marital fertility levels, regardless of whether they had a tradition of childbearing outside marriage. But as the Golden Age of Marriage came to a close, these historical patterns may have re-emerged, affecting both the timing of the onset of the trend towards higher levels of non-marital fertility, and the intensity of this trend. However, a re-emergence of historical differences required that at least some of the factors that had contributed to spatial variation in non-marital fertility prior to the Golden Age of Marriage were still important in subsequent decades.

One factor that might be relevant is variation in how childbearing outside marriage was perceived. In the regions where non-marital fertility had been widespread prior to the Golden Age of Marriage, it might have been easier for this behaviour to spread again in the decades that followed. Evidence that this is the case has, for example, been presented for regional patterns in Sweden, where the vanguard regions in the 1960s and 1970s were those that also had historically high levels of non-marital fertility (Tomasson, 1976). There is also evidence that the strength of family ties has long differed in Southern and in Northern Europe (Reher, 1998). In regions with weak family ties, such as Scandinavia, lower levels of intergenerational control might have made it easier for younger generations to deviate from the behavioural patterns of their elders. Thus, in both past and present times the diffusion of deviant family formation behaviour might have occurred more quickly in Northern than in Southern Europe.

Another factor that may have contributed to the continuity in patterns is variation in secularisation levels. Secularisation processes gained momentum in the eighteenth century, with spatial variation between and within countries often displaying quite substantial path dependencies over time (Kaufmann, Goujon, & Skirbekk, 2012; Lesthaeghe & Lopez-Gay, 2013 on Belgium; Klüsener & Goldstein, 2014 on Germany). As religious couples are less likely to have a child outside marriage (Klüsener & Goldstein, 2014; Lappegård, Klüsener, & Vignoli, 2014), temporal continuity in spatial secularisation patterns might also contribute to continuity in spatial non-marital fertility variation.

In addition, the institutional context might contribute to the persistence of historic patterns. Family law is one of the oldest areas of law, and the regulations governing families vary substantially across European countries (see Perelli-Harris & Sánchez Gassen, 2012). Most countries exhibit path dependencies in the development of their family legislation. This is also the case for the general principles of welfare state organisation, the foundations of which were first laid in many European countries in the late nineteenth century. In the German-speaking countries, for example, welfare support has long been linked to the family via the married (male) breadwinner, as, based on subsidiarity considerations, the family was seen as the principal unit for dealing with issues related to bringing up children. Scandinavian countries, by contrast, have a long history of implementing individualistic support schemes and encouraging female employment (Kolbe, 2002). These policies strengthened the economic position of women, and may have contributed to the forerunner status of Scandinavian countries in the recent increase of non-marital fertility.

In most European countries family legislation and welfare state institutions are organised at the national level. According to Watkins (1991), this has contributed to a decrease in regional differences in family formation patterns within countries in the twentieth century – an argument for which she has provided empirical support. Regional convergence in demographic behaviour within nation states was not, however, fostered only by family policies and the harmonisation of family legislation. The establishment of national education systems, which often promoted the use of a common state language, as well as investments in national transport infrastructures tended to facilitate more intense communication within countries, rather than across country borders. As a result, shifts in family formation patterns might diffuse more quickly in space and time within countries than across national borders (Decroly & Grasland, 1993).

Discontinuities in spatial patterns might occur for a number of different reasons. First, there might be dramatic changes in the composition of the population. For example, in the territory of historic Austrian Galicia the Jewish population was virtually eliminated during the Holocaust. Thus, even though this group had a higher propensity than the general population to avoid registering their marriages with the authorities, we would not expect this historic pattern to substantially affect current non-marital fertility levels in this area, which is now located in western Ukraine.

Another possible reason for these discontinuities is spatial variation in how views on childbearing outside marriage have changed over time. Stigmatisation or toleration of childbearing outside marriage has in historical studies frequently been linked to spatial variation in agricultural inheritance patterns (see, e.g., Khera, 1981; Klüsener & Goldstein, 2014; Shorter, 1978). But because the share of the population who are involved in agricultural activities is much smaller than in the past, this association may no longer have a large impact. The degree to which people perceived access to marriage as a privilege might have also varied spatially over time. In addition, discontinuities can occur as a result of policy reforms. Governments might implement reforms that create incentives for couples to abandon traditional customs, and thus make societies more open to childbearing outside marriage. This seems to have occurred in Bulgaria, a case I will discuss in more detail below.

3. Data and methods

3.1. Data and choice of years

To investigate variation in non-marital fertility, I focus in this study on the non-marital fertility ratio, which is defined as the number of non-marital live births divided by the total number of live births. This measure is a rather crude indicator of non-marital fertility, as it does not allow me to control for age structure, migration background, educational attainment, or differences in the numbers of married and unmarried women between regions or in a region over time. The data also cannot be used to identify childbearing among non-married cohabiting couples, or to investigate how this behaviour has become more prevalent in recent decades (see Perelli-Harris et al., 2012). Yet the big advantage of using the non-marital fertility ratio is that it is available at a high degree of geographic detail for almost all European countries over long periods of time.

The data for the analysis were collected by the statistical offices of the observed countries. For the period around 2007 I obtained the data directly from these primary sources. For earlier periods some of the data were derived from secondary resources (see the 'Demographic data' section in the references for details). The secondary resources used in compiling the historical state-level time trends over the past several centuries (presented in Appendix 1) included a publication on international long-term trends in vital statistics by Statistics France (SGF, 1907), publications of the *Office Permanent de l'Institut International de Statistique*, and a data handbook edited by Flora, Kraus, and Pfenning (1987). In addition, I downloaded data from the *Developed Countries Demography* database (INED, 2015) and the *Human Mortality Database* (UCB & MPIDR, 2015).

Some of the data used for the period around 1910 were prepared by the collaborators on a project that is investigating the decline in infant mortality across Europe at a high level of geographic detail, who kindly agreed to share their data with me.[4] The regional data for the developments since 1960 were mostly derived from a data collection compiled by the *Atlas de la Population Européenne* project (Decroly & Vanlaer, 1991). These data were complemented by annual country data for the period 1960 to 2007, which were obtained from Eurostat, the Demographic Yearbook of the Council of Europe (2005), and *Demoskop Weekly* (2015).

The years I have chosen to focus on in the analysis were selected in part based on the availability of data. It is important to note that 1910 was selected primarily because regional data for that year are available for almost all of the European countries. Data are much more difficult to obtain for the period following World War I, as, for example, the Soviet Union did not publish information on whether births occurred within or outside marriage for some time. Attempts to assess the extent to which the 1910 pattern is indicative of patterns that existed prior to the Golden Age of Marriage are complicated by the fact that, by 1910, some parts of Western and Northern Europe were already in the middle of the demographic transition, and thus were experiencing substantial fertility declines. This transition affected both marital and non-marital fertility, as well as marriage timing. Unfortunately, data limitations do not allow me to study detailed spatial patterns prior to 1910. But in Appendix 1 I provide long-term data for a large number of countries and bigger sub-regions of countries over the last three centuries. Thus, at least at this cruder level of spatial detail, I can investigate to what degree the levels observed in 1910 are still representative of the nineteenth-century patterns in different parts of Europe.

The graphs in Appendix 1 show that in a number of countries the non-marital fertility ratio declined in the decades prior to 1910. The Western and Northern European countries where this occurred include England and Wales, Scotland, the Netherlands, and Iceland. In Central Europe, non-marital fertility decreased dramatically in a number of German states in the late 1860s, largely because marriage bans were lifted (Knodel, 1967). In Southern Europe, non-marital fertility increased in Italy in the late nineteenth century, but had returned to mid-nineteenth-century levels by 1910. This temporary increase seems to be largely a registration artefact, as a significant share of couples did not register their church marriages with the civil authorities during the conflict between the Italian state and the Vatican which occurred in this period (Kok & Leinarte, 2015). Except in England and Wales and in Scotland, the declines found in European countries prior to 1910 did not affect whether a country had a high, medium, or low level of non-marital fertility relative to other European countries. This provides me with some assurance that at least at this crude level of spatial detail, the 1910 levels capture quite well for most of Europe the degree of variation in non-marital fertility that existed prior to the Golden Age of Marriage.

When we look at the more recent years covered in the analyses, we can see that the year 1960 represents the heyday of the Golden Age of Marriage. The year 1975 constitutes an intermediate point in the departure from the Golden Age of Marriage, as some vanguard countries were already experiencing an increase in non-marital fertility. The year 1990 marks the beginning of the transition in Eastern Europe. Non-marital fertility rose rapidly in many post-communist countries in the period that followed. The year 2007 is the most recent year for which data have been obtained.

When considering the 1910 data, it is important to note that at that time the quality of population statistics varied substantially across Europe (Edge, 1928; SGF, 1907). While the countries of Northwestern Europe, including Germany, had very reliable registration systems in 1910, many countries in Eastern and Southern Europe had problems with the under-registration of vital events, especially of births in which the child died within the first days of life. Children who were born outside marriage were at higher risk of dying in infancy than children who were born within marriage. This gap might have contributed to a downward bias in the reported rates of these countries. Another challenge is variation in registration standards within Northwestern Europe: e.g., in countries such as France and the Netherlands a live birth was registered as a stillbirth if the child died before the birth was registered (Klüsener et al., 2014). These problems may also have affected the long-term time trends presented in Appendix 1.

As any attempts to correct for variation in registration standards would be based on bold assumptions, I decided to use the data without modifications, while assuming that in areas where having a childbirth outside marriage was more accepted, a non-marital birth was more likely to be reported. Nevertheless, in interpreting the outcomes it is important to keep in mind that the analysis presented in this paper examines the persistence of the past in the share of *registered* births that occurred outside marriage.

The demographic data were matched to GIS-shapefiles, which provide information on the administrative boundaries of the regions for which the demographic data were collected. These shapefiles were derived from the *MPIDR Population History GIS Collection* (MPIDR, 2014a, 2014b, 2014c), national historical GIS projects (see the 'GIS data' section in the references for details), and the *GADM Database of Global Administrative Areas* (GADM, 2012).

3.2. Generating estimates for a time-constant regional division of Europe

When researching the persistence of past spatial variation patterns in Europe, the substantial changes in national borders and regional administrative boundaries over the last 100 years pose a major challenge. This is particularly the case for Central and Eastern Europe. To facilitate the comparison over time, efforts have been made to derive estimates for a time-constant regional division of Europe. For the period 1960–2007, this study benefits from the fact that such a data-set has already been derived by Klüsener et al. (2013) for a paper on regional aspects of non-marital fertility trends since 1960.[5] This data-set covers for most European countries the current regional administrative divisions, while in some exceptional cases other divisions which existed at some point in time during the period 1960–2007 are used.[6] This data-set was complemented with data for the year 1910.

In estimating the non-marital fertility levels for the time-constant regions in 1910, a simple spatial interpolation method based on area weighting is used (Goodchild & Lam, 1980).[7] The central assumption of this method is that marital and non-marital births are homogenously distributed, both in the so-called *source regions* for which data are available for a given year, as well as in the time-constant *target regions* for which estimates have to be produced. This sounds like a strong assumption, as it is not reasonable to expect that either the population or the births were homogenously distributed across a regional territory. However, it is important to point out that the bias produced by such an estimation is largely dependent on the geographical extent of the source regions relative to the target regions. The smaller the source regions and the larger the target regions, the smaller the bias that is introduced by this spatial interpolation technique. In this case, data on live births and non-marital live births were available for more than 5000 source regions for the year 1910, and these data were used to derive estimates for 604 target regions. Thus, the bias introduced by this approach was expected to be rather low.[8] The estimates were derived by intersecting a GIS-polygon file with the boundaries of the source regions with a GIS-file of the target regions to obtain the smallest common polygons. The area information from these polygons in turn allowed me to generate the estimates for the target regions.

3.3. Analytical strategy

The analysis is divided into three parts. In section 4.1 I provide an overview of the non-marital fertility trends in European macro regions since 1960, followed by a geographically detailed account of present spatial variation in non-marital fertility across Europe. In section 4.2 I explore to what degree the persistence of past spatial variation patterns might be relevant for understanding present-day spatial variation across Europe. To address this question, I examine how the current spatial variation patterns correspond with the patterns observed 100 years ago and at other points in time over the last 100 years. Finally, in section 4.3, I discuss potential future pathways of spatial non-marital fertility variation across Europe.

Throughout the analysis, I make use of descriptive methods and cartographic representations. In the second part of the analysis, the correlations between regional non-marital fertility levels in the years 1910, 1960, 1975, 1990, and 2007 are presented.

For the years 1960–1990 these correlations apply to a reduced sample, as I lack regional data for a number of Eastern European countries in this period.[9] As most of the variables are positively skewed, Spearman's rank order correlation coefficient has been chosen to derive the correlations. If the persistence of the past plays a role, it may be generally expected that a positive association would be found between past and present spatial non-marital fertility variation in different years. This part of the investigation was inspired by an analysis of temporal continuity in non-marital fertility variation at the national level by Kok (2009). In his paper, Kok used a sample that consisted primarily of Western European countries to examine non-marital fertility levels in the period 1900–2000.

As the persistence of the past is likely to vary spatially across Europe, I have also chosen to explore the statistical associations between historical and present-day patterns for different sub-regions of Europe. This analysis compares the levels of variation in 1910 and in 2007. To determine whether and to what degree the association between non-marital fertility levels in these two periods varies across different sub-regions of Europe, I use a Geographically Weighted (GW) Spearman's rank order correlation coefficient (Fotheringham, Brunsdon, & Charlton, 2002). This implies that I will calculate the coefficient for sets of local samples. For each region i in the sample, a local Spearman's rank order correlation coefficient is obtained, which includes values of the variables of interest for the region i itself, and for neighbouring regions j situated in the adjacency of region i.[10] This implies that for the derived European sample of time-constant regions in 1910 and 2007, a total of 604 local correlations will be obtained. For the calculations I used the R-package *GWmodel*.

In deciding which of the neighbouring regions to include in the local correlation statistics, Geographically Weighted statistical approaches provide the user with the option of working with either fixed or adaptive bandwidths. A fixed bandwidth is defined as a distance radius, while an adaptive bandwidth is based on a k-nearest neighbours approach. For my analysis, I have chosen to use an adaptive bandwidth, as it allows me to better account for the considerable variation in the sizes of the regions across the European sample. The implication of the bandwidth can differ depending on what kind of spatial weighting functions are chosen (see below). In most cases, the bandwidth implies that no information for regions beyond that bandwidth of k-nearest neighbours will be included. Geographically Weighted statistical approaches offer optimisation-based procedures for deciding how many nearest neighbours should be used as bandwidth. But as this is just an explorative analysis, I decided to keep things simple by working with arbitrarily chosen bandwidths. To show the sensitivity of the choice of the bandwidth on the outcomes, I will present the results for 20 and 30 nearest neighbours.

In addition to using a bandwidth, GW-based methods include the option to work with spatial weighting functions to give neighbouring regions j, which are closer to the region i for which a local statistic is derived, more weight than more distant regions j. Different options for deriving these weights are available. I present the outcomes for two different weights, as provided in the R-package *GWmodel*, which allow me to carve out different dimensions of the existing spatial variation patterns in the correlation between spatial non-marital fertility patterns in 1910 and in 2007. I will refer to them as 'intermediate' and 'localised' weighting schemes. For the intermediate scheme, which is based on a Gaussian-shaped kernel weighting function,[11] the weights for neighbouring regions slowly decrease with distance, which allows me to look at shifts in the association at an intermediate spatial scale across Europe. By contrast, the localised weighting scheme, which is based on a bisquare-shaped kernel weighting function, gives nearby neighbouring regions a much higher weight than more distant regions. Thus, this scheme is more sensitive to small-scale deviations in the association between past and present non-marital fertility levels from patterns that exist at higher spatial scales.[12]

4. Spatial variation in non-marital fertility across Europe in historical perspective

4.1. Recent trends and present variation

4.1.1. Non-marital fertility trends in European macro regions since 1960

In presenting the results, I will first discuss non-marital fertility trends for broad European macro regions over the last 50 years. This will allow me to describe regional variation in the timing and pace of the departure from the Golden Age of Marriage of the mid-twentieth century. The categorisation of European countries into macro regions was based on similarities in their welfare state systems (Esping-Andersen, 1990), and on other parallels in political developments over time. The macro region of Northern Europe represents the Nordic countries, which have extensive welfare state support systems (Esping-Andersen, 1990). The Western European region is comprised of countries that either have quite liberal welfare states (the United Kingdom, Ireland, the Netherlands), or have long provided very high levels of child care support (France and Belgium). The availability of child care may be assumed to have positive effects on the economic independence of women. The third region of Central-Western Europe includes the German-speaking countries, which, apart from the former German Democratic Republic, have rather conservative welfare states (Esping-Andersen, 1990). These conservative welfare regimes are characterised by family support geared towards married couples and a temporal delay in the implementation of policies aimed at supporting the reconciliation of family and work. The Central-Eastern and Eastern Europe categories cover all of the former communist countries except for the German Democratic Republic.[13] All of the former Soviet republics that are not currently part of the European Union[14] are in the Eastern Europe category, while the other post-communist countries are in the Central-Eastern Europe category. The region of Southern Europe is comprised of countries that have populations with strong family ties (Reher, 1998), and that, at least until recently, had rather conservative welfare states (Esping-Andersen, 1990). In addition to data on the non-marital fertility trends for these six macro regions, data for Europe as a whole have been derived. The resulting numbers are shown in Figure 1, in which the small map in the upper-left corner indicates which European country has been linked to which macro region.[15]

The time series starts in the heyday of the Golden Age of Marriage. Around 1960, all six macro regions except for Eastern Europe had a non-marital fertility ratio below 10%. The first region to report a strong increase in this ratio was Northern Europe; there the transition started in the 1960s and gained additional momentum in the 1970s. By the late 1970s, non-marital fertility had also started to rise in Western and in Central-Western Europe. But unlike in Western Europe, the increase in Central-Western Europe was initially short-lived, and was mostly driven by developments in the German Democratic Republic (GDR) and Austria. The regions that made up these two countries had historically been hot spots of non-marital fertility (see below). Thus, their populations may have been particularly susceptible to reverting to higher levels of non-marital

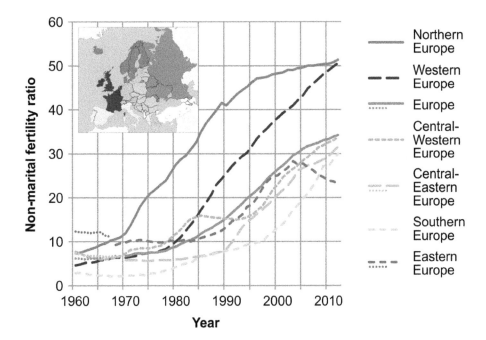

Figure 1. Development of the non-marital fertility ratio in European macro regions 1960-2012. Note: The ratio is derived by dividing the sum of the non-marital live births reported by countries belonging to a specific macro region by the sum of the total number of live births of these countries. Numbers for Eastern Europe exclude Ukraine until 1968 (dotted line) and Moldova until 1971. The data for Central-Eastern Europe do not cover Romania until 1970 (dotted line). From 1970 until 1992 the data for Romania have been linearly interpolated based on the available data for the years 1970, 1975, 1980, 1985, 1990, and 1993. For Bosnia and Herzegovina data are missing for 1992–1995, for Kosovo for 2000–2003, and for Montenegro for 2010–2012. Source: Statistical offices; Eurostat; UN statistical yearbooks; Decroly and Vanlaer (1991); Council of Europe (2005), own calculations.

fertility. After rather generous support schemes for single mothers were introduced in the 1970s in the GDR and in Austria,[16] the shares of births that occurred outside marriage started to rise in both countries. However, in the mid-1980s these support schemes were extended to married mothers (GDR) or restricted to non-married mothers without a partner (Austria). After these reforms were implemented, the increase in non-marital fertility came to a halt in both countries, at least temporarily (see also Klüsener & Goldstein, 2014; Kytir, 1992).[17] The decline in non-marital fertility in Central-Western Europe in the 1980s and the early 1990s was also related in part to compositional factors: i.e., eastern Germany, which had rather high shares of non-marital births, went from having fertility rates which were close to replacement level in the early 1980s, to having extremely low fertility rates in the 1990s (Goldstein & Kreyenfeld, 2011). As a result of the temporary decline, Central-Western Europe went from being a forerunner in the transition to being a laggard.

In the Central-Eastern and the Eastern European regions, the average non-marital fertility levels changed very little between 1960 and the mid-1980s. Southern Europe, on the other hand, had on average the lowest non-marital fertility ratio of all of the macro regions in 1960, and the ratio continued to decline until the 1970s. But in the

1970s, the non-marital fertility ratio started to increase in Southern Europe as well, and has been rising ever since. However, the increases in the late 1970s and the 1980s were still quite small.

Thus, by the 1980s, the non-marital fertility ratios of Northern and Western Europe were on a clear upward trajectory, while the other regions were lagging behind. The economic collapse of the Eastern Bloc in the late 1980s resulted in trend changes in these countries. During the crisis period that followed, non-marital fertility started to increase substantially in Central-Eastern and Eastern Europe. In Central-Western and Southern Europe, the trend towards higher non-marital fertility ratios also accelerated in the mid- to late 1990s. In some of these countries, such as in Germany, the acceleration of the increase occurred parallel to the enactment of legislative reforms that substantially reduced the remaining legal discrimination of children born outside marriage.

In the 2000s, the developments in Eastern Europe were probably the most remarkable of the trends that were unfolding across Europe. While all of the European macro regions had rapidly increasing non-marital fertility ratios in the late 1990s and the early 2000s, Eastern Europe started to deviate from this general trend from around 2003 onwards. Since then, non-marital fertility levels have been on a downward trajectory in this macro region. This trend is detectable in Russia, Belarus, and Moldova, while Ukraine has just experienced a levelling off of increases in non-marital fertility (see Appendix 1). There seem to be two main explanations for why this trend is occurring in Eastern Europe. First, it has been argued that non-marital fertility rose in Eastern Europe in the 1990s partly in response to insecure economic conditions (Perelli-Harris & Gerber, 2011). This provides support for the view that the economic stabilisation of the 2000s might have contributed to the subsequent decrease in non-marital fertility levels. Second, scholars have observed that Eastern Europe appears to be entering a period characterised by a reversion to traditional norms. This trend is reflected in de-secularisation trends (see, e.g., Evans & Northmore-Ball, 2012, on Russia) and the enactment of legislation designed to limit non-traditional family formation behaviour (e.g., in Russia).

The countries of Northern Europe have registered smaller increases in non-marital fertility in recent years, which suggests that the transition to higher non-marital fertility levels might be close to completion in this part of Europe. In four of the other five regions, non-marital fertility ratios are continuing to rise. Thus, with the exception of Eastern Europe, a convergence of non-marital fertility levels can currently be observed across Europe. When we look for evidence of the persistence of the past in the current trends, Eastern Europe again stands out. While this part of Europe had the highest non-marital fertility ratio in the early 1960s, it had the lowest in 2012. Another region that experienced substantial shifts in its relative position is Western Europe. While this macro region was in the second-last position in 1960, current trends suggest that it will soon overtake Northern Europe to become the macro region with the highest non-marital fertility.

4.1.2. A geographically detailed view of non-marital fertility variation across Europe in 2007

In order to study present-day variation in non-marital fertility levels at a high level of geographic detail, I compiled information on the non-marital fertility ratio for more than 2300 European regions and localities for the period around 2007. The resulting

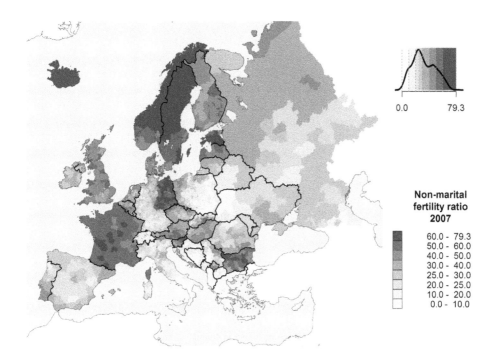

Figure 2. Non-marital fertility ratio 2007.
Note: The regional boundaries considered for this map are shown in Appendix 2. The density curve in the upper-right corner provides additional information to the legend given in the lower-right corner by showing how the chosen colour categories relate to the distribution of the mapped variable.
Source: Statistical offices; Eurostat, own calculations.
Base Map: MPIDR (2014a), partly based on EuroGeographics for the administrative boundaries; GADM (2012).

map is displayed in Figure 2. When interpreting the map, it is important to keep in mind that the level of spatial detail varies across countries, as I tried to obtain for each country the information with the highest level of detail available.[18]

The map shown in Figure 2 also supports the view that the spatial variation in non-marital fertility levels across Europe is far from random. In Northern Europe, hot spots with very high levels include Iceland and large parts of Sweden and Norway. Within Central-Eastern Europe, Estonia is by far the country with the highest non-marital fertility levels. In Western Europe, France reports the highest levels, with relatively little internal variation across its subnational regions. Other hot spots include the territory of the former German Democratic Republic in eastern Germany, and an area encompassing the southern part of Austria and eastern Slovenia. In Southeastern Europe, Bulgaria has exceptionally high non-marital fertility levels.

In many instances the patterns appear to be closely linked to national borders, even though in recent decades regional non-marital fertility variation has become less associated with the territories of nation states (Klüsener et al., 2013). There is, for example, a strong dividing line in non-marital fertility between France and Switzerland, despite the fact that the populations east and west of the border speak the same language. Existing research suggests that the non-marital fertility divide along this border is largely a result of differences in the family policies and the family legislation of France and Switzerland (Le Goff & Ryser, 2010; Perelli-Harris & Sánchez Gassen, 2012).

A number of countries exhibit a significant degree of internal regional variation in non-marital fertility levels. Some of these patterns appear to have first emerged long ago. In Germany, for example, Klüsener and Goldstein (2014) showed that differences in non-marital fertility levels between the eastern and western parts of Germany can be traced back to the eighteenth century. Poland is also an interesting case, as large parts of the regions of the country that were part of Germany until World War II, and that were resettled after the war, today have much higher non-marital fertility levels than the other regions of Poland (see also Brzozowska, 2011). In Slovakia, there are stark differences between the northern and the southern parts of the country, even though the north–south stretch of this country is quite small: along Slovakia's border with Poland, the levels of non-marital fertility are, at 7% to 20%, rather low; whereas in the southern part of Slovakia, the non-marital fertility ratios are, at 35% to 55%, quite high. Another country with clear regional differences is Serbia: in that country, non-marital fertility levels are lowest in the mountain areas of the western Balkans along the border with Bosnia-Herzegovina and Montenegro, and are highest in the Danube region along the borders with Romania and Bulgaria (Stanković & Penev, 2012).

In Kosovo, the area populated by the Serbian minority stands out from the rest of the territory. However, the high levels of non-marital fertility reported in the Muslim-dominated part of Kosovo appear to be an artefact, as a large number of the births in this area are to couples who are perceived as being married within their community, but who have not officially registered their marriage (see Klüsener et al., 2013; for details). This tendency to avoid the civil registration of marriage seems to have emerged in the second half of the twentieth century, when Kosovo was still part of Serbia (see Appendix 1). If only the births for which the father could not be determined are treated as non-marital (classified as illegitimate by Statistics Kosovo), the non-marital fertility ratio in Kosovo is as low as the ratio in neighbouring Albania. Some minority regions in other countries also stand out. In Italy, for example, South Tyrol exhibits levels that are very similar to those observed in neighbouring Austrian Tyrol.

There are also a number of clusters with similar non-marital fertility levels that extend across country borders. For example, there is an area with rather low non-marital fertility levels which stretches across the southeastern part of Poland and the western parts of Belarus and Ukraine. This area of quite low levels roughly corresponds to the state boundaries of interwar Poland. Historical boundaries also seem to show up in other cases. In Italy, the areas with rather low levels of non-marital fertility are concentrated within the boundaries of the former Kingdom of Naples. These findings lend support to the argument that we should seek to determine to what degree current spatial variation patterns correspond with past patterns.

4.2. Persistence of the past?

In examining the potential *longue durée* of regional patterns, I compare the spatial variation in 2007 with the patterns that existed around 1910. Figure 3 provides a geographically detailed view of non-marital fertility variation in 1910, based on data for 5000 historical regions and localities. The spatial patterns in 1910 were also far from random. However, in virtually all of Europe, the non-marital fertility ratios were much lower in 1910 than in 2007. In line with the theoretical considerations of Watkins (1991), we can see that the state borders in the 1910 map are less meaningful than

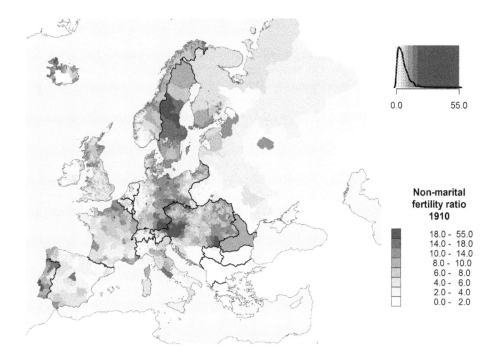

Figure 3. Non-marital fertility ratio 1910.
Note: The regional boundaries considered for this map are shown in Appendix 3. The density curve in the upper-right corner provides additional information to the legend given in the lower-right corner by showing how the chosen colour categories relate to the distribution of the mapped variable.
Source: Statistical offices; Ekamper and van Poppel (2008); Devos (2014); Klüsener et al. (2014), own calculations.
Base Map: MPIDR (2014a, 2014b, 2014c), partly based on EuroGeographics for the administrative boundaries; National Historical GIS projects: Boonstra (2007); Dansk Center for Byhistorie (2008); Gregory, Bennett, Gilham, & Southall (2002); Guttormsson & Garðarsdóttir (2002); Historical Database of Local Statistics [Lokstat] (2014); Norwegian Social Science Data Services [NSD] (2013); Riksarkivet (2013); da Silveira, Alves, Lima, Alcântara, & Puig (2011).

those of the 2007 map for explaining the spatial patterns, because in the early twentieth century nation states were just starting to have a significant influence on the demographic map of Europe. Thus, specific patterns are often not aligned with the boundaries of empires or nation states. This is, for example, the case for an area with rather low non-marital fertility levels which covered the Netherlands, the adjacent territories in western Germany, and, to some degree, Belgium. Similarly, there was a hot spot of non-marital fertility in Central Europe which covered southern Bavaria and the neighbouring territories of today's Austria. In these two territories high non-marital fertility was linked to inheritance practices and accompanying legislation (Khera, 1981; Shorter, 1978). While Austria of today is also a non-marital fertility hot spot, the level of non-marital fertility in Bavaria has 'converged' towards the levels reported in other parts of western Germany (see Figure 2). It is likely that this convergence trend was fostered by discontinuities in Bavarian civil legislation that resulted from the introduction of a unified civil code in Germany in 1900. While Bavarian civil legislation had given children born outside marriage quite substantial rights, the German civil code explicitly stated that a child born outside marriage was not related to the father (see Klüsener & Goldstein, 2014).

In the map of 1910, in a number of countries those areas that include capitals or other big cities stand out as non-marital fertility hot spots within the country. Among these hot spots are Madrid in Spain, St. Petersburg and Moscow in Russia, and Rome in Italy. It seems that particularly in conservative countries such as those mentioned above, (reported) non-marital fertility was largely restricted to the relatively anonymous large urban centres.

I will now compare the non-marital fertility levels for the 604 time-constant regions for which I obtained published data and/or estimates of non-marital fertility levels for 1910 and 2007. For a reduced sample of 482 regions, which excludes a number of Eastern European countries,[19] estimates for the years 1960, 1975, and 1990 are also available (Appendix 4 provides an overview which regions are included in the full and the reduced sample).

The obtained global (i.e., not spatially weighted) Spearman's rank order correlation coefficients are displayed in Table 1. The table provides correlations for regional non-marital fertility variation in 1910 and 2007 for the full sample, and a matrix of correlations of variation for the reduced sample in 1910, 1960, 1975, 1990, and 2007. The table shown here was constructed in a manner similar to that of a table presented by Kok (2009), in which he displayed the outcomes of a correlation analysis of non-marital fertility in 15 (mostly Western) European countries in 1870, 1900, 1930, 1960, and 2000. Kok also used Spearman's correlation coefficient. Although the correlations presented here cover a much larger part of Europe at a higher level of detail than those of Kok (2009), the obtained coefficients and trend patterns have many similarities. All of the correlation coefficients in Table 1 are in the expected positive direction. However, the correlation between 1910 and 2007 is rather low, with the obtained correlation coefficients being 0.29 for the full sample and 0.30 for the reduced sample.

Table 1. Rank order correlation (Spearman's rho) of regional non-marital fertility ratio (NMFR) in 1910, 1960, 1975, 1990, and 2007.

	NMFR 1960 N = 482	NMFR 1975 N = 482	NMFR 1990 N = 482	NMFR 2007 N = 482	NMFR 2007 N = 604
NMFR 1910	0.59	0.51	0.43	0.30	0.29
NMFR 1960	–	0.80	0.53	0.40	–
NMFR 1975	–	–	0.83	0.69	–
NMFR 1990	–	–	–	0.89	–

Note: The reduced sample excludes Belarus, Romania, Russia, and Ukraine, for which no regionally detailed data are available for the years 1960, 1975, and 1990. Both the full and the reduced sample exclude an area in Southeastern Europe which is today covered by the countries Albania, Greece, Kosovo, the former Yugoslavian republic of Macedonia, Montenegro, and Turkey; as no data on the non-marital fertility ratios in this area are available for 1910 (see also Figure 4). For the same reason some regions in the east and southeast of European Russia also had to be excluded from the full sample. All of the European micro states – such as Andorra, Monaco, Liechtenstein, and San Marino – are also excluded.
Source: Statistical offices; Eurostat; UN statistical yearbooks; Decroly and Vanlaer (1991); Council of Europe (2005); Ekamper and van Poppel (2008); Devos (2014); Klüsener et al. (2014); own calculations.

The comparison of the correlations that were obtained between the regional non-marital fertility levels in 1910 and the years 1960, 1975, 1990, and 2007 for the reduced sample show that the correlation with the 1910 values decreased over time. Similar trends of declining correlations are observable for the correlations of the regional levels in 1960 and 1975 on the one hand, and the levels in later periods on the other. These trends, which are also visible in the numbers presented by Kok (2009), suggest that the patterns of the past persist, but are fading over time.

The correlations for Europe as a whole might hide large- and small-scale variations in the association between non-marital fertility levels in 1910 and 2007 in different sub-regions of Europe, which I will now explore with the Geographically Weighted Spearman's rank order correlation coefficient. The input data and main outcomes of the Geographically Weighted correlation analysis are displayed in Figure 4. Figure 4a shows the non-marital fertility ratio in 2007; and Figure 4b displays the log-transformed values of the non-marital fertility ratio in 1910.[20] Unlike the maps in Figures 2 and 3, these maps display the non-marital fertility ratio for the 604 time-constant regions. This method of presentation lacks spatial detail, but might facilitate the comparison of the regional levels in 1910 and 2007.

Figures 4c–f show the outcomes of the Geographically Weighted correlation analysis. In Figures 4c and 4d I present the results obtained with the 'intermediate' spatial weighting function, which allows me to study shifts in the association between past and present patterns across Europe on a broader spatial scale for both a smaller and a larger bandwidth (20 vs. 30 nearest neighbours). Figures 4e and 4f display the outcomes based on a more 'localised' spatial weighting function that is more sensitive to small-scale deviations from larger-scale patterns. The results for the 20 and the 30 nearest-neighbours bandwidths are also compared in these figures. Figures 4c–f demonstrate that the choice of weights and the number of neighbours change the outcomes considerably. Nevertheless, the four maps have many similarities.

When we look at the outcomes for spatial shifts in the correlation between non-marital fertility levels in 1910 and 2007 at an intermediate level of spatial detail across Europe (Figures 4c and d), we can see that also at this scale the analysis returned a positive association in almost all of the regions. However, some areas deviate from this pattern. The most prominent exceptions are found in Southeastern Europe. Bulgaria has shifted from having extremely low to having extremely high non-marital fertility levels, while the regions that today make up Romania had comparatively high levels in the past and quite low levels today.[21] A second area for which negative correlations are obtained is England and Wales: in 2007 the low values were centred on London in the southeast, whereas in 1910 they were more dispersed.

Studies that have attempted to explain the large discontinuities in Southeastern Europe have noted that Bulgaria has a long tradition of government intervention in family formation patterns. This tradition started after Bulgaria became independent in the late nineteenth century. At that time, legislators did not develop civil legislation based on existing customs. Instead, for various reasons, they directly transferred legal norms from western civil legislation to the Bulgarian legal code (see Todorova, 2000; for details). During the communist era as well civil legislation had a substantial influence on family formation patterns. For example, in an effort to preserve traditional family formation behaviour and to incentivise marriage, the government imposed a bachelor tax on non-married individuals (see also Brunnbauer & Taylor, 2004). As a result of these policies, the decision to marry may have become decoupled from social norms, and more closely linked with economic considerations.[22] These developments might have contributed to the sharp

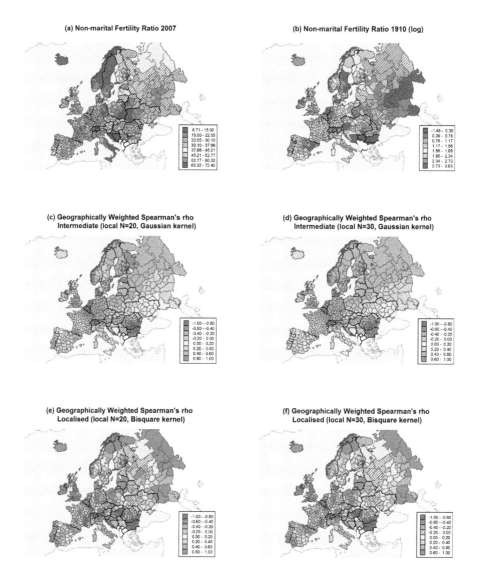

Figure 4.   Geographically Weighted rank order correlation (Spearman's rho): non-marital fertility ratio in 1910 vs. in 2007.
Source: Statistical offices; Eurostat; UN statistical yearbooks; Decroly and Vanlaer (1991); Council of Europe (2005); Ekamper and van Poppel (2008); Devos (2014); Klüsener et al. (2014), own calculations.
Base Map: MPIDR (2014a, 2014b, 2014c), partly based on EuroGeographics for the administrative boundaries; National Historical GIS projects (see also the 'GIS data' section in the references for details).

increase in non-marital fertility in Bulgaria during the economic instability of the 1990s and the 2000s, when the bachelor tax was no longer in effect.

Parts of Southeastern Europe and England and Wales also show negative associations in Figures 4e and f, which display the outcomes for the more localised weighting function. However, the obtained negative coefficients are even higher than those shown in Figures 4c and d. Other regions with negative coefficients also show up. In Western

Europe, these areas include large parts of France and parts of northwestern Spain and Portugal. The more localised analysis of Eastern Europe indicates that there is a rather big area with negative correlations covering the central part of European Russia, substantial parts of western and central Ukraine, and southern Belarus. In the Ukrainian and the Belarusian territories in particular, this negative association might be linked to the drastic changes in the composition of the population as a result of the Jewish Holocaust. Another difference in the maps with the more localised pattern is that the negative correlations in the border region between Hungary and Romania are more pronounced. Last but not least, there is also a small area with negative coefficients in Central Europe that covers parts of eastern Germany and the Czech Republic.

While the more localised weighting function returns negative correlations for a larger number of regions, it also provides much higher positive correlation coefficients for many regions. First, however, I will discuss the areas that show high positive associations in the analyses based on the intermediate weighting scheme (Figures 4c and d). One hot spot with high positive correlations can be observed around the Baltic Sea. In this area, the regions with predominantly Catholic populations (Poles and Lithuanians) had comparatively low levels of non-marital fertility in both 1910 and 2007. By contrast, many of the Baltic Sea regions with mainly Protestant populations, such as Sweden, Finland, and the territory of present-day Estonia, had much higher levels. This broader area with very high positive correlations extends west to include Denmark, the Netherlands, Belgium, Switzerland, large parts of Germany, northeastern France, and western Austria.

When we look at the outcomes for the more localised weighting scheme, we can see that the picture changes (Figures 4e and f). For the Baltic Sea region, the areas with high positive associations are now concentrated in Poland, Lithuania, and Latvia, as well as in a border zone between Sweden, Norway, and Finland. In Germany, the areas with high positive associations are mainly found in the border zone between eastern and western Germany. The long-standing non-marital fertility divide between east and west in that country has been described by Klüsener and Goldstein (2014). In France, the zones with high positive associations are mainly clustered along the regions bordering Spain in the southwest and Belgium, Germany, Switzerland and Italy in the east. In both 1910 and 2007, these French border regions tended to have higher levels of non-marital fertility than the adjacent regions in neighbouring countries. The outcomes for the French border zones are in line with the findings of Bocquet-Appel and Jakobi (1996, p. 121) who showed that these borders constituted at least temporary barriers to the spatial diffusion of the fertility decline as part of the demographic transition. The fact that these boundaries also show up in my analysis seems to underline their importance as demarcations between distinct zones that differ in terms of their family formation behaviour patterns and the timing of their transitions to new patterns. Other areas that are shown to have a pronounced positive correlation in the more localised analysis include Ireland, Iceland, an area comprising southern Portugal and southern Spain, the eastern part of European Russia, and a rather large area stretching from southeastern Germany to the western Balkans.

Overall, the analysis of the persistence of past non-marital fertility variation patterns suggests that while there is some degree of continuity from a pan-European perspective and at an intermediate level of spatial detail, the outcomes become more nuanced if approaches are used that are more sensitive to local deviations from the general patterns. However, even in the analysis that returns the highest number of negative correlations (the one presented in Figure 4e), for the majority of regions a positive

Geographically Weighted correlation coefficient is obtained (62%); and the share of regions with correlations above 0.3 (40%) is far larger than the share of regions with a correlation below –0.3 (19%).

4.3. Potential future pathways

4.3.1. Future patterns of between-country variation

The discussion of future pathways is divided into two parts: potential variation across countries, and potential variation within countries. Existing research by Lappegård et al. (2014) provides support for the view that between-country variation of childbearing in cohabitation across Europe is linked to secularisation processes, as well as to the economic autonomy of women. Patterns of disadvantage seem to be more relevant for understanding variation between individuals and across subnational regions (Lappegård et al., 2014). Projections by Kaufmann et al. (2012) indicate that the secularisation process has levelled off in the predominantly Protestant countries that were the forerunners in this development,[23] and is continuing in the predominantly Catholic countries. Thus, the secularisation levels of European countries with Protestant and Catholic traditions are currently converging, and this process may in turn contribute to a convergence in the levels of non-marital fertility. However, as was mentioned above, the situation is different in a number of Eastern European countries with an Orthodox tradition. Since these countries broke with their secular communist past, religiosity has grown (see, e.g., Evans & Northmore-Ball, 2012, on Russia). If this tendency towards increasing religiosity prevails in Eastern Europe, the already visible trend towards a divergence of non-marital fertility levels in Eastern Europe on the one hand and the rest of Europe on the other might continue into the future.

The economic autonomy of women is heavily influenced by welfare state institutions (McLaughlin & Glendinning, 1994). Societies in Northern and Western Europe seem to have been forerunners in providing women with higher levels of autonomy through legislative action. There are indications that other countries are currently enacting similar measures (Ostner, 2006), in part because autonomy for women is supported by European institutions such as the European Court of Human Rights (Goldhaber, 2007) and the European Union. In the future, this trend might contribute to a convergence in the economic status of women across Europe. However, the non-EU part of Eastern Europe might again constitute an exception to this general trend. In the development of their welfare state and family policies, these countries seem to be less influenced than other countries by European institutions, although they may be affected to some extent via their membership in the Council of Europe. In general, it appears that the non-EU part of Eastern Europe is the area of the continent which is least likely to follow the trend towards convergence in family legislation and welfare state development. Thus, current indications that Eastern Europe is no longer making the general transition towards high non-marital fertility ratios are, perhaps, not so surprising. There is also no evidence that non-marital fertility is increasing strongly in European countries with a Muslim tradition. The only exception is Kosovo, but, as discussed above, the increase there appears to be a statistical artefact. Thus, the non-EU countries with an Orthodox or a Muslim tradition seem to be the European countries that are most likely to revert to or to continue to have rather low non-marital fertility levels.

4.3.2. *Future patterns of within-country variation*

As I noted in the introduction, the exploration of potential future within-country variation patterns will focus on Denmark, which was the first European country to complete the transition from having rather low to having high levels of non-marital fertility. Figure 5 displays the non-marital fertility ratio for the 99 Danish municipalities in the period 2007–2010. Interestingly, the highest non-marital fertility ratios were registered in the most central and the most marginal areas of Denmark. The first group of areas with high levels of non-marital fertility consists of the municipalities in the centre of the metropolitan area of Copenhagen, while the second group is made up of the small Danish islands and the northern part of Jutland, which constitutes the continental part of Denmark. In both clusters of municipalities, more than 50% of all births were to non-married mothers. Meanwhile, the lowest levels of non-marital fertility were reported in the outer core and suburban belt of the Copenhagen metropolitan area.

For the island of Zealand, on which Copenhagen is located, and the smaller islands to the south of Zealand, the non-marital fertility patterns are reminiscent of those of

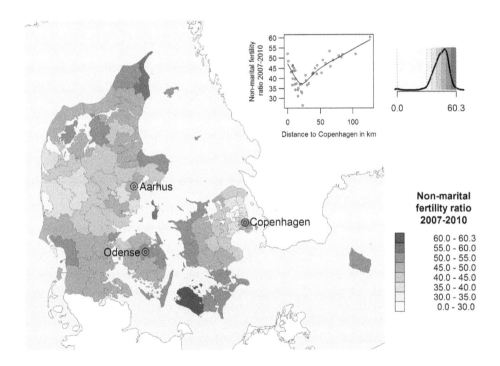

Figure 5.   Non-marital fertility ratio in Danish municipalities (2007–2010).
Note: The non-marital fertility ratio was derived based on the birth counts for the period 2007–2010. The scatter plot displays the non-marital fertility ratio of regions within a distance of 120 km around the city of Copenhagen by the distance to the geographical centre of the city of Copenhagen. The fitted line is a polynomial regression line obtained with a locally weighted scatterplot smoother (LOWESS) (Cleveland, 1979); the density curve in the upper-right corner provides additional information to the legend given in the lower-right corner by showing how the chosen colour categories relate to the distribution of the mapped variable.
Source: Statistics Denmark, own calculations.
Base Map: Dansk Center for Byhistorie (2008); MPIDR (2014a), partly based on EuroGeographics for the administrative boundaries.

classical spatial distribution models, such as the land use model suggested by Thünen (1826) or the city model by Burgess (1925): i.e., the non-marital fertility levels seem to vary systematically with the distance to the centre of the Copenhagen metropolitan area. To show this pattern more clearly, a scatter plot has been added to the upper-right corner of Figure 5 that displays the non-marital fertility ratios for areas within a distance of 120 km around Copenhagen by the distance to the centre of the city of Copenhagen. This plot benefits from the fact that the Copenhagen metropolitan area is made up of several independent municipalities. Through these observations, a polynomial regression line was fitted using the locally weighted scatterplot smoother (LOWESS) as suggested by Cleveland (1979). This line exhibits a steep negative gradient, from the rather high non-marital fertility levels in and around the city of Copenhagen, to the substantially lower levels in the outer core and suburban belt of the metropolitan area. However, starting at a distance of around 20 km from the city centre of Copenhagen, the levels increase. At around 60 km from centre, levels similar to those in the city of Copenhagen are reached.

Around Aarhus, the second biggest Danish city, the municipalities in the suburban belt around the city again tend to have lower levels of non-marital fertility than the city of Aarhus itself or the more peripheral areas. A challenge I faced in assessing whether this pattern is specific to Denmark was the fact that most of the other countries either have not completed the transition to high non-marital fertility levels, or do not provide the kind of fine-gridded data needed to distinguish between the inner and the outer cores of large cities and their suburban belts. However, it is possible to observe that in, for example, the United Kingdom and France, the metropolitan areas of London and Paris are among the regions with the lowest non-marital fertility ratios in an intra-country comparison (see Figure 4). At least for Paris and its surrounding regions, the pattern was the exact opposite in 1910.

The low non-marital fertility levels in the outer cores of the city centres of metropolitan areas and their suburban belts are probably to some degree the result of selective migration processes. Research has shown that metropolitan areas attract people with high levels of educational attainment (Buch, Hamann, Niebuhr, & Rossen, 2014), who often have a lower propensity to have a child outside marriage (Perelli-Harris et al., 2010). The outer core of the city centre is also frequently an in-migration destination for foreigners. Members of these groups tend to have a lower tendency to give birth to a child outside marriage (see, e.g., Klüsener & Goldstein, 2014; for Germany). This may be partly because a large share of the people who migrate to Europe are from regions with more conservative social norms regarding family formation behaviour, and partly because family reunion migration is facilitated in some European countries if a couple were married (for an overview, see Wray, Agoston, & Hutton, 2014). Moreover, the social values of individuals might affect their migration decisions. For individuals who care about the traditional family formation norms which were most prominent during the Golden Age of Marriage in the 1950s and 1960s, suburbia – which tends to be associated with access to well-paying jobs in the city and comparatively low housing prices – might provide the ideal spatial context for living in accordance with these family ideals (see also Fagnani, 1991; Kulu, 2013). Meanwhile, people who favour alternative, non-traditional lifestyles, including childbearing outside marriage, might prefer to live in the city centre.

5. Conclusion

In this article, I explored the continuities and discontinuities in spatial variation in non-marital fertility across Europe over the last 100 years. Non-marital fertility has increased substantially since the temporal minimum in the Golden Age of Marriage in the 1950s and 1960s. The comparison of the spatial variation patterns in 1910 and 2007 suggests that the persistence of the past is relevant for understanding today's spatial variation in non-marital fertility levels. This is particularly the case when we look at variation across all of Europe or at an intermediate level of spatial detail. However, the outcomes are more mixed in my analyses that are capable of carving out local deviations from these general patterns. In addition, the results indicate that the persistence of the past not only varies spatially; it also seems to fade over time.

In terms of the future pathways of between-country variation, both the theoretical considerations and the observed trends suggest that most European countries will converge at rather high levels of non-marital fertility. The European integration process may be expected to contribute to this convergence, as it tends to promote the harmonisation of family legislation and the elimination of any remaining legal discrimination of children born outside marriage. However, the non-EU part of Eastern Europe might constitute an outlier in this convergence trend, as it is currently the only European region that has declining non-marital fertility ratios. This development reflects a reactionary trend in the non-EU former Soviet republics: in these countries, religiosity has been rising and many people appear to be rejecting a wide range of family formation behaviours that are not in line with traditional norms. Another group of potential outliers might be the European countries with a Muslim tradition, as non-marital fertility levels in these countries have so far been very low – with the exception of the statistical artefact in Kosovo, which was discussed above. Thus, a dichotomy in non-marital fertility levels might emerge between the non-EU countries with Orthodox Christian or Muslim traditions on the one hand, and the rest of Europe on the other. However, it is also likely that different levels will continue to exist between EU countries even after they have completed the transition. For example, in Finland the process levelled off in the early 2000s at a non-marital fertility ratio of around 40%, while in France the transition is not yet complete, but is currently at a level of 56% (see Appendix 1). Within countries, it seems that in the future the outer cores and suburban belts of big metropolitan areas might become the last strongholds of marital fertility. Tendencies in this direction are already visible in a number of countries in Northwestern Europe, including in Denmark, as was shown in this paper.

Disclosure statement

No potential conflict of interest was reported by the author.

Notes

1. See Hägerstrand (1965) and González-Bailón and Murphy (2013) for general considerations.
2. Since 2011, Denmark has again registered an increase in the non-marital fertility ratio (see Appendix 1). However, this has no impact on my analysis of the spatial non-marital fertility pattern as I focus on the period 2007–2010.
3. In 1895, for example, the share of births in Austrian Galicia that were outside marriage was 78.92% among the Jewish population, but just 12.98% among the non-Jewish population (Nathansohn, 1910; cited by Lowenstein, 1994, p. 170).

4. See Klüsener et al. (2014) for detailed source information.
5. The shapefiles and the data are available on the following webpage: http://www.demogr. mpg.de/de/ausbildungkarriere/was_ist_demografie_1908/kinder_ja_ehe_nein_daten_3010/def ault.htm.
6. At either the NUTS-2 or the NUTS-3 level, depending on which division is historically and/or politically more meaningful (see Klüsener et al., 2013, for details).
7. Klüsener et al. (2013) used the same approach to derive the data-set for the period 1960–2007.
8. However, in the 1910 file the geographic detail varies to some degree across countries. Thus, the estimates are better for some parts of Europe than for others. I will come back to this issue in the presentation of the results.
9. Details will be given when the results are presented.
10. The spatial distances between regions are derived by calculating the spherical distances between the regional geographical centroids.
11. The Gaussian-shaped weighting function is in the *GWmodel* package specified as a continuous weighting function, which implies that observations beyond the bandwidth are also included. Thus, the bandwidth choice just affects the shape of the weighting function. This property of the Gaussian-shaped weighting function contributes to make the outcomes less localised.
12. For details on the weighting functions, see Gollini, Lu, Charlton, Brunsdon, and Harris (2014).
13. The latter has been included in the Central-Western Europe region, as its territories became part of the Federal Republic of Germany in 1990.
14. The numbers for Russia cover all of Russia, including the Asian part.
15. See also the annotations to Figure 1. National-level trends can be obtained from Appendix 1.
16. When I point in this paper to the temporal coincidence of legislative reforms and trend changes in non-marital fertility in specific countries, this does not imply that the trend changes are caused by these legislative reforms. Causality can also exist in the opposite direction, as shifts in family formation strategies can lead to the adoption of legislation that conforms to the newly emerging patterns of behaviour.
17. Interestingly, in France as well the increase in non-marital fertility gained momentum in the 1970s after a substantial support scheme for single mothers had been introduced (Knijn, Martin, & Millar, 2007). However, unlike the GDR and the Austrian governments, the French government did not later enact legislation designed to limit the increases in non-marital fertility.
18. As including the boundaries of the regions in the maps shown in Figure 2 and Figure 3 would have substantially affected their readability, I decided to display in the maps only the country boundaries, and to include maps with the regional boundaries in Appendices 2 and 3.
19. See annotations to Table 1 for additional details.
20. The log-transformation accounts for the fact that the 1910 data are positively skewed. Using this transformation allows me to take the same categorisation (standard deviation categorisation centred on the mean) for the 1910 and 2007 maps in order to carve out variation in terms of the rank in 1910 that will be considered by Spearman's rank order correlation coefficient.
21. The estimation of non-marital fertility levels in 1910 for the time-constant regions in those areas that already belonged to Romania in 1910 was limited by the fact that the available data for the source regions only allowed me to distinguish between Bucharest and the rest of the country. Thus, the rather homogenous 1910 estimates in southern and eastern Romania are an artefact of this limitation. However, as the discontinuity in the trend patterns is mainly driven by the developments in Bulgaria, this should not affect the general outcomes of the Geographically Weighted correlation analysis for this Southeastern European area.
22. Salles (2006) argued in a similar vein with regard to the German Democratic Republic.
23. France also belonged to this group of forerunners, even though it was predominantly Catholic. This pattern is linked to early secularisation trends resulting from the French Revolution (Lesthaeghe & Neels, 2002).

References

Literature

Abrahamson, M. (2000). Case studies of surges in nonmarital births. *Marriage & Family Review, 30*, 127–151. doi:10.1300/J002v30n01_09

Berlin, I. (1958). *Four essays on liberty.* Oxford: Oxford University Press.

Bocquet-Appel, J.-P., & Jakobi, L. (1996). Barriers to the spatial diffusion for the demographic transition in Western Europe. In J.-P. Bocquet-Appel, D. Courgeau, & D. Pumain (Eds.), *Spatial analysis of biodemographic data* (pp. 117–129). Montrouge: John Libbey Eurotext.

Brunnbauer, U., & Taylor, K. (2004). Creating a 'socialist way of life': Family and reproduction policies in Bulgaria, 1944–1989. *Continuity and Change, 19*, 283–312. doi:10.1017/S0268416004005004

Brzozowska, Z. (2011). Przestrzenne zróżnicowanie urodzeń pozamałżeńskich w Polsce w latach 2002-2010 [Spatial differentiation of non-marital births in Poland, 2002-2010]. *Studia Demograficzne, 2*, 59–84.

Buch, T., Hamann, S., Niebuhr, A., & Rossen, A. (2014). *How to woo the smart ones? Evaluating the determinants that particularly attract highly qualified people to cities.* Hamburg: Hamburg Institute of International Economics. HWWI Research Paper 159.

Burgess, E. W. (1925). The growth of the city: An introduction to a research project. In R. E. Park, E. W. Burgess, & R. D. McKenzie (Eds.), *The city: Suggestions for investigation of human behavior in the urban environment* (pp. 47–62). Chicago, IL: University of Chicago Press.

Cleveland, W. S. (1979). Robust locally weighted regression and smoothing scatterplots. *Journal of the American Statistical Association, 74*, 829–836. doi:10.1080/01621459.1979.10481038

Cutright, P. (1971). Illegitimacy: Myths, causes and cures. *Family Planning Perspectives, 3*, 25–48. doi:10.2307/2133953

Decroly, J. M., & Grasland, C. (1993). Boundaries, political systems and fertility in Europe. *Population: An English Selection, 5*, 101–119.

Edge, P. G. (1928). Vital registration in Europe: The development of official statistics and some differences in practice. *Journal of the Royal Statistical Society, 91*, 346–393. doi:10.2307/2341602

Esping-Andersen, G. (1990). *The three worlds of welfare capitalism.* Princeton: Princeton University Press.

Evans, G., & Northmore-Ball, K. (2012). The limits of secularization? The resurgence of orthodoxy in post-Soviet Russia. *Journal for the Scientific Study of Religion, 51*, 795–808. doi:10.1111/j.1468-5906.2012.01684.x

Fagnani, J. (1991). Fertility in France: The influence of urbanization. In J. Bähr, & P. Gans (Eds.), *The Geographical Approach to Fertility* (pp. 165–173). Kiel: Geographisches Institut der Universität Kiel. Kieler Geographische Schriften 78.

Fotheringham, A. S., Brunsdon, C., & Charlton, M. (2002). *Geographically Weighted Regression: The analysis of spatially varying relationships.* Chichester: John Wiley & Sons.

Goldhaber, M. D. (2007). *A people's history of the European Court of Human Rights.* New Brunswick: Rutgers University Press.

Goldstein, J. R., & Kreyenfeld, M. (2011). Has East Germany overtaken West Germany? Recent trends in order-specific fertility. *Population and Development Review, 37*, 453–472. doi:10.1111/j.1728-4457.2011.00430.x

Gollini, I., Lu, B., Charlton, M., Brunsdon, C., & Harris, P. (2014). GWmodel: An R package for exploring spatial heterogeneity using geographically weighted models. *Journal of Statistical Software, 63*, 1–50. doi:10.18637/jss.v063.i17

González-Bailón, S., & Murphy, T. E. (2013). The effects of social interactions on fertility decline in nineteenth-century France: An agent-based simulation experiment. *Population Studies, 67*, 135–155. doi:10.1080/00324728.2013.774435

Goodchild, M. F., & Lam, N. S.-N. (1980). Areal interpolation: A variant of the traditional spatial problem. *Geo-Processing, 1*, 297–312.

Hägerstrand, T. (1965). A Monte Carlo approach to diffusion. *European Journal of Sociology, 6*, 43–67. doi:10.1017/S0003975600001132

Kaufmann, E., Goujon, A., & Skirbekk, V. (2012). The end of secularization in Europe? A socio-demographic perspective. *Sociology of Religion, 73*, 69–91. doi:10.1093/socrel/srr033

Khera, S. (1981). Illegitimacy and mode of land inheritance among Austrian peasants. *Ethnology, 20*, 307–323.

Kiernan, K. (2004). Unmarried cohabitation and parenthood in Britain and Europe. *Law & Policy, 26*, 33–55. doi:10.1111/j.0265-8240.2004.00162.x

Klüsener, S., & Goldstein, J. R. (2014). A long-standing demographic East-West divide in Germany. *Population, Space and Place* [Early View]. doi:10.1002/psp.1870

Klüsener, S., Perelli-Harris, B., & Sánchez Gassen, N. (2013). Spatial aspects of the rise of non-marital fertility across Europe since 1960: The role of states and regions in shaping patterns of change. *European Journal of Population, 29*, 137–165. doi:10.1007/s10680-012-9278-x

Klüsener, S., Devos, I., Ekamper, P., Gregory, I. N., Gruber, S., Martí-Henneberg, J., van Poppel, F., da Silveira, L. E., & Solli, A. (2014). Spatial inequalities in infant survival at an early stage of the longevity revolution: A pan-European view across 5000+ regions and localities in 1910. *Demographic Research, 30*, 1849–1864. doi:10.4054/DemRes.2014.30.68

Knijn, T., Martin, C., & Millar, J. (2007). Activation as a common framework for social policies towards lone parents. *Social Policy & Administration, 41*, 638–652. doi:10.1111/j.1467-9515.2007.00576.x

Knodel, J. (1967). Law, marriage and illegitimacy in nineteenth-century Germany. *Population Studies, 20*, 279–294. doi:10.1080/00324728.1967.10409964

Kok, J. (2009). Family systems as frameworks for understanding variation in extra-marital births, Europe 1900–2000. *Romanian Journal of Population Studies, 3*, 13–38.

Kok, J., & Leinarte, D. (2015). Cohabitation in Europe: A revenge of history? *The History of the Family*. doi:10.1080/1081602X.2015.1067240

Kolbe, W. (2002). *Elternschaft im Wohlfahrtsstaat: Schweden und die Bundesrepublik im Vergleich 1945–2000* [Parenthood and the welfare state: A comparison of Sweden and the Federal Republic 1945–2000]. Frankfurt am Main: Campus-Verlag.

Kulu, H. (2013). Why do fertility levels vary between urban and rural areas? *Regional Studies, 47*, 895–912. doi:10.1080/00343404.2011.581276

Kytir, J. (1992). Unehelich, vorehelich, ehelich - Familiengründung im Wandel: Eine empirische Analyse der Erstgeburten österreichischer Frauen 1950 bis 1990 [Out of wedlock, pre-marital, marital - family formation in transition: An empirical analysis of first births among Austrian women 1950-1990]. *Demographische Informationen, 1990–1991*, 29–40.

Lappegård T., Klüsener, S., & Vignoli D. (2014). *Social norms, economic conditions and spatial variation of childbearing within cohabitation across Europe*. Rostock: Max Planck Institute for Demographic Research. MPIDR Working Paper WP-2014-002.

Laslett, P. (1980). Introduction: Comparing illegitimacy over time and between cultures. In P. Laslett, K. Oosterveen & R. M. Smith (Eds.), *Bastardy and its comparative history: Studies in the history of illegitimacy and marital nonconformism in Britain, France, Germany, Sweden, North America, Jamaica and Japan* (pp. 1–70). Cambridge, Ma.: Harvard University Press.

Le Goff, J.-M., & Ryser, V.-A. (2010). Meaning of marriage for men during their transition to fatherhood: The Swiss context. *Marriage & Family Review, 46*, 107–125. doi:10.1080/01494921003648654

Lesthaeghe, R. (2010). The unfolding story of the Second Demographic Transition. *Population and Development Review, 36*, 211–251. doi:10.1111/j.1728-4457.2010.00328.x

Lesthaeghe, R., & Lopez-Gay, A. (2013). Spatial continuities and discontinuities in two successive demographic transitions: Spain and Belgium, 1880-2010. *Demographic Research, 28*, 77–136. doi:10.4054/DemRes.2013.28.4

Lesthaeghe, R., & Neels, K. (2002). From the first to the second demographic transition: An interpretation of the spatial continuity of demographic innovation in France, Belgium and Switzerland. *European Journal of Population, 18*, 325–360. doi:10.1023/A:1021125800070

Lowenstein, S. M. (1994). Ashkenazic Jewry and the European marriage pattern: A preliminary survey of Jewish marriage age. *Jewish History, 8*, 155–175. doi:10.1007/BF01915912

McLaughlin, E., & Glendinning, C. (1994). Paying for care in Europe: Is there a feminist approach? In L. Hantrais & S. Mangen (Eds.), *Family Policy and the Welfare of Women* (pp. 52–69). Loughborough: Cross-National Research Group.

Nathansohn, H. (1910). Die unehelichen Geburten bei den Juden [Births out of wedlock among Jews]. *Zeitschrift für Demographie und Statistik der Juden, 7*, 102–106.

Ostner, I. (2006). Paradigmenwechsel in der (west)deutschen Familienpolitik [Paradigm shift in (West) German family policies]. In P. A. Berger & H. Kahlert (Eds.), *Der demographische Wandel: Chancen für die Neuordnung der Geschlechterverhältnisse* [Demographic Change: Opportunities for the reorganization of gender relations] (pp. 165–199). Frankfurt am Main/ New York: Campus Verlag.

Perelli-Harris, B., & Gerber, T. P. (2011). Nonmarital childbearing in Russia: Second Demographic Transition or pattern of disadvantage? *Demography, 48*, 317–342. doi:10.1007/ s13524-010-0001-4

Perelli-Harris, B., & Sánchez Gassen, N. (2012). How similar are cohabitation and marriage? Legal approaches to cohabitation across Western Europe. *Population and Development Review, 38*, 435–467. doi:10.1111/j.1728-4457.2012.00511.x

Perelli-Harris, B., Sigle-Rushton, W., Kreyenfeld, M., Lappegård, T., Keizer, R., & Berghammer, C. (2010). The educational gradient of childbearing within cohabitation in Europe. *Population and Development Review, 36*, 775–801. doi:10.1111/j.1728-4457.2010.00357.x

Perelli-Harris, B., Kreyenfeld, M., Sigle-Rushton, W., Keizer, R., Lappegård, T., Jasilioniene, A., Berghammer, C., & Di Giulio, P. (2012). Changes in union status during the transition to parenthood in eleven European countries, 1970s to early 2000s. *Population Studies, 66*, 167–182. doi:10.1080/00324728.2012.673004

Reher, D. S. (1998). Family ties in Western Europe: Persistent contrasts. *Population and Development Review, 24*, 203–234. doi:10.2307/2807972

Ruggles, S. (2015). Patriarchy, power, and pay: The transformation of American families, 1800– 2015. Presidential Address at the Population Association of America Annual Meeting in San Diego, May 1, 2015.

Salles, A. (2006). The effects of family policy in the former GDR on nuptiality and births outside marriage. *Population (English Edition), 61*, 141–151. doi:10.3917/popu.601.0141

SGF [Statistique Générale de la France]. (1907). *Statistique internationale du mouvement de la population d'après les registres d'état civil: Résumé rétrospectif depuis l'origine des statistiques de l'état civil jusqu'en 1905* [International vital population statistics according to the civil registers: Retrospective summary since the origins of vital statistics until 1905]. Paris: Imprimerie national.

Shorter, E., Knodel, J., & van de Walle, E. (1971). The decline of non-marital fertility in Europe, 1880–1940. *Population Studies, 25*, 375–393. doi:10.1080/00324728.1971.10405813

Shorter, E. (1978). Bastardy in south Germany: A comment. *The Journal of Interdisciplinary History, 8*, 459–469. doi:10.2307/202916

Stanković, B., & Penev, G. (2012). Rađanje van braka: Neki prostorni aspekti [Births outside marriage: Some spatial aspects]. *Demografija, 9*, 181–199.

Thünen, J. H. v. (1826). *Der isolierte Staat in Beziehung auf Landwirtschaft und Nationalökonomie, oder Untersuchungen über den Einfluß, den die Getreidepreise, der Reichthum des Bodens und die Abgaben auf den Ackerbau ausüben* [The isolated state in relation to agriculture and political economy, or investigations concerning the influence which grain prices, the richness of the soil, and taxes, exert upon tillage]. Hamburg: Friedrich Perthes.

Todorova, V. (2000). Family law in Bulgaria: Legal norms and social norms. *International Journal of Law, Policy and the Family, 14*, 148–181. doi:10.1093/lawfam/14.2.148

Tomasson, R. F. (1976). Premarital sexual permissiveness and illegitimacy in the Nordic countries. *Comparative Studies in Society and History, 18*, 252–270. doi:10.1017/ S0010417500008227

Trost, J. (1978). A renewed social institution: Non-marital cohabitation. *Acta Sociologica, 21*, 303–315.

Watkins, S. C. (1991). *From provinces into nations: Demographic integration in Western Europe 1870–1960*. Princeton: Princeton University Press.

Wray, H. E., Agoston, A., & Hutton, J. (2014). A family resemblance? The regulation of marriage migration in Europe. *European Journal of Migration and Law, 16*, 209–247. doi:10.1163/15718166-12342054

Data

Demographic data

Council of Europe. (2005). *Recent demographic developments in Europe 2004*. Strasbourg: Council of Europe Publishing.

Decroly, J. M., & Vanlaer, J. (1991). *Atlas de la population européenne* [Atlas of the European population]. Brussels: Editions de l'Université de Bruxelles.

Demoskop Weekly. (2015). *15 novyx nezavisimyx gosudarstv: Dolja vnebračnyx roždenij (na 100 rodivšixsja), 1960-2012* [15 newly independent states. The share of non-marital births (per 100 births), 1960-2012]. Moscow: National Research University Higher School of Economics. Retrieved March 15, 2015 from http://www.demoscope.ru/weekly/ssp/sng_emb.php

Devos, I. (2014). *HISSTER-Database*. Ghent: Ghent University, History Department.

Ekamper, P., & van Poppel, F. (2008). Zuigelingensterfte per gemeente in Nederland, 1841-1939 [Infant mortality by municipality in the Netherlands, 1841-1939]. *Bevolkingstrends, 56*, 23–29. http://publ.nidi.nl/output/2008/bt-56-01-ekamper.pdf

Flora, P., Kraus, F., & Pfenning, W. (1987). *State, economy, and society in Western Europe 1815-1975: A data handbook in two Volumes: Volume II: The growth of industrial societies and capitalist economies*. Frankfurt am Main/New York: Campus Verlag.

INED. (2015). *Developed Countries Demography Database*. Paris: INED. Retrieved July 20, 2015.

UCB [University of California, Berkeley] and MPIDR [Max Planck Institute for Demographic Research]. (2015). *Human Mortality Database*. Berkeley/Rostock: UCB/MPIDR. Retrieved July 20, 2015 from http://www.mortality.org

SGF [Statistique Générale de la France]. (1907). *Statistique internationale du mouvement de la population d'apres les registres d'etat civil: Resume retrospectif depuis l'origine des statistiques de l'etat civil jusqu'en 1905* [International vital population statistics according to the civil registers: Retrospective summary since the origins of vital statistics until 1905]. Paris: Imprimerie national.

GIS data

Boonstra, O. W. A. (2007). *NLGis shapefiles*. Retrieved March 31, 2013 from https://easy.dans.knaw.nl/ui/datasets/id/easy-dataset:44426/

Dansk Center for Byhistorie [Danish Centre for Urban History]. (2008). *Danmarks lokaladministration 1660-2007* [The local administration of Denmark 1660-2007]. Århus: Dansk Center for Byhistorie. Retrieved March 15, 2015 from http://dendigitalebyport.byhistorie.dk/kommuner

GADM. (2012). *GADM database of global administrative areas*. Davis: University of California Davis. Retrieved March 31, 2012 from http://www.gadm.org

Gregory, I. N., Bennett, C., Gilham, V. L., & Southall, H. R. (2002). The Great Britain Historical GIS project: From maps to changing human geography. *The Cartographic Journal, 39*, 37–49. doi:10.1179/caj.2002.39.1.37

Guttormsson, L., & Garðarsdóttir, Ó. (2002). The development of infant mortality in Iceland, 1800–1920. *Hygiea Internationalis, 3*, 151–176. doi:10.3384/hygiea.1403-8668.0231151

Historical Database of Local Statistics [Lokstat]. (2014). *Belgian Historical GIS* (supervised by Vanhaute, E., & Vrielinck, S.). Ghent: Ghent University, History Department.

MPIDR [Max Planck Institute for Demographic Research]. (2014a). *MPIDR Population History GIS Collection*. Rostock: MPIDR. Retrieved March 31, 2014 from http://censusmosaic.org/web/data/historical-gis-files

MPIDR [Max Planck Institute for Demographic Research]. (2014b). *MPIDR Population History GIS Collection – Austria 1910* H. Rumpler, & M. Seger (Eds.) (2010). *Die Habsburgermonarchie 1848–1918, Band IX, Soziale Strukturen, 2. Teilband* [The Habsburg monarchy 1848–1918, Volume IX, Social structures, 2nd subvolume]. Wien: Verlag der Österreichischen Akademie der Wissenschaften). Rostock: MPIDR. Retrieved March 31, 2014 from http://censusmosaic.org/web/data/historical-gis-files

MPIDR [Max Planck Institute for Demographic Research]. (2014c). *MPIDR Population History GIS Collection – Serbia 1865-1895* (based on files by Gruber, S.). Rostock: MPIDR. Retrieved March 31, 2014 from http://censusmosaic.org/web/data/historical-gis-files

Norwegian Social Science Data Services [NSD]. (2013). *Norwegian Historical GIS*. Bergen: NSD.

Riksarkivet. (2013). *Historical GIS of Sweden*. Stockholm: Riksarkivet.

da Silveira, L. E., Alves, D., Lima, N. M., Alcântara, A., & Puig, J. (2011). Population and railways in Portugal, 1801–1930. *The Journal of Interdisciplinary History, 42*, 29–52. doi:10.1162/JINH_a_00204

Appendix 1. Long-term trends in the non-marital fertility ratio for European countries and regions

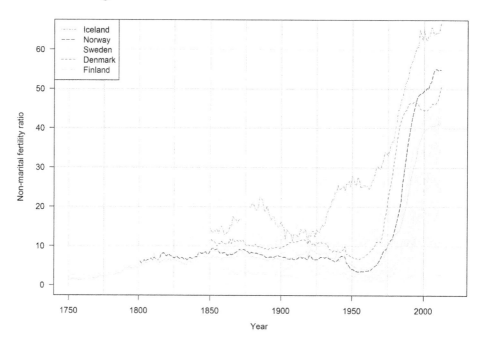

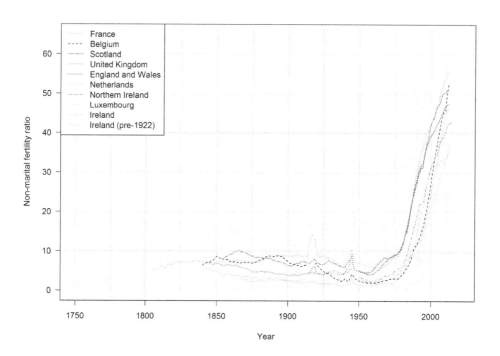

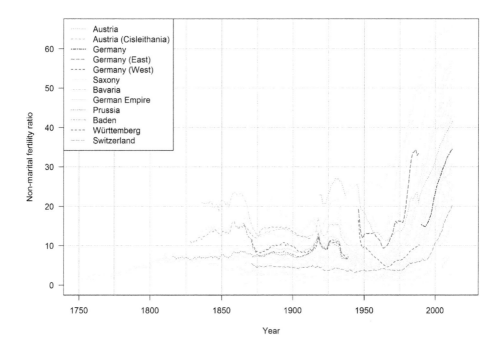

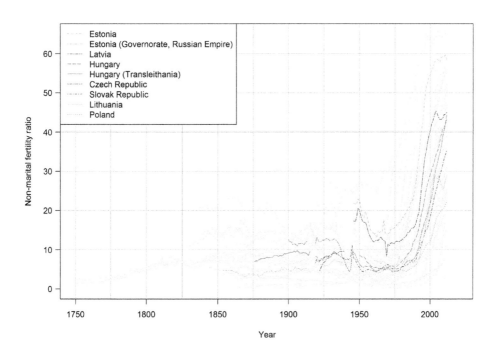

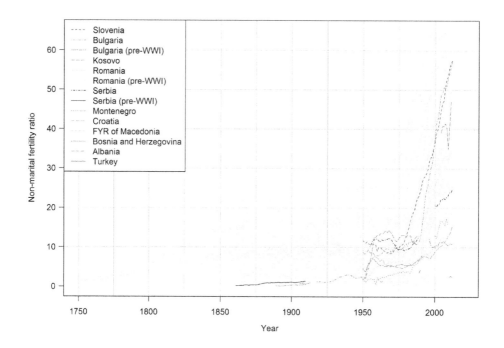

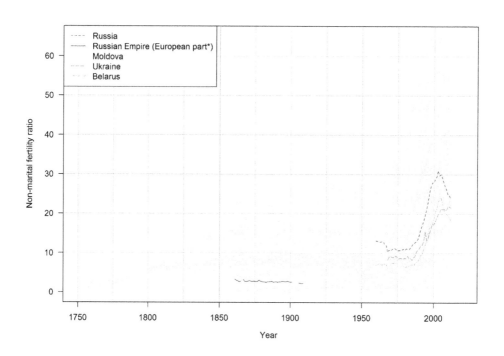

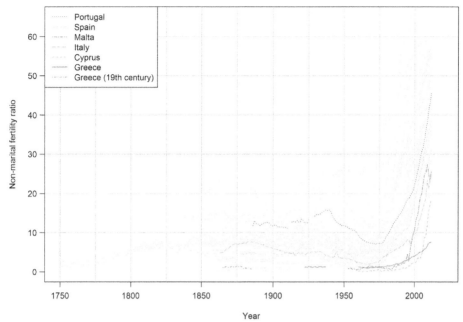

Note: Lines represent countries and subnational regions in the existing boundaries of the specific times. For historical periods, in which boundaries differed significantly from present-day boundaries, separate lines are drawn. For some of the historical data it was not clearly stated in the source whether the data cover live births only, or all births including stillbirths. The data for Austria (Cisleithania) refer until 1855 to the period 1 November of preceding year – 31 October; the data for Bavaria refer until 1870 to the period 1 October of preceding year – 30 September. Russian Empire (European part) includes the European part of the Russian Empire without the Kingdom of Poland and the Grand Duchy of Finland.

Source: Statistical offices; Eurostat; UN statistical yearbooks; publications of the Office Permanent de l'Institut International de Statistique; SGF (1907); Flora et al. (1987); Decroly and Vanlaer (1991); Council of Europe (2005); Klüsener et al. (2014); INED (2015); UCB and MPIDR (2015), own calculations.

Appendix 2. Administrative boundaries 2007

Base Map: MPIDR (2014a), partly based on EuroGeographics for the administrative boundaries; GADM (2012).

Appendix 3.   Administrative boundaries 1910

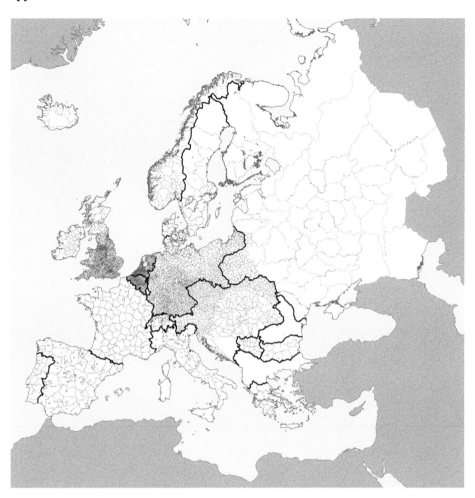

Base Map: MPIDR (2014a, 2014b, 2014c), partly based on EuroGeographics for the administrative boundaries; National Historical GIS projects (see also the 'GIS data' section in the references for details).

Appendix 4. Time-constant boundaries 1910–2007

Note: The reduced sample used in the correlation analysis excludes the regions that are high-lighted with shadowlines.
Base Map: MPIDR (2014a, 2014b, 2014c), partly based on EuroGeographics for the administrative boundaries.

Index